Pulling Back the Curtain

Pulling Back the Curtain

Rollin Russell

SANTOS BOOKS

Endorsements

Rollin Russell is a gifted storyteller and theological guide. His reflections extend from the shared faith within a congregation and the shared life of congregations over the past six decades. You will recognize the stories and appreciate his interpretations.

Rev. Richard Edens, Parish Pastor, Retired

A compassionate and candid storyteller, Rev, Dr. Rollin Russell offers a fascinating glimpse behind the scenes as he navigates challenging and often humorous situations in local congregations during his time as a young pastor. Later, his perspective as a denominational leader within the United Church of Christ gives us an insider's view of an era that included social issues of national significance – civil rights, the advancement of women in ministry, ecumenism, and the ordination of gay ministers. This book will especially appeal to clergy and laypeople who have lived through those extraordinary times. It is a compelling and authentic testament to justice, community, and the transforming power of an inclusive faith.

Rev. Denise Cumbee Long, J.D., Pastor and Non-profit Administrator

Rollin Russell changed my life one day with a simple but public act of courage and humility. He made me want to be a better man. Reading his memoirs gave me deeper insight into how such a moment came to be. The story of his personal journey is not only an interesting one, it is an inspiring one. Enjoy and savor it.

Rev. John C. Dorhauer, retired President of the United Church of Christ

Ministers, churches, and small and large organizations can benefit from Dr. Russell's experiences and his amazing ability to articulate those events that shaped him and through him shaped others. The memories and recollections in this memoir will show how he used his wisdom and skills to bring people together, to lead people and congregations in the right direction with minimal rancor and with a spirit of Christian community building.

Mr. Larry K. Small, Textile Industry Executive

This memoir is not only an honest, insightful and very personal reflection on a life well lived, but readable, scholarly commentary on ecumenical and social justice issues that will resonate with the reader on personal, professional, spiritual and cultural levels.

Rev. Bruno Schroeder, Parish and Institutional Pastor, Retired

My dad's memoir is a reflection on family, faith, friendships and profession. It's the story of his commitment to the church as it changed with social movements over more than a half-century. Dad was finishing this book at the time of his 88th birthday, in January 2025, just as the world was being up-ended. In such times, the themes of his story come into sharp focus. The book invites us to consider family, faith, friends and profession – in the world and in our lives – in times that have changed and in the changing times ahead.

Dr. Stephen T. Russell, Regents Professor, University of Texas at Austin

Southern reared "PK" shares his steps (and mis-steps) in a rapid learning curve as he navigates his own path in ministry from local churches to UCC Conference ministries. This memoir offers a chronicle of the Civil Rights movement, narrates character building jobs, recounts vocational development, and acknowledges a spouses' intuition. It's a great read.

Rev. C. L. "Curly" Stumb, Pastor and Outdoor Ministry Leader

First Printing, 2025
Published by Santos Books, Elizabethtown, PA
ISBN: 9798992890709

For my parents, who made my life possible and set me on this path;
For the many parishioners, pastors and colleagues, who made it an adventure;
For my beloved wife, children, family and friends who supported me through thick and thin:
Thanks be to a loving, inspiring and forgiving God.

Growing up in a parsonage, a preacher's kid, set me on a path of family, social, educational and religious experience which has been formative. Those experiences have shaped the way I still see and understand events, the way I judge and evaluate situations, and the choices I have presumed were open to me.

Growing up in Indianapolis till age eleven, then in New Orleans through High School graduation were significant as well, as were my college and seminary experiences in Kentucky and Tennessee respectively. The intersection of those four very different local and educational cultures with each of the four elemental early patterns of experience forms a matrix that has been foundational for my life ever since.

In retrospect I can trace most of my decisions, actions, perspectives, and relationships to the interactions of that eight-dimensional Rubix cube. When a medium or tough decision stares me in the face I can imagine those eight dimensions of my experience spinning, bouncing off each other, looking for a right or even a decent answer.

That web of experience and the values that they instilled have served me well in many instances as I pondered a range of problems in family, ethical, relational and professional situations. Unfortunately, it also put a set of blinders on me that I did not begin to shed for decades. The Civil Rights movement and later the movement for women's equality began to give me a broader perspective, and later the gay rights movement added to it.

But none of that has prepared me for the new set of issues that I and many others face late in life. Several wise and presumably old people have said that "Life is lived forward, but understood backward." That's why memoirs are often very interesting. They are usually written in the later years of life and, even if started earlier, are revised in retrospect with the benefit of hindsight and further experience.

While writing this memoir I frequently reflected on difficult situations as well as seemingly minor incidents and thought, "How could I have done that?" "How could I have been so insensitive?" "Why did I fail to understand that?" The temptation is to leave all those sins of commission and omission out, and some of them I have. Others will be obvious.

One of the classical Confessions of Sin nails it: "We have left undone the things we ought to have done; and we have done those things we ought not to have done. But thou, O Lord, have mercy upon us" (Book of Worship of the Evangelical and Reformed Church, 1947). That confession is followed by an Assurance of Pardon, and it is comforting to believe in a forgiving God, though that assurance comes with a *caveat*, "That we may hereafter live a godly, righteous and sober life . . . ." I like to think I tried, though I had a fairly loose understanding of each of those three admonitions.

One of the blessings of a pastoral career is that I have all those liturgical phrases, which I repeated so often, as well as cherished scriptures and hymns, rattling around in my head and causing me to reflect on what I do and what I have done and adding additional dimensions to my constantly spinning mental Rubix cube. That may be one of the most important gifts of trying to live as a Christian and the unique benefit of having been a pastor. All that experience has prepared me in a general way for what I assume will be the challenges of the last decade

But it has not prepared me for some of the more perplexing specifics. Things I have seen in the lives of others and, in many cases, tried to help them cope with, I am now dealing with myself. The deaths of loved ones; the anticipatory grief of watching the person closest to me decline; the knowledge in my bones, literally, of my own decline; the failure of agency in the face of global crises; they all weigh on my heart. What I am still able to do is write, communicate, worship, send modest checks for important causes, and pray: pray that I can keep that up as I pray for justice, equality, unity and peace.

I hope that this memoir will help some church folks better understand the things that their pastors rarely share with them. And will perhaps help pastors know that their ministries often have unanticipated and wonderful results. My years in UCC Conference Ministry and my constant involvement in ecumenical efforts toward Christian and interfaith unity, like so many other clergy in those positions, are usually little reported or understood. My intention is to pull back the curtain on pastoral ministry in parish, denominational and ecumenical settings so readers can see "how the sausage is made."

All of the following reflections come from my well-worn memory bank and may not be as accurate as others recollect. You have my sincere apology for any such error and an honest invitation to let me know what I got wrong . . . and to forgive me. I will try to "Stay Calm and Carry On."

---Rollin Russell

1

BORN IN A SNOWSTORM

The stories my parents told about my birth are exaggerated, I hope. It was a snowy day in late January 1937. My parents, Ed and Eleanor Russell, were living in Beech Grove, Indiana where my dad served as the pastor of Beech Grove Christian Church. Snow had accumulated on the streets and when my mom was close to being ready to deliver they were afraid they could not make it to the hospital across town. They called Dr. Roger Blackford, their family doctor, a church member and friend. He said he would be right over and deliver the baby at their house.

The doctor arrived and it was an anxious, "quick, boil some water" kind of moment, right out of a movie. I was born with the umbilical cord wrapped around my neck, so it was dicey for a few moments, then it was nip and tuck, literally, as Dr. Blackford cleaned me up and put my mother back together. I was healthy and intact.

Just as Mom and Dad started to relax a little, Roger told my dad to take off his sweater and roll up his sleeve. Much to Ed Russell's astonishment, Dr. Blackford took a large hypodermic needle from his black bag and prepared to draw a significant amount of blood from my dad's arm. While engaged in this procedure he explained that he had a theory that a strong dose of the father's blood would make a baby stronger and healthier in the long run.

He proceeded to pinch the skin on my little baby back, inserted the needle, and slowly inject the blood. He then massaged the lump it created until my back was smooth. Sounds crazy, and it probably was. I survived, of course, and for all I know my subsequent good health may be attributable to that whacky theory and late-night injection.

Of course, Roger Blackford was no ordinary doctor, or person for that matter. In the lore frequently told in our family, he would always greet women he knew, whether at church, in his office or on the street, by raising the index and middle finger on his right hand and saying, "Dr. Roger Blackford, at your cervix, ma'am." He would be hauled before the state medical review board on ethics charges a generation later. Women did not think it was a bit funny, but he would always laugh heartily, and so would any men who happened to be nearby.

But the best story about Dr. Blackford had to do with his response to a potentially career-ending accident. He was working with some lab equipment when a glass implement broke and severely cut his right hand and wrist, severing some tendons. He was told he would probably never be able to do surgery again. He went out the next day and bought a baby grand piano, had it placed in his living room, and began to learn to play. It was a matter of many months, but the strenuous exercise of his hand had him back in the operating room, plus, he became a very good pianist. He was our family doctor until we moved to Indianapolis two years later, and he and his family continued as friends and frequent visitors for a decade.

My father was called to be the pastor of Eighth Christian Church in Indianapolis in 1939. The Church building was located at 14th St. and Belleview Ave on the West Side of the city, just north of Washington Ave. and near the factories where most of the men in the congregation worked, Diamond Chain and Link Belt. Our family moved from a rental house in Beech Grove to another on Mount Street, two and a half blocks from the church and right across the street from School #75.

I hung out at the school yard across the street and all spring and summer long watched "the big kids" play baseball, all the time thinking forward to the day when I would get to play too. The school yard was gravel, small crushed, so that it was not too hard on anyone who fell. But you did not want to slide into third base or home.

Behind our house was an alley, and on the other side of the alley were some houses that faced Tremont Street and several adjoining vacant lots which were the impromptu neighborhood trash dump. There were mounds of dirt and gravel, lots of rusty paint cans, old car parts, fallen and pruned limbs and brush, old tires and occasional "finds," like casters off an old wash tub or a piece of an inner tube that could be used to make a sling shot.

It was a great place to play, especially cops and robbers or cowboys and Indians. Jerry, a year older than I, and who lived two doors down, had a b-b-gun. He was the owner and expert: only he was allowed to pour the b-bs into his mouth from their package and spit them into the tube on his Red Ryder pump action carbine. And, of course, he got the most turns at shooting at the tin cans we set up on mounds. I got to set up the cans.

Indianapolis was a good place to grow up. The annual 500 mile race at Speedway, just a couple miles out Highway 52 from our home on the West Side, was more than just a yearly event, it was an obsession. I never went to the race on Memorial Day: all the kids thought it was long and boring. But the time trials were a must each year for the week before the big race. You could get in cheap, and the cars went at top speed, trying to qualify, but almost as important, to secure a good starting position. The fastest car on the first day of qualifying got to start in the "pole position:" inside car on the first row. That day was the most fun.

For weeks prior to the race, and especially on the big day, all the neighborhood kids would work on their model race cars, eight to twelve inches long, carefully carved to look like an Indy racer, numbered and painted with the colors of each kid's favorite driver. Each car had a string attached to the front and the race was really a foot race, we pulled the cars around the "track."

There were strict rules: if your car turned over on a curve the owner had to go back and set it up right before proceeding. If someone kicked or stepped on another kid's car, it was a one lap penalty. The racecourses were up and back on one of the neighbors' paved driveways, or around a paved area in the playground at School 75. We would qualify for starting positions just like the big guys, and the longest race would be on Memorial Day.

I also loved going to Riverside Park. Indianapolis surely had other parks, and maybe some of them were just as nice, but Riverside was close, and it is where we always went. The White River runs through the city and the park occupies a large tract of land on its banks. In the summer it's where we picnicked, rode the roller-coaster and the ponies, and after I got my first bike, it's where we headed after school.

What I remember most vividly, however, was how beautiful it was in the evening, streetlights aglow and totally deserted after a fresh snowfall. Dad loved to drive around after it had snowed and stop to rejoice in the glistening elegance of his favorite spots, the drive through Riverside Park being at the top of the list.

We lived on Mount Street through my second-grade year when we moved to a larger house one block over on Belleview. I suppose that offerings were up and church officers could afford a little nicer place for the pastor. I know that my mom was happy about the move and had probably lobbied for it. That's the house I remember best. There were two upstairs bedrooms with a connecting bathroom.

I had the back bedroom, and it had a large closet on one side under the eaves of the roof, and a cubby-hole den on the other where I had a desk. I spent hours in my little den making model airplanes and carefully painting them with "dope," a thick glossy paint made especially for that purpose, and boy, did it smell good. I am sure I and thousands of kids like me could have gotten high on that stuff if we even had a clue as to its potential.

These were the years of World War II, and all the airplane models were of Air Force and Navy fighters and bombers. The model kits came with a block of balsa wood which had the shape of the fuselage printed on it, plus a longer, flatter piece with the printed shape of the wings and other parts. I had a set of three X-acto knives that I used to cut out the shapes, trim them into some resemblance of the pictures on the plans and then sand them into smooth surfaces, ready to paint. Each one took several days to complete. These were often among the gifts I received for Christmas and birthdays.

That all sounds pretty militaristic now, but at the time every young man in the church and the neighborhood was in the military and the war was constantly on our minds. Every second or third house had a white banner with a red border hanging on the wall or in a front window, and the banners had one or more blue stars to represent the number of men or women in that household who were in the military. Every Sunday's worship included news from "our men in uniform," though there were women in uniform, too. Whenever there was a death, a huge outpouring of support ensued, and the blue star was replaced with gold.

In addition to my model airplanes, I was a member of the Junior Civil Air Patrol. It sounds official, but I think I sent off for my membership certificate and included a cereal box top. With my membership came a spotter's guide which had the silhouettes of German and Japanese aircraft. It was not clear what members were to do if we spotted one . . . in Indiana. I studied that booklet with eager intensity and could distinguish a Messerschmitt from a Junker, or a Mitsubishi from a Zero. Every time an airplane went overhead all the neighborhood kids would look up, anxiously, straining to see if it was the enemy.

One of the big changes when we moved to the new house was a victory for my Mom. We got an electric refrigerator. On Mount Street we had an ice box on the back porch next to the kitchen. It was wood on the outside and had metal faced insulation on the inside, with four doors, two large ones for food, and two small ones at the bottom for ice. The ice man came twice a week and brought a fifty pound block of ice which he chipped in half with an ice pick and put half in each of the small compartments. We had our own ice pick stuck in the door jamb to use when anyone wanted to chip off some ice to put in a drink or in a pitcher of lemonade.

There was careful financial planning involved in getting that new, top of the line Crosley Shelvador refrigerator, so called because it was the only brand on the market with (you guessed it) shelves in the door. The result of the financial planning was scrimping on everything for several months, plus $100 from my college fund, with my enthusiastic consent. Now we had ice from an ice cube tray, though I was sad to see the ice pick disappear, it having had a sort of silent aura of menace about it.

Most of my life in those years, when I was aware of it and when I wasn't, centered around the church in one way or another. On Sundays there was church school and worship in the mornings, and worship again in the evening. On Wednesday evenings: prayer meeting; on Thursday mornings: the Christian Women's Fellowship.

Some of my earliest memories were reciting verses or singing songs for the women. They seemed to dote on me, and my mother lapped it up. I especially remembered the day when it dawned on me that something was not right about that. The other kids at church did not get taken to the women's meetings, much less get up and recite or sing.

The moment of crisis occurred when one of the women decided to surprise my mother by having me recite a sweet little poem about mothers at the meeting one week. She invited me to her house down the street and Mom let me go. She drilled me on the poem and made me swear to keep the secret. I guess the secret keeping was too much for me and when the fateful, appointed moment came I disappointed and embarrassed one and all by barfing. When Mom found out what had happened she was so angry that, thank heaven, the performances stopped. I am not sure what she said to the offending woman, but everyone got the message.

On Sunday evenings after the worship service we would go home, and friends would start arriving. Four other pastors and their wives from neighboring churches of our denomination would arrive to do postmortems on the events of the day in their respective congregations. They all came to our house each Sunday evening because the Russells were the only ones who had a kid, namely, me. The men had all been seminary classmates at Butler University School of Religion, and they were all eagerly seeking to build up their church memberships. So, most of the conversation was a sort of ecclesiastical pissing contest.

"How many new members did you take in today?"

"Well, it was a slow day and I only had two 'additions' this morning."

"Well, we took in three this morning and one tonight."

"Hey not bad: that's eight for the month so far at your place."

It was a congenial competition. They were all in it together and relished each other's successes. Coffee was the drink of preference. Of course, I was hugged and kidded by all of them until my bedtime. One of the happy features of the new house on Belleview was that, after being sent to bed, I could sneak down to the landing on the stairway and eaves drop unobserved until even later. That's when the jokes and stories about weird or obstreperous church members were told, each greeted with uproarious laughter.

Bob Lewis was a big, rotund man with a great sense of humor and a deep baritone voice. One of his stories is a classic. "I have been trying for months to get folks to be quiet during the organ prelude on Sunday mornings. They come in talking and keep on talking and waving at their friends even after Mabel starts the prelude. She tried upping the volume for a couple of Sundays, but no one seemed to notice. I tried getting up and solemnly saying, 'Let us prepare our hearts *in silence* during the organ prelude.' But they kept right on talking."

"So this morning I asked Mabel to play a long, quiet number and I went around the building, up the stairs to the balcony before the people started coming in, and when they were talking away I shouted in my deepest voice, 'Be still and know that I am God!' Then I snuck back down, went around the building, and casually went into the chancel. It was deathly quiet." Three weeks later Bob reported that the trustees had voted to paint "Be Still and Know That I Am God - Psalm 46" on the proscenium arch over the chancel.

It was on one of those Sunday night occasions, with me listening in secret on the landing, that I learned that my best friend's father was driving my Dad crazy. Don McLain was a character in his own right.

Even in 1946 and '47 he still drove his old Ford Model A sedan. He kept it polished and in good repair and, though it smelled a little musty, it ran smoothly and he clearly intended to drive it indefinitely. His theology was of the same vintage, and he likewise had no intention of updating it either. He taught a men's Sunday school class, and every Sunday morning he would dissect and contradict Dad's sermon of the week before. That, of course, would be dutifully reported to Dad by one of his friends in hushed tones between Sunday school and worship.

The conflict was probably inevitable. My dad was deeply committed to social justice, was a 1930's Social Gospel liberal in his theology, and didn't mind challenging traditional, conservative perspectives in his sermons. His final dissertation in seminary was written in 1936 under the guidance of the professor of Old Testament and was titled, "The Idea of Social Justice in Hebrew Prophesy." In that thesis he pointed out the over-emphasis on personal salvation of most Christian writing and preaching of the time, to the extreme detriment of the Old Testament prophets' clear emphasis on social justice and ethics.

Don McLain apparently wanted to hear about getting saved, avoiding the fate of the damned, and going to heaven. Instead, he was hearing about poverty, working conditions and a Messiah who would "execute justice in the land." I am sure he wanted his pastor to "stay off politics and preach the Gospel," a challenge pastors have heard for generations.

I had been clueless about all that, but I suddenly understood from comments my Dad made at one of those Sunday night sessions that my best friend, Dickie McLain's dad was in running conflict with mine. I spent many hours at the McLain's house and he spent many at mine. We each had a large collection of toy soldiers which we kept in boxes, easy to carry one block away to play soldiers on the living room floor at the friend's house. We also put in many hours playing pitch and catch with a baseball in one or the other of the back yards or hitting and fielding ground balls.

I particularly liked him because my other two good, close-by friends were fun to be with, but were a little awkward. They had a hard time catching or hitting a ball, so we didn't play ball. Scotty Bartlett lived right across the street and his family was also part of our church. His dad was an auto mechanic, a real grease monkey, and had a shop in the garage behind their house. Scotty and I could hang around in the garage and mess with the tools his dad wasn't using. His dad would periodically remind us to "put them back where you got them and don't step in the grease."

The main attraction to going to Donny Dixon's house was that his dad was a parts manager at one of the local Ford dealerships, and there was usually a brand new car parked in front of the house. In addition, his mom, Kathryn, was a happy jokester and always had something good to eat. She was the only one of the mothers, except mine, who drove a car.

I went to Dixons' a lot. It was the one place I was allowed to spend the night. Maybe it was because they had a bigger house and I was invited, or maybe because they were good friends with my folks. Or just maybe, Mr. Dixon looked down a little on Mr. Bartlett, convinced that everyone should bring their cars to the dealership for authorized service, and also on Mr. McLain, for not trading in his old Model A. How very easily kids learn the subtle social dynamics of adults and conform to the expected behaviors.

I was baptized at Eighth Christian Church on my eleventh birthday, which happened to fall on a Sunday that year, 1948. In the Christian Church at that time there were no confirmation classes or educational preparation except for whatever a kid got in Sunday school. Baptism was administered by immersion: the person baptized was lowered into the water . . . and brought back up, of course. For that the church needed a baptistery, a large tank with steps down into it that could be filled and drained as needed. Eighth Church had one in the back of the chancel with a red drape covering it which was opened only when there was a baptism.

I had told my Dad that I was going to join the church that morning, and told my three friends during Sunday school. None of them had joined the church or been baptized yet; it was usually done when a person was twelve years old, a loose imitation of St. Luke's story of young Jesus in the Temple at Jerusalem. All three of my friends looked at one another and decided on the spot to join up too.

A new boy had moved into the neighborhood that month, and he came to church that Sunday and sat with the rest of us. At the end of the service, when the last hymn was being sung and the invitation to "accept Jesus Christ as your personal Lord and Savior" was offered, we started walking down the aisle, and he apparently thought he was supposed to do that too. Dad knew I was coming but he did not expect anyone else, and certainly not a kid he'd never seen before. Everyone else seemed convinced that the Holy Spirit had struck mightily and for certain. I am sure that the other parents nearly fainted.

Dad led us through the confession of faith, and I saw a tear start down his cheek. I had never seen him cry, and did not understand it then. He welcomed us as members of the church and announced that we would be baptized during the evening service that night. That afternoon was an education for me and an ordeal for him. He had to hustle back to the church to start the water running in the baptistery. He had to get one of the deacons to go over and make sure the tank did not run over and that the water was warm, it being January. He called one of the women and asked her to make sure the white baptismal robes were clean and ready. Then he called the church families to make sure they were OK with baptizing their kids that evening, ready to give them an out if not. They were.

Then he had to find out where the new boy lived and visit the house to tell his folks what had happened. He wanted to let them know that this was not some weird cult that was trying to get a hold on their son and that it would be wonderful if he were baptized that evening, but he certainly did not have to be. I had walked home from school with the boy a time or two. He lived on the way, so I knew which house he lived in.

I waited on the sidewalk while Dad went to the door. I could see him explaining what happened, with gestures toward me. He was not invited inside, but was listened to politely, then came back down their steps and we walked home. Four of us were immersed in the waters of baptism that evening, accompanied by the enthusiastic singing of an extra-large crowd. We did not see that boy again, nor his family.

We left Indianapolis and Eighth Christian Church within a month of my eleventh birthday and baptism and moved to New Orleans, Louisiana. Dad had interviewed with the Search Committee at St. Charles Avenue Christian Church in New Orleans in late December when the Eighth Church folks thought we were on vacation visiting relatives in Ohio. We moved in February. The moving van left on Saturday, Dad preached a farewell sermon on Sunday, there was lunch at the church, and then we went back to the house to finish packing the car.

The last stop we made before leaving town was to say a cordial and conciliatory goodbye to Don McLain. The usually aloof and distant deacon actually walked out to the curb to bid us farewell. I know he was glad to see us go, but though Mom gritted her teeth and bit her tongue, he and Dad were apparently glad they parted that way. Though I was not conscious of it at the time, I learned something important that day.

2

RICE AND BEANS AND SLOT MACHINES

Being a Preacher's Kid, a P. K., was no fun . . . except when it was. I will never forget the snowy Christmas Day in 1947 when we packed up the old Chevy and snuck out of town. We were living in Indianapolis where my Dad was pastor of Eighth Christian Church. He was going to interview to be the pastor of a Church in New Orleans, LA, and Mom and I were going too. No one in the church was supposed to know we were going and that he was considering another church. Only my folks' close friends, Bob and Hazel Lewis knew about it. Bob was the pastor at Seventh Christian Church, about a mile away, and they had been friends since they were in seminary together. We went by their house to say goodbye, and the snow started falling heavily as we left there and headed south.

Dad figured that if we could make it to Louisville the snow would turn into rain and from there it would be easy going. Wrong. The windshield defroster had not been invented yet, or if it had, we didn't have one on that old Chevy. What we had was a little fan mounted on the dashboard which blew air on the driver's side windshield. You had to keep the heater on full blast and hope that the fan blew enough warm air on the windshield to keep it from freezing and keep the wipers fairly free of ice. So, it was drive 20 miles, stop and scrape the windshield, drive 20 miles, stop and scrape the windshield. It made for a long evening. I fell asleep in the back seat.

I was ten years old. I vaguely remember being carried through the rain into a motel somewhere in Tennessee. This was 1947. No Marriotts or Holiday Inns, no Courtyard Suites or Sheratons, they were more like Motel Six in a deep funk. But I was asleep again before I hit the roll-away bed. The next morning, we woke to a clear and beautiful day; sunshine and blue sky. Mom and Dad liked to drive a while before stopping for breakfast, so we stopped in northern Mississippi and ate at a diner, one of those old railroad passenger cars tricked up with a kitchen, several tables and a couple farmers having their coffee. Lunch was in Hattiesburg, MS where we got on US 11 and made it to New Orleans by late afternoon. Mom consulted the directions we had been sent and got us to the home of the Chairman of the Search Committee of St. Charles Ave. Christian Church.

It was still light when we drove to the church to get a first look. The parsonage was next door. We were blown away, or at least, I was. St. Charles Avenue was and is a wide boulevard with a grassy median, huge oak trees with Spanish moss and palm trees in the yards on both sides and in the median, and with stately houses set well back from the street. Trolley cars ran on tracks in the center of the median, and I soon learned that I could ride for seven cents and go all the way down town and back; it took an hour and a half to do the full circuit. The church and parsonage took up an entire block between Henry Clay and John C. Calhoun Streets. The next street over was Daniel Webster: the three great pre-Civil War Congressional debaters. Maybe growing up between them is why I have always been one to relish a good, spirited argument.

The church building was a huge brick structure with stone columns and a dozen steps in the front. The parsonage was a two-story Victorian with wide porches around two sides, a bay window in the living room, and poinsettias in bloom, front and back. The house had four fireplaces, each with elegant tile facings and carved mantle pieces. The ceilings were fourteen feet high, which made it cooler in the summer. I had never seen such a house, much less ever imagined living in one. Thank heaven we did not have to burn wood in those fireplaces to heat the place. There was a large floor furnace downstairs and gas heaters in the upstairs bed-room fireplaces.

Dad took the job, and we moved in February. I was so glad to be in warm, sunny New Orleans I thought I'd never stop grinning. That is, until my first day at school. I was in the sixth grade, and everyone knows how sixth graders are. For one thing, nobody told me that students were supposed to say: "yes, ma'am," and "no ma'am" to the teachers. So, the first time I innocently answered, "uh huh," the room got deathly silent and the teacher slowly turned from the blackboard, fixed me with a withering stare, and through clenched teeth, sent me to the principal's office. As I stood up and walked to the door, trying to look invisible, the other kids whispered things like "boy, are you gonna get it," and "you are in deep shit now." The principal's secretary ushered me into the inner office, the principal looked up and said, "So, what did you do?" I didn't have a clue. He was probably thinking: this kid's only been here a couple hours, how'd he get into trouble so fast?

The mystery was cleared up when the bell rang at the end of class and the teacher arrived at the office. She divulged the horrifying crime that I had committed: when asked a question I had responded, "uh huh." Then she left, and the principal, visibly relieved, told me in his wisest voice: "Son, you're in the South now, and here we say, yes ma'am and no ma'am, yes sir and no sir. You understand?" I nodded enthusiastically and said, "yes, sir." Then he hustled me off to my next class.

The other initial problem was with the boys in my class and in the next class higher, "the big guys." None of them had ever seen a Yankee before. They didn't know that damn Yankee was two separate words. And, I had never heard of the Civil War, or as I soon learned, the War of Northern Aggression. Guess we hadn't gotten to that part in social studies in Indianapolis. But boy, they had heard about it, and in great detail. They especially took some pleasure in telling me all about the damn Yankee occupation of New Orleans and the cruelty of General Benjamin Butler: Beast Butler to them. Now they had 'em a damn Yankee right there in LaSalle School.

It's amazing how danger can sharpen your instincts. I picked out the biggest, strongest looking kid in the next grade higher, Charlie Bayles. He didn't seem to be all that interested in the Civil War, or in anything else he might have been taught, or ever would be taught in school. And thank goodness it was February, because what we did at recess was play basketball out in the school yard, and Charlie could really play basketball and every other sport as well. Well, I told him how good he was, and it didn't hurt that I could play fairly well myself. Every kid in Indiana grew up with a basketball in his hand, a hoop nailed to the garage, and listening to the State High School Playoffs every year. So, with Charlie to tag along behind at recess and lunch time I was able to escape certain annihilation.

It wasn't long till they also learned that my dad was a preacher. Talk about confusing. Except for one kid who was a Presbyterian and another who was Jewish, almost all the rest were Catholics or, as they said, Cat'lics. Priests did not have children! These were the Catholic kids whose families couldn't afford or didn't want to send them to Catholic school, but most were thoroughly indoctrinated anyway, especially about Protestants. So, I was their chance to win a few points for the Blessed Virgin by converting a preacher's kid. I guess that's where I got my initial experience in theological debate.

Plus, as a PK, I was supposed to be, if not totally righteous, at least marginally virtuous. For the teachers that took the form of "I know your father would be SO disappointed." For the kids it took a much more interesting and educational form, like, "hey, Russ, did you hear the one about the traveling salesman that got lost and had to spend the night at the convent?" Or, "hey, Russ, my brother knows a guy that can get us in the side door to see Evelyn West and her Treasure Chest in the Quarter." Or, "hey, man, have you seen this Tijuana Bible? Don't let the teacher see it." You can't imagine the new and interesting things to which I was introduced. As I said, being a PK was no fun . . . except when it was.

That was half my life. The other half was at church, and I was just as indoctrinated as anyone. The Christian Church was part of the Disciples of Christ. That denomination has a very open theological perspective: no real doctrine at all. Instead, we had a series of mottos: "No creed but Christ, no book but the Bible, no name but Christian." "Where the Bible speaks, we speak and where the Bible is silent, we are silent." And then there was: "In essentials, unity; in non-essentials, liberty; in all things, charity." Not a bad basis for theological debates among sixth graders. The "Disciples" are like the Episcopalians in that they have the Lord's Supper every Sunday, and they are like the Baptists in that they baptize believers by immersion. For that a fair size pool, a baptistery, was needed in the sanctuary, and St. Charles Ave. Church had a nice big one.

St. Charles Ave. Christian Church was the only Disciples church in the city. The next nearest was in Baton Rouge, and there were only a dozen or so in Louisiana. My folks felt like they were missionaries: not "holier than thou," but different: in that New Orleans world but not of it. My Dad used to joke to his friends up north about being "in New Orleans, the land of dreams, with collard greens, rice and beans and slot machines."

Casino gambling had only been illegal for a few years. The French Quarter was hopping till dawn most nights, with Dixieland jazz, exotic drinks and exotic dancers, the official term for strip tease dancers. Plus, every filling station and lunchroom had a row of slot machines: "one armed bandits."

My folks really felt like missionaries and foreigners when the issue of race, usually ignored in white New Orleans, reared its head. Mom came home from a Women's Fellowship meeting one day so angry she was ready to pack and head north immediately. The church had an African American man as janitor, and his wife did some cleaning and serving when there were group meetings. Mom made the shocking mistake of referring to her in one meeting as "the colored lady." She was given icy stares from one and all and informed that there is no such thing as a "colored lady." They are colored women. Only white women are ladies. My Dad's long suit was social justice. It kicked into high gear at that moment and things started getting more than a little dicey. He was a genuine, certified Liberal and didn't mind saying so.

And, of course, there was Mardi Gras. We had never seen or imagined anything like it. The parades started in February and, in the two weeks before Mardi Gras Day, parades ran every night. Tens of thousands of dollars were spent on extravagant costumes, floats and elaborate formal balls. Pastors who moved there from out of state usually hated it for the first three or four years thinking about what could be done with all that money and energy, then finally acquiesced and went along with the festivities. Most, like my parents, tried to be "in that world but not of it," a fairly uncomfortable posture when that's all the church folks, like everyone else, seemed to talk about for two months.

As a kid I had no such misgivings. What a great time it was! I could get on the streetcar in front of the house, head downtown, get off at Washington Ave., and work my way through the crowd. I would find a place near the street and spend the evening hollering, "throw me something, mister!" as the elaborately decorated floats went by. Dukes of the "Crewe" rode on prancing horses, the king rode on the first and most elaborate float, followed by a dozen other floats with masked revelers throwing beads and trinkets. There were high school bands, street bands and clowns, all doing the "Mardi Gras shuffle:" trying to keep from stepping in the horse manure. I always headed home with pockets full of junk, which was hoarded and stashed away in a box, to be added to the next night.

Mardi Gras, Fat Tuesday, was the day before Ash Wednesday, the beginning of Lent, when the Catholics began their Lenten fast. All the Catholic kids would come to school, having been to early Mass, with ashes on their foreheads. The guys would rub it off as soon as they got out of sight of the church or their parents. The girls wore the ashes with an air of piety and like a badge of their sanctity, or at least their good intentions. So, who gets sixth grade girls, anyway?

That's the way my life went through elementary and high school. Go to school, play ball, get a late supper, hang out with friends at the sno-cone stand and go to bed. I played sandlot baseball in the spring and summer, usually on an open field at Audubon Park, or at Tulane University. Both were just down the street on St. Charles Ave. In the fall it was touch football with the same guys who lived in that neighborhood, and on the same fields. But in the winter when I was in high school it was basketball, and that was the most fun. I would jump on the streetcar in front of the house as soon as I got home from school, get off at Lee Circle, with its statue of Robert E. Lee, perched atop a high stone column, looking North -- defiantly, we all assumed. The YMCA was right across the street, and I was on one of its teams.

The other guys on the team were from Downtown and its rougher neighborhoods. They were tall and fast and could shoot the lights out, or so it seemed to me. As the coach said, "I was small, but I was slow." My role was to bring the ball up court, pass off, then back pedal to half court and guard against a fast break. I didn't score much. But one day we were winning big and the coach called a play for me. As soon as the other team shot the ball on the next possession I was to run toward our basket. Our guys were bigger, so we almost always got the rebound; whoever did was to throw the ball the length of the court to me for a layup. They did, I got the ball and was so excited I missed the bunny shot. Oh, the humiliation! The other guys laughed and laughed. But they got a kick out of it, and the play became a kind of ritual whenever we were way ahead. So, I did end up scoring once or, if we were lucky, twice each game. I was the snowbird, in more ways than one.

The best part was that after evening games on the weekends, we could catch the streetcar the rest of the way downtown, get off on Canal Street, the main drag through the shopping district, and hang out in the French Quarter and on Bourbon Street. I was obviously not old enough to go into the strip clubs, but if I was with one of the taller guys the doormen would usually open the door and give us a tantalizing peek at the dancer bumping and grinding on stage. Sometimes I could slip into the jazz clubs when a lot of people were going in and out. They could only admit people 18 or older because liquor was sold inside. But once inside it was dark and I could find a place in the back, order a bourbon and coke, and go unnoticed. That's how I fell in love with Dixieland Jazz.

My favorite club was the Famous Door where the Dukes of Dixieland played every weekend night. Frank Asunto played the trumpet and his brother Freddie was on the trombone. They were awesome. They later became the best-known Dixieland group in New Orleans, or anywhere, and made several bestselling records. The clarinet player sometimes doubled on tenor sax, but mostly it was classic Dixieland: trumpet, trombone, clarinet, banjo, piano, bass and drums. The place rocked till the early morning hours, though I had to catch the streetcar and be home by midnight. Looking back, it is amazing what all of us teenage boys were able and allowed to do during those years.

Of course, those glimpses inside the strip joints were stimulating and memorable. There was a kind of sexual electricity in the air in New Orleans, whether you spent time on Bourbon Street or not. It may have been the same in Indianapolis and everywhere else among teenagers, but I don't think it was quite so palpable. I was rarely without a girlfriend, or if so, I would be fantasizing about one or the other of the girls at school. It was all about "making out," or trying to. We all got our driver's licenses on, or soon after, our sixteenth birthdays, and it was always a challenge: who could get the family car, and could we arrange a double date, and who was having a party at their house that weekend.

The parties were usually for someone's birthday and would always be held in the ground floor "rec room" of that kid's house. There are no basements in New Orleans, it being below sea level and surrounded by levees, and most living rooms, dining rooms and bedrooms were on the second level. The birthday kid's parents would periodically come halfway down the stairs to check things out, smile wanly, and quickly withdraw. They clearly had been instructed that if they came all the way down there would be hell to pay the next morning: a screaming fit is the humiliated teenage girl's ultimate weapon against parents. The room would be in semi-darkness, Johnny Mathis or Nat King Cole blaring from a hi-fi set, a punch bowl and cookies available, and cokes in the cooler. Some couples danced, others made out in the corners, but the main event was the gossip and speculation of who liked who, who was going to try to get who to do what, and how successful that might be. It was a hormone city.

New Orleans' music fixation was not lost on me either. I started trumpet in the seventh grade, played in the junior band at Fortier High School in the ninth, and made senior band, last chair trumpet, in the tenth grade. We were known for our accomplishments as a concert band and had superior ratings each year in the state competitions. That was our director's strong suit. We marched at football games, but never in Mardi Gras parades. We were the Uptown public high school. Easton was the Downtown school, and they had a large flashy marching band and were in every parade. We were both envious and disdainful of our cross-town rivals. I moved up through the chairs in our trumpet section until I got to be second chair for part of my senior year, but the first and third chair guys were clearly better. I was good enough to get a music scholarship to college and thank heaven for that.

After graduation from high school I went away to college, all the way to Lexington, Kentucky on a Greyhound bus to Transylvania College. The music scholarship and a job at the dining hall waiting tables made it all possible. There I discovered that being from New Orleans was a novelty, and that my new friends, most of them from Kentucky, Ohio and Tennessee, were eager to drive me home for Christmas or spring vacation and stay a couple days in that huge parsonage on St. Charles Ave. No more Greyhound buses, and lots of fun with college friends in the Big Easy.

It was during my senior year at college that the big crisis happened. The church burned down! The fire started in the electrical wiring in the attic and the roof burned and fell into the sanctuary, leaving nothing but the hollow shell of the brick walls. The fire was discovered in the middle of the night and dozens of fire trucks from all over the city raced to the scene and pumped thousands of gallons of water into the building. The next afternoon, after the flames were extinguished, the Fire Chief arrived to inspect the damage. He went into the smoldering building while firemen rolled their hoses, and the press waited outside. He emerged a half hour later, soaked, water sloshing out of his boots. He had fallen into the totally full baptistery! He said to the reporters, good Irish Catholic that he was, "I don't know who these people are, but I think I am one of them now." One of the firemen who had accompanied him remarked, "When he came up out of the water, he was not saying Glory Halleluia!" New Orleans . . . what a city!

3

BAT BOY FOR THE PELICANS

"Want to Be the Pelicans' Batboy?" The headline on the sports page of the Times-Picayune newspaper one day in March of 1951 jumped out at me. I was fourteen years old and loved baseball. My dad and I had gone to the New Orleans Pelicans ball games several times each summer and I loved to play and watch baseball. The "Pels" were the AA farm team of the Pittsburgh Pirates and played in the Southern Association. Dad and I had also gone to see the Indianapolis Indians when we lived there, and they were the AAA farm team of the Pirates. In fact, one of my favorite players from the Indians, Stan "the Man" Wentzel, was now with the Pels. He was a power hitter and a hero of every kid in Indianapolis and now in New Orleans. He was one of the "veteran players," and it never occurred to me that that meant he was on his way down the professional baseball ladder.

The headline that day was followed by an article that invited kids to write an essay on "Why I Want to be the Pelican Bat Boy." Dad showed me the story and suggested that I enter the contest. I sent in my essay and won. That was the beginning of one of my most delightful youthful adventures. A sketch of me surrounded by cartoons of a bat boy getting in the park free, handing a bat to one of the sluggers and getting autographed baseballs appeared on the front page of the sports section in April. I was an instant celebrity at school. Even the older guys started hanging around, mainly wanting me to get them a broken bat or a scuffed-up ball that was going to be thrown out. We would nail brads in the bat handle and put yards of tape around it to hold it firm. That and the scuffed balls saw a lot of action from that time on in my neighborhood.

Dad took me to the ballpark several days before Opening Day to meet the General Manager of the team and with the trainer, Tiny Tunis, who showed me what I was to do. They gave me the smallest size Pelicans ball cap they had, and Mom had to alter it so it would fit. They told me I was going to get a small uniform with BB on the back where the players' numbers were. In the meantime, I was to wear my jeans and a white tee shirt; I already had a pair of spiked shoes. I had to be at every home game unless I was sick, in which case the manager's son, Robbie, would fill in. *And,* I would get to go on one road trip with the team. I was so pumped and full of myself by the sudden celebrity that I nearly floated to the park every evening. Pelican Stadium was at Carrolton Avenue and Tulane Avenue, and I could get on the streetcar in front of our house on St. Charles Avenue and ride all the way there.

Tiny Tunis, the team trainer, was intimately familiar with all the players. He was the one who massaged their sore shoulders and wrapped their banged-up knees and twisted ankles. There was a training table in his room and a steel whirlpool tub. The shelves were stocked with various liniments, different sizes and kinds of tape, rubbing alcohol, aspirin: everything to try to make and keep the players functional. He had a bucket of ice water, laced with ammonia in the dugout for each game. The ammonia made it super cold, and it was there in case anyone sprained an ankle. They could put it in the bucket immediately and stop the swelling. Tiny took me under his wing. I had a bench outside his training room and a couple hooks on the wall to hang a shirt or jacket, and a place under the bench for my spikes. He would warn the players to watch their language around "the preacher's kid," and I would wince, figuring I had heard it all by that time at school and in the French Quarter.

By the time I got to the ballpark on game days the players were already dressed and out on the field taking batting practice. Each player had his own bats; all Hillerich and Bradsby Louisville Sluggers, but made to order in various lengths and weights, and with some slight variation in shape. There were bats by other companies, but I never saw any professionals at that time who used anything but Louisville Sluggers. Each guy had his own preference in bats, and his number was painted on the end of the bat handle. My job before the game was to make sure that each player's bats were in the proper place in the bat rack with the numbers outward. During the game I sat on the top step of the dugout, by the bat rack and retrieved the bats after each hitter headed for first base or back to the dugout.

Tiny was adamant that I pay attention to the game on every pitch: "We don't need you to get hit in the head by a line drive foul ball." And, "Watch out for our guys after a strike out; sometimes they get mad and throw the bat." Neither foul ball nor thrown bat ever came close, though his admonitions made me uncharacteristically attentive.

Most of the players were young hopefuls, with a few veterans mixed in, like Stan the Man. The player who was kindest to me was Norman Morton, a right-handed pitcher. He let me hang around his locker and kidded with me a lot. In 1951 he was in his second professional season, having been drafted by the Pirates organization and played his first year in Single A ball in 1950. New Orleans was a step up and many thought he was on his way to the "big dance." The next year was his best and he was the opening day pitcher, an honor reserved for the best guy coming out of spring training. Our catcher was Larry Dorton, and in papers that week the sports writers wore out the line, "Morton and Dorton, the Pels' opening day battery." Norm pitched a four-hit shutout, and we won.

The biggest star was Frank Thomas. He played left field and led the league in batting average, runs-batted-in and home runs. He was big, strong and fast, and was the only player on the Pelicans team that year that did well in the major leagues, and boy did he do well. He was called up to the majors by Pittsburg in 1953 to replace the legendary Ralph Kiner whom the Pirates traded that year to the Chicago Cubs. Thomas did not make the Pirates fans forget Kiner, but he played well and was a

National League All-Star in 1954, '55 and '58. He played with or against some of the Hall of Fame greats of his day: Ernie Banks, Hank Aaron, Roberto Clemente and Eddie Matthews. He finished second to Banks in RBI's and home runs in several seasons. Thomas was on the first New York Mets team in 1962, batted clean-up in that infamous initial year, and led the team in RBI's and home runs.

There were, of course, no African American players on teams in the Southern Association in 1951. We had one Mexican player in the outfield, Felipe Montemayor. He was tall, lanky and lightning fast, and he played center field. He was a good hitter and could steal bases. He was called up to the Pirates the same year that Frank Thomas was, but did not do well in the "Bigs." His English was not very good, though certainly better than anyone else's Spanish, and that made him a sort of loner on the team. In one game he misjudged a routine fly ball, and it dropped in for a double. When the inning was over and the team came back off the field and into the dugout, the manager growled, "What the hell happened out there?" Monty responded, "The sun got in my eyes." The manager exploded, "It's a *night game*, dumb ass!" Monty shrugged and said, "Must have been the moon."

That manager was Rip Sewell, the famous blooper ball pitcher. He had pitched for the Pirates for most of his career and had compiled a strong win/lost record. Along with the usual array of pitches he mixed in an occasional "eephus" pitch, which was lofted about 15 to 18 feet in the air and came down with uncanny frequency right over the plate. Batters who were looking for the fastball or curve had their timing so badly thrown off they would often fall down swinging. In addition, they took it as a kind of insult, a crank pitch, and would try to knock it a mile. Of course, the harder they swung, the less likely they were to connect. As a manager he was surly, and Tiny tried to keep me out of his path. Rip always had a huge chew of tobacco in his cheek and was the all-time champ at spitting tobacco juice. He was famous for his raging anger at a bad play in the field, at which times he would look for something to kick, his usual target being the ice bucket.

All summer long I looked forward to my road trip with the team, and the time finally came in early August. Dad took me to the new Union Passenger Terminal downtown late one night where I boarded the train for Nashville with the team. Tiny Tunis and Norm Morton were looking out for me and assured Dad that everything would be fine. It was an overnight train, so we got on the Pullman cars, and I was assigned to an upper bunk above Tiny. I was so pumped and full of myself: off on a road trip with a pro baseball team! That's when I began to learn how much fun those guys were having: constant traffic up and down the corridors all night, loud jokes and bawdy songs: ". . . oh, roll your leg over, the Man in the Moon." They loved baseball and were good at it, but they also loved the jock culture.

This was also my first introduction to the pro baseball daily schedule. We woke up late, rolled out for breakfast in the dining car before arriving at Nashville's old gothic train station on Broadway a little after noon. Then it was off to the hotel. Everyone unpacked in their room -- my roommate was Norm Morton – then they hit the streets to see what they could find to do in Nashville. There was plenty. I went to a movie with Norm and two other guys, still feeling like a hot shot. Then at 4:00 pm we looked for a place to eat. Game time was at 7:30, batting practice and warm-ups started at 6:30, and everyone was expected at the ball park by 6:00. After the game is when it really got interesting.

We ate dinner after the game, usually around 11:00 pm, and it was a big dinner, steak or chops and potatoes. These guys could pack it away. I noticed a lot of people waiting outside the locker room after games. Some were the older players' wives who made the trip, but there were a number of attractive young women who seemed to know some of the players and who apparently went to dinner with them. I was clueless. I went straight to bed after getting in from dinner, under the watchful eye of Tiny Tunis. I was aware that there were card games going on in other rooms and in the lobby. Then it was up in the morning around 10:00 am for a late breakfast, usually in a greasy spoon near the hotel, and the routine started all over again.

The ballpark in Nashville was even more dilapidated than Pelican stadium. Locals claimed that it had been a ball field since 1870 and that the park was built in 1901. It looked like it. It was referred to as Sulphur Dell because it had been built on a sulfur spring that supplied the city at the turn of the 20th Century with supposedly medicinal waters. The right field fence was short 262 feet from home plate, some 40 or 50 feet nearer than in most ballparks. To compensate somewhat, the wall was extra high in right field, like the "Green Monster" in left field at Fenway Park in Boston. At Sulphur Dell the right field wall had a fence on top and totaled 30 feet high. The Nashville Vols loaded their roster with left-handed hitters who specialized in golfing low, inside pitches over that wall.

To complicate matters for opposing teams there was a four-foot em-bankment that ran along the base of the right field wall at a 45-degree incline and with a narrow, ten-foot-wide ledge at the top, a unique con-figuration which made outfielders nervous as they thought about field-ing drives off the wall or running up the bank to try to catch one. The embankment made for some crazy caroms off the wall and numerous extra bases for the Vols. We lost two of the three games there.

The next stop was Chattanooga to play a three-game series with the Lookouts. In contrast to Sulphur Dell, the ballpark in Chattanooga had typical dimensions: 377 feet down the left field line and 330 down the right. It was a good place to play, and, after Nashville, the team relaxed and played well, winning two of three games. We caught the train the morning following the last game of the series, bound for Birmingham and a four game weekend series with the Barons.

The last two games in Birmingham were a Sunday doubleheader, and one of the big attractions all around the league was a blooper ball demonstration by Rip Sewell between games. One of the sluggers for the Barons was the younger brother of the famous Charlie "King Kong" Keller. His little brother was known by opposing teams, of course, as "Ping Pong." He did not like that too much. He had the gorilla build of his brother, and the bluster to go along with it, so there was a lot of shouting back and forth. He was going to try to hit Old Rip's blooper ball, and he intended to smash it.

Sewell started him off with a couple medium fast balls and a curve, all of which he knocked a mile. So, he started taunting Rip to throw the "eephus" pitch. It finally came, and Ping Pong swung for the fence, missed by a foot, and fell on his behind, to the delight of all the Pelicans. After a couple more pitches Rip reached unnoticed into his back pocket and pulled out his special ball. Tiny Tunis had rigged it up with a small parachute, and on the way up it looked like all previous bloopers, but when it started down it floated slowly down halfway to home plate. Ping Pong ran toward the mound and must have swung three times before it hit the ground, producing laughter from the crowd and both teams. If he was acting and going along with the joke, he was superb.

The trip back to New Orleans that night was by bus. The team had won enough games on the trip to stay in first place in the league, so it was a happy and raucous ride. Some slept, or tried to, but most hollered back and forth and, when necessary, broke into a familiar chant: "Driver, driver, don't we rate; stop this bus let's urinate." Thank goodness there were a few opportunities to do so on U. S. 11 at that hour, though I am sure the driver was frustrated with how long it took, especially if food could be purchased on site or across the highway. It was Tiny's job to make sure that everyone was back on board to continue the ride. I fell asleep and was awakened when we pulled into the parking lot at Pelican Stadium in New Orleans where my folks and all the families were waiting to take us home. I had a lot to tell my friends in the next few days.

The "big boss" of the entire Pittsburgh Pirates organization was the legendary Branch Rickey. Rickey was most famous for having broken the color line in major league baseball by bringing Jackie Robinson to the Brooklyn Dodgers in 1947. He had previously developed the first minor league farm system for the St. Louis Cardinals, an organizational innovation that established the Cardinals as winners for years. Rickey became the General Manager of the Pirates in 1950 and was viewed as a genius and guru. He is credited with bringing the great Roberto

Clemente to Pittsburgh. Everywhere Branch Rickey worked his magic he produced World Series contenders within a few years. He was on a tour of the minor league farm teams when he came to New Orleans and watched several Pels games. Everyone was in awe.

One of the results, though he probably had it in mind much earlier, was calling Frank Thomas up to the Pirates. Another was of much less note. He told the Pelicans general manager that they could not have a 14-year-old batboy on the field; the team could not get liability insurance in case I got hurt. Tiny Tunis gave me the bad news and told me what a good job I had done. Then he told me that they would like me to be the Press Box Boy. I made the change without a lot of enthusiasm and spent the rest of the season hustling up and down long flights of stairs to get food for the sports writers and announcers, and to keep the cooler of drinks iced and full. It turned out to be a lot of fun, and the best part was that they offered me the job for the next year too. Now I had to go to the General Manager's office and fill out the forms to get a paycheck; they paid me! It was not a lot, but I felt that I was now a working guy, hanging out with the sports writers, and I had a key to the press box so I could get there early and get everything set up.

The regular crowd in the press box included journalists from the (then) three New Orleans daily papers, guys who carried on a friendly rivalry over who got their stories in fastest, had the best accounts of the game, and got good headline placement. There were usually a couple stringers who lived in New Orleans but wrote for the opposing teams' local papers: piece work. The writers had the largest area, a long line of chairs at a shelf-table looking out over the field. Above and behind them on a platform were the official scorer and the public address announcer. The former kept the official score card for the game, and on any disputed or questionable calls (was it a hit or an error?) he made the final decision. In those cases, there would be animated arguments among the writers as to how it should have been scored. The official scorer had the panel of switches that controlled the lights on the score board. When he flipped the switch for the error light on the big board, someone was sure to groan, "It was a bad hop; base hit, bad call."

On the first base side of the press box was a partition, and beyond it a small area for the broadcast guys. In 1951 that included a telegraph operator who sent the play by play by Morse Code to the eight cities of the Southern Association where local announcers would describe the game over local radio. Next to him was the Pelicans' own radio play-by-play announcer, "Rooster" Andrews, "the Old Redhead." When the team was playing away games Rooster would sit in a small broadcast studio downtown at WDSU, take the play by play off the teletype and, complete with a sound effects machine which had a dial for the roar of the crowd and one for a bat hitting a ball, would announce a dramatic play by play of the game. He had his own versions of "It's going, going, gone," and "Here comes Rip out to the mound; looks like Morton will get an early shower."

There was a special section down the left field line, halfway to the fence, for the "Negro Patrons" who were, of course, not admitted to the grandstand. There were no Black players on any of the Southern Association teams, but with Branch Rickey as our big boss and with him having brought Jackie Robinson to the majors just a few years before, there was much speculation. Would the Pels have to take a Black player, and if so how would the city and the league respond? The issue never appeared in any story that I know of, nor was it raised in any broadcast, but it was the subject of animated discussion in the clubhouse and press box. Yet, the situation, though tinged with trepidation, was entirely abstract. The same old racist assumptions continued, unexamined. The Old Redhead still would call out for his radio audience, "There's a high fly ball into left field; it's curving foul, and it's into the Coal Bin. Look at 'em scramble!"

In retrospect, though I clearly remember the chatter all around, I am embarrassed at how oblivious I was to the tension which underlaid the prospect of dramatic and radical change to the status quo in the South. Clueless, as ever, I had a great time at the "*old* ball game."

4

NICE THROAT

T he Trailways bus left New Orleans late, of course. It was early September and Brucene Cook and I were off to enroll for our freshman year at Transylvania College in Lexington, Kentucky. We had been friends ever since my family moved to New Orleans in 1948 when my dad became the pastor of St. Charles Avenue Christian Church. Brucene's family was very active in the church, and the two of us had been in Sunday School classes and youth groups since we were eleven years old. Her older brother, Bobby, was a senior at Transy and was already in Lexington. It was a church related college and about half of the kids there were from Christian Churches, mostly in Kentucky, Tennessee and Ohio. It was a long and boring ride, and though we had been friends for years we soon ran out of conversation.

We reached Birmingham in the afternoon, Nashville in the evening, and Lexington late that night. Bobby met us at the bus station, loaded our luggage in the back of a borrowed car and took us to the campus. I slept only sporadically on the bus, and was glad to finally arrive, and get some sleep. Bobby let me into the men's dorm, Ewing Hall, gave me a key to a room on the second floor of the freshman wing and helped me drag my luggage upstairs. He then hustled back to the car to take his sister to Hamilton Hall, the women's dorm. His room was downstairs on the first floor of Ewing, and he said he'd see me in the morning and we'd get breakfast.

To say that Ewing Hall was Spartan would be more than kind. It was seedy and bare. The hard wood floors had not been refinished in decades, if ever, and the beds were iron bunks. There was a sink in the room, two desks, each with a goose neck lamp, two desk chairs and two chests of drawers, all of which had long since seen their better days. There was a single light fixture in the ceiling, a frosted white globe with two bulbs and a brown ring inside the globe, a feature whose meaning I was soon to learn. There was a closet with a rod for hanging clothes and with hooks on both sides of the door. The showers, urinals and toilets were down the hall and resembled a locker room lavatory. I was not put off or particularly disappointed. It was college; it was 1954; what did I know?

My luggage consisted of a Samsonite suitcase and a medium-sized footlocker. They had been high school graduation presents. I had to get in the footlocker to find sheets and a blanket to make up the bed. I chose the top bunk (easier to make up) and figured that when a roommate arrived, we could decide on a permanent arrangement. I found a pillow on a shelf in the closet, made up the bed and climbed in. There was a deep sag, but it did not deter my sleep. I woke up early the next day and started to unpack. Bobby knocked on the door a little later and we walked down to the Transy Den to get breakfast. It was a "greasy spoon" and soda shop on the corner across from the gymnasium. He had already walked two blocks to get Brucene at Hamilton Hall, and she was waiting in a booth. After breakfast we got a quick tour of the campus before Bobby had to leave us to begin greeting and helping other arriving freshmen. It was quick, not because we were in a hurry, but because the campus was small, just four-square blocks, with the girls' dorm down the street. We returned to our respective dorms to finish settling in.

Brucene and Bobby Cook both had dark hair and eyes, and both were energetic and outgoing. Brucene was tall and pretty. Bobby was short, funny, a perpetual motion dynamo and a born leader. I always looked up to him, and it was because of him, in no small measure, that we both went to Transy. Bobby was voted Mr. Pioneer his senior year, a big deal, and Brucene was voted a Crimson Beauty several years in a row.

They were great friends to have when you show up on a strange campus, far from home, and more than just a little bewildered.

The college had been founded in 1780, chartered by the Virginia General Assembly as the first college west of the Allegheny Mountains, hence, the name, Transylvania, which means "across the woods." It was the sixteenth college founded in the U. S. and among its first contributors were George Washington, John Adams and Thomas Jefferson. Famous graduates included Stephen F. Austin, John C. Breckinridge, and Jefferson Davis, along with 50 United States Senators and 101 Congressmen. It had been named Kentucky University for several decades, and had a law school, medical school and divinity school since 1818. When the land grant colleges were established in 1878, Kentucky Agricultural and Mechanical University was formed and moved across town to the present location of the University of Kentucky. The old campus was left in the hands of the church trustees and the original name was restored.

Ok, that's sort of interesting, but "how do I get out of having an 8:00 class?" That history was told to freshmen with great flair and feeling, though it did not mean much at the time. What it meant in practical terms was that we had some very old buildings. The most prominent was Old Morrison which had been built in 1833, a classic Greek revival building of stucco over brick, gleaming white and at the head of the circular drive, which was the main entrance to the campus, a drive which, of course, no one ever used except for parking. Old Morrison is where the venerable Lexington native, Henry Clay taught law school classes. Its east pediment contained the tomb of Constantine Samuel Rafinesque, a well-known botanist of the 19th Century, who wrote and published the earliest scientific classifications of the region's flora. He was not a popular professor and was relieved of his duties when accused of an affair with the college president's wife. In parting he placed a curse on the school. He was buried in Old Morrison anyway. Go figure.

Since the college is named Transylvania, which is also the name of the region in Hungary that is the fabled home of Count Dracula, one of the big events each year was Halloween. Ghosts and goblins, vampires and hideous creatures roamed the campus after dark, especially frequenting Rafinesque's tomb in Old Morrison. There were ghoulish parties, ghastly treats and horrific tales, all climaxing in the staging of the play, "Dracula," by the drama department at midnight.

The title role my freshman year was played by a tall, dark-haired theatre major who seemed born for the part. It was carried off with as much faux seriousness and dramatic overacting as the occasion demanded and the raucous audience would allow. There were numerous intimate moments that night when a guy would gaze at his date and murmur, "Hmmm, you hav-a ze nize-a throat." The festivities ended after the final curtain, in the early morning hours, with a weary but noisy revel around the tomb and, of course, an invoking of the curse.

We freshmen trudged back to Ewing Hall and turned on our lights to get ready for bed. After about ten minutes a strange smell began to emanate from several of the rooms, and guys started looking out into the hall, sniffing the air, only to discover that the smell was coming from inside our rooms. The more they looked the worse it got, until someone shouted, "Holy Shit! It's in the light globe!" The victim residents looked up at their ceiling lights and saw to their disgust that piss was just starting to simmer in the fixtures.

By then it was 2:30 am, not a time to try to unscrew the fasteners holding the globes in place, especially since they were hot as hell, much less try to get a globe with a substantial amount of hot piss down from the ceiling and to the bathroom at the end of the hall. Most just gave up, turned out the light and figured they would deal with it in the morning. The mystery of the brown ring was solved.

I was at Transy thanks to a music scholarship, which paid half my tuition, plus a job in the dining hall that paid for my meals. I needed to make enough money doing summer jobs to pay the balance of tuition and for my dorm room. My folks provided money for books, travel and ready cash. The music scholarship had been awarded on the basis of a letter of recommendation from my band director at Fortier High School in New Orleans. I don't know what he said, but it could not have been too positive and still been truthful. I was not a particularly good trumpet player and the highest I ever got in that section was second chair. So, Bob Bricker, the conductor of the wind ensemble at Transy, took a chance in giving me a scholarship. I was very nervous the first few days of band practice as we read through the music we were eventually to play in the fall concert. He started me off as second chair, first trumpet, and on the third day he apparently decided to find out what I could do.

We were playing a suite by Gustav Holst, and the second movement began with a trumpet solo that was fairly difficult. There was an initial chord by the woodwinds, then the trumpet played the melody alone and it had an octave jump that our first chair player had some trouble with. Bricker said, "Let's take it again from the top of the second movement and, New Orleans Sam, play the trumpet solo." I figured that was me. I nearly wet my pants, but didn't have time to really get nervous. He immediately gave the downbeat, the clarinets and saxes played the opening chord, I came in on cue and I nailed the solo. I could see his eyebrows arch upward as his face said, "Whoa, OK." We finished the piece and the session, and I walked out on a cloud. I would be brought back down to earth, but not for a while.

In my sophomore year I was first chair, and the next year I picked up a little extra scholarship reduction by also being band manager. That meant that I made sure that the drums and bass horns made it to all ball games and concerts and back again to the band hall. The reality check came on the first day of band practice my senior year. A freshman on scholarship was placed in second chair next to me, and it became apparent within fifteen minutes that he could play circles around me. He had better range, better articulation, and was a better sight reader. I was blown away and embarrassed to be sitting a chair ahead of him. I wasn't in that spot for long. I hope Verle Pennington became a professional musician, a conductor if not a trumpet player. He was the best musician I had met to that point. He knew that I knew how much better he was, and he took it very casually, so I could do that too. We switched chairs within the week.

One of my friends from the first week of school in my freshman year was Russ McClure. He was a trombone player and a very laid back, funny character. We got particularly close when he started dating Brucene, and by the end of the year that relationship was serious. So serious was it that Russ came home with me that summer so he could continue to date Brucene. His dad was the parts manager at a dealership in their hometown and had provided a repainted and fixed up Plymouth coupe for him. Russ and I took turns driving and drove the three of us straight through to New Orleans. Hey, who had money to stay at a motel, especially since we would need two rooms.

Russ stayed in one of the upstairs bedrooms, ate with the family, and he and I went to work every morning with my old buddy, Paul Wilson. All three of us had gotten summer jobs at the American Radiator and Standard Sanitary Corporation plant out on the lake front on Lake Pontchartrain.

It was the first experience for all of us working in a huge factory. We made toilet bowls and tanks. Every time I go to the bathroom at someone's house or in a public restroom I look to see if it says "Standard" on the back rim of the bowl. For several years, if it did, I could look inside the tank and find a number stamped into the porcelain that indicated which of the guys we worked with had made it. I don't think anyone ever saw me checking out their toilets.

All the guys who made and finished the molds and the actual products, and made good money, were White. All the guys who swept the floors, pushed the racks of molds, tanks and toilets to the dryer or the kiln, were Black. Except for Russ, Paul and me. I worked mostly in the mold shop, getting the plaster molds from which the actual molds for the bowls and tanks were made back and forth to the skilled guys who poured and trimmed them. I would later be called to pull the new molds on their wooden flats into the dryer. I monitored the dryer four times a day to make sure it was at the right temperature.

Russ and Paul worked in the next phase of the process, getting molds out of the dryer, taking them to the shop floor, then taking the "green," still soft products to the kiln to be fired. They had the hardest job. Several racks of bowls, rims, tanks or lids would be stacked on a large, framed, steel dolly and they were very heavy to push and very hard to stop once they got going. Only twice did one of the racks get out of control and crash into a door, smashing all the freshly formed bowls. There was hell to pay: the guys who made them would not be paid for their day's work, which was on a "piece work" basis. Russ and Paul had the harder job because they were both stocky and stronger than I. I was tall and skinny, and not to be trusted with a rack of new toilets.

Water fountains were conveniently located throughout the factory. In every case there was an ordinary upright cooler labeled, "White," and a smaller one beside it labeled, "Negroes." After the first couple weeks, Russ started drinking from the latter. When anyone pointed out his error he would feign ignorance, shrug and smile. But he kept on doing it. It got to be a standing joke on the floor: "the dumb ass kid from Kentucky doesn't know whether he's white or Black." I was not so brave, and, having grown up in New Orleans, it would never have occurred to me to do it anyway.

One day six of the guys grabbed Russ, lifted him off the ground and held his face in the flowing water of one of the "Negro" fountains, he and they laughing all the time. No one talked about it after that, he continued to drink from the "wrong" fountain and it was clear that the Black guys who worked with him looked at him a little differently, with a measure of appreciation, mixed with the fear: "that white boy gonna get himself some trouble."

That summer ended with Russ and Brucene getting married by my dad at St. Charles Ave. Christian Church. Paul and I were groomsmen, Brucene was her beautiful self, Russ was a nervous wreck, and the place was packed with well-wishers. Then it was back to Transy, Russ and Brucene in the old Plymouth. I don't remember how I got back.

Transylvania was a very small college, slightly fewer than four hundred students while I was there, and there were thirty faculty members. It was an eerily contained society, a kind of Petri dish of intense interaction. It certainly never occurred to me at the time, but I had been born in 1937, one of the lowest birth-rate years in the 20th Century. The reason for that, no doubt, was that the country was still in the depression years, jobs were scarce and incomes low; many folks could not afford to have kids. One of the results was a very low enrolment of freshmen for several years in a row, more than adequate facilities in every college, and low student–faculty ratios. We probably got better instruction than we might otherwise have gotten, and solicitous attention from the faculty who had a stake in our making good enough grades to stay in school.

There were four sororities and four fraternities on campus, and each had a chapter room in the basement of the respective dormitories. The social life of the campus was organized around them, with each having a dance in the spring and fall, most in the Hamilton Hall Ball Room on the first floor of the women's dorm, and most students came to all of them. Intra-mural athletics was a big deal, with each season, football, basketball and softball, being six games long, and each fraternity played the other three twice, followed by a tournament.

Basketball was the big intercollegiate sport; hey, this was Kentucky! Everyone went to all the home games. All the students who lived in the dorms also ate in the same dining room in Hamilton Hall, and all at the same time every day. So, we all knew each other well and pretty much knew who was doing what to and with whom.

There were three "dating rooms" on the main floor of Hamilton Hall. The rules were simple: the door must stay open; both parties must have both feet on the floor at all times. Mom Franks made regular and frequent, usually unobtrusive passes by each of the rooms as the enforcer. There was a lot of making out in the halls and in the corners after a date and before curfew by those who were not lucky enough to get a Rose Room.

There was more of the same going on in the parking lot behind foggy car windows. None of the girls had cars and only a few of the guys did. So, it was advantageous to have a friend who lived in town and could get his parents' car for a weekend double date. Again, we knew each other pretty well, and what we didn't see we heard about. There were a number of marriages between couples that met at Transy. Only a few were rushed. This was before the pill, of course, so, to put it delicately, a high level of personal discipline was exercised, mostly by the women.

Working in the dining hall was where I learned some of my most valuable lessons. 1) If you are late, everyone else has to work harder and they don't appreciate it; 2) if you don't hustle, everyone else is slowed down and they, like wise, don't appreciate it. And we all knew each other well enough that the signals were clear; be on time, work hard, and we will all do well and have fun.

A lot of the fun was in the back, around the dish washer, out of sight of the diners. The dish washing crew, aka, the Slop Slingers, had an *esprit d' corps* that was manifested in raucous joking and singing. Plates were scraped into the garbage, racked and shoved into an ancient, clanking, institutional size dish washer, removed, dried and put away till the next meal. The garbage was carried out back to be picked up by the chef's cousin who raised hogs. It was a nice ecological cycle. I always wondered if he sold us pork and ham.

The chef was Marshall and he and all the cooking staff were Black and, needless to say, the only ones on campus who were. Everyone else on the dining hall staff was a student: all white. In retrospect it is embarrassing that none of us even noticed or thought it was worth noting. There was a lot of laughing and joking with Marshall and the four women who helped him in the kitchen, but no one knew where they lived or had any contact outside the confines of our dining hall.

My job for four years was as a waiter, busboy and drier of plates and silverware after the tables were cleared. During my senior year I was the head waiter, which meant that instead of waiting and bussing two tables of eight students, I had one student table and the front-and-center table of the two Hamilton Hall house mothers. The two house mothers always entered last, and the doors were closed behind them, with everyone standing till they were seated. They would then signal for me to lead a musical table grace: "For health and strength and daily food we give Thee thanks, O Lord. Amen." Everyone sang, and when the house mothers were seated, everyone sat and the meal was served. Serve from the left, pick up from the right; just like Emily Post decreed. In retrospect it seems unbelievably quaint, but it was probably not atypical of that era in a small, Southern college.

I actually learned some valuable lessons in my classes. The most important thing was how to write well. Only in a small college like Transy and maybe only at that time could someone like me have as a professor of Freshman Composition, English 102, a Harvard PhD. John Harrison was a remarkably able and patient teacher. Why he was at a small, undistinguished college in Kentucky is a mystery to me, and I chalk it up to the vicissitudes of academic life in that decade. Whatever the reason, I learned to write. His teaching also awakened me to the vast and interesting world of English literature, and I became an English major.

The English faculty had only four professors, so I was able to take at least one class each year with Dr. Harrison. There were two other memorable teachers in that department. Harold Douglas, who specialized in American literature, was a recent master's degree graduate of University of Tennessee, and we all saw him as very urbane; he just had that air about him. Verna Mitchell Clarke taught Shakespeare and Elizabethan Literature, and she looked the part, a tiny woman with a thin face and carefully coiffed white hair, who always, *always* wore high laced collars tied at the neck with ribbons. Both, like Dr. Harrison, were good classroom teachers who wanted us to do well. My big "take away" learning was, 1) learn to write well and creatively; 2) learn to sense what is most important to the professor and always be prepared to speak or write extensively on that dimension of the course. Those lessons got me through college and seminary.

My graduation took place on a Friday morning in early June of 1958. I had already been accepted at Vanderbilt Divinity School and had a job lined up for the summer so that I could afford to enroll at Vandy. It was a hectic day. Brucene and Russell McClure graduated with me, and Bobby Cook, Brucene's brother, who had been a senior when we were freshmen, graduated that same day across town at College of the Bible, one of our denomination's seminaries.

All the Cooks, McClures and Russells came to Lexington for the festivities, and after the ceremonies went to nearby Shaker Village for dinner. Then the Russells were off to Indiana, where my dad was to receive an honorary degree, Doctor of Divinity, from his seminary *alma mater*, Christian Theological Seminary, which had been the Butler University School of Religion when he attended. That evening he became Edward E. Russell, D.D. He always said the D. D. meant "donated dignity."

The next day Mom and Dad drove me back to Lexington, then made the long drive on to New Orleans as they had in 1948, ten years earlier. And who could have guessed the turmoil that would engulf us and the nation in the next ten years. A few did, but we were oblivious to the gathering storm that had already begun to break in the United States Supreme Court and then at Central High School in Little Rock, Arkansas.

5

SOUTHERN WHITE BOY GETS A WAKE UP CALL

Following my college graduation in June 1958, I needed a car. My old buddy, Russ McClure's dad was a shop manager at a dealership in Somerset, Kentucky. He found a 1948 Chevy that was in good condition, made all the needed repairs, serviced the car and sold it to me for $400.00. Dad and I went to Somerset to pick it up on the day after my graduation from Transylvania. He and mom then went back home to New Orleans while I stayed an extra day in the dorm at Transy, then loaded up all my stuff and headed south and home.

That summer I worked as an office boy and gofer at the local Hyster dealership. Hyster made, sold and serviced forklift trucks and other heavy equipment for the factories and warehouses along the Industrial Canal and on the Mississippi River docks, as well as for loggers in the Delta area. I had a corner desk in the large front office with the secretaries and salesmen. The manager's office was a separate room beyond that front area, and the shop was in the back. The manager was a member of the church, and my dad had gotten the job for me. I felt like a really hot number, riding the St. Charles Ave. streetcar downtown to work every morning. I read the morning paper on the way, folding it length ways, the way I had seen businessmen do on the streetcar. I don't remember actually reading anything but paying close attention to who was noticing how cool I was.

At work I mostly ran errands, driving a company car to pick up parts for the guys in the shop from businesses that made bearings, machine replacement parts and industrial equipment. I also folded, stuffed, stamped and mailed advertising brochures for new models of our forklifts, or other equipment to send to our various customers and potential customers. The manager, who was a particular friend of dad's, took me to lunch several times and tried to explain the business, including interesting conversations on business ethics. I think he could see that I was marginally interested at best, but he was patient and indulgent.

I did get a kick when one of the brochures I sent out produced a batch of orders and made the company some profit. The secretaries took calls for the orders and forwarded them on to the supplier. I sold a hundred or so Little Bull Winches and never even left the office. Most days I walked to a greasy spoon down the street for lunch and had po'boys with guys from the other shops in the area. I heard some great jokes and learned some new levels of swearing that had never been dreamed of in college or at the toilet bowl factory where I had worked previous summers. The summer passed quickly.

I had been accepted at three seminaries for the entering class, fall of 1958. All of my classmates from college who were preparing for seminary, except one, were going across town to College of the Bible (now renamed, Lexington Theological Seminary). I did not want to spend the next three years with the same guys (and it was all guys, of course). I leaned toward going to Pacific School of Religion in Berkeley, California, a beautiful campus overlooking San Francisco Bay, and I had lots of relatives in northern California. But I loved my old Chevy, and I was not at all sure it would make it over the mountains. So, I decided to go to Vanderbilt Divinity School. Two friends from Transylvania were already there and vouched for it. That was a half-assed way to make a decision, but it turned out to be a very good one. I would later think of it as providential.

When the day came to leave for Nashville, Tennessee and the beginning of my seminary education, I packed up the Chevy with all my accumulated goods, including my Samsonite two-suiter and my footlocker, and headed north. I arrived in Nashville in the early evening and found the Disciples Divinity House where I would live for the next year and a half. It was a recently constructed two story building two blocks from the Vanderbilt campus, and it provided several double and single rooms for single students, and a number of apartments for married students. It was operated by the Christian Church (Disciples of Christ), the denomination of my youth, and was about the best housing option in the area. The "Disciples" had four graduate seminaries that served the denomination, and several Divinity Houses at ecumenical seminaries, Yale, Chicago and Vanderbilt among them, where students from that tradition could live while in seminary.

I got my key from the house manager, unpacked my belongings in my room and then wandered the halls and hung out in the lobby which was equipped with a ping-pong table. That's where I met George. George Depee was from Pampa, Texas, a graduate of Texas Christian University, a fellow Disciple, and a pretty good ping-pong player. We bonded immediately, and took in the orientation sessions together, routine and dull events where we met the faculty and acted impressed. At several of the sessions we each stood, told our names, where we went to college and our denominational affiliation, smiled and tried to look studious and pious. But it became clear who was and who was not the pious type. We found each other. We started referring to ourselves as "the heretics," and it stuck. Some on the faculty were not amused, but others were solicitous, hoping someone in their classes would actually ask challenging questions at some point.

One of the happy realities of seminary life was intra-mural sports. It was September, and we were recruited by upper class seminarians to play on the Divinity School's touch football team. I had never played high school or college ball as some of these guys had, and I wasn't very big or fast, but I could catch a football. So, I went to a practice on a field near the campus and that's where I met Bob Keck. I much later learned that Bob had been a small college All-American, and he could throw the perfect pass.

We played the Med School, the Law School, the Engineering School teams and the B-teams of the fraternities. We won about half of our games, mainly because Bob was such a good passer; in touch football every down is a pass play. If Clay, the other receiver, and I ran the right route and turned at the right time the ball would be there. It is hard to express how much fun it is to catch a pass, elude a defensive player and make a good gain or, best case, a touchdown. Bob would become an important part of my life decades later.

* * * * *

The full significance of the fact was not apparent initially, but one of our entering classmates was James Lawson, the second African American student ever admitted to Vanderbilt Divinity School. He was part of a very cautious effort by the university to begin admitting black students, one at a time, in graduate programs. We soon learned that Jim was not only one of the brightest students among us, but he had spent several years following college in prison as a conscientious objector to the Korean War. After his release he became a Methodist missionary to India, spent three years there, including months at an ashram with Mohandas Ghandi, learning the disciplines of non-violent resistance. The Methodist Board of Missions then encouraged him to enroll at Vanderbilt Divinity School to get his seminary training.

Though none of us students knew of his background, the Divinity School administration and faculty must have known and had some idea of his purpose, in addition to completing his seminary studies. Jim was soon put in contact with students at Fisk and Tennessee A & I Universities, both Black schools. The Nashville Christian Leadership Council, an affiliate of Martin Luther King, Jr.'s SCLC, had made the contact. Jim began meeting with the students in the winter of 1958-59 and teaching them the principles and disciplines of non-violent resistance.

The US Supreme Court decision in Brown vs. Board of Education had been handed down on May 17, 1954. It stated, "We conclude, unanimously, that in the field of public education the doctrine of 'separate but equal' has no place. Separate educational facilities are inherently unequal." Years of editorial posturing and much consternation and uncertainty followed. Southern school boards tried to figure out what this meant for their schools and how they might respond, and citizens groups were organized to oppose desegregation. But no definitive action took place for several years, and day-to-day schooling continued pretty much as usual in most southern communities.

The action and the news soon shifted to the bus boycott in Montgomery, Alabama. Rosa Parks got on the Cleveland Avenue bus on December 1, 1955, sat down in a seat near the middle of the bus, which was permitted under the bus company's rules. But when the front of the bus filled with white patrons further along the route, she was required to move back. She did not. After a tense exchange with the driver, the police were summoned, and Ms. Parks was arrested and taken to the police station. Local Black leaders were contacted and they began to organize a boycott. A young pastor, Rev. Martin Luther King, Jr., who was fairly new to town, was recognized as a resolute and steady voice, and he was encouraged to assume leadership. The boycott went on for weeks and provided a protracted news story that was carried all over the nation.

I had ridden on segregated public transportation in New Orleans since I was eleven years old and thought it was weird but paid no further attention. No one else in the city thought it strange in the least. Every streetcar and bus had an ironically worded wooden sign which fit into holes in the back of each seat. It said, "Colored Patrons Only Behind This Sign," as though it was for their benefit. As white riders boarded the signs would be moved toward the rear if the seats were full in front. As "colored patrons" got on and vacant seats were in the front, the sign would be moved forward, unless, of course, a white person was sitting in that particular seat. It was a flexible arrangement, sort of, but the clear message was: "We do not sit together, and white folks have precedence." Black people usually got up and moved back without comment if a white person needed a seat and moved the sign back. It was just the way it was done. With the news from Montgomery, it began to dawn on me that the system was not just weird, it was not fair.

Another significant event then grabbed the headlines. The Brown vs. Board of Education ruling was first manifested in concrete action in Little Rock, Arkansas. The Board of Education there was the first in the nation to issue a statement of compliance with the federal law. It was a phased program, and the first step was to be the limited desegregation of Central High school, scheduled for September 1957. That was the beginning of my senior year in college, and the daily news from Little Rock was a constant specter in the background while my classmates and I went through the normal *sturm und drang* of the final year of our undergraduate studies. But, by the time I began my first year at Divinity School the next fall, the issue was on everyone's mind, especially our faculty members' and that of our classmate, Jim Lawson.

The sit-in movement burst on the scene in February 1960 when four students at North Carolina A. and T. University in Greensboro took seats at the lunch counter at the F. W. Woolworth store downtown and refused to move when ordered to do so. Within two weeks there were sit-ins in eleven cities (Juan Williams, *Eyes on the Prize*), including Nashville. The students who had been organized and trained by Lawson for the previous year mobilized 200 classmates and friends for sit-ins at several downtown lunch counters beginning on February 18. It was stunning. As each group of students was arrested and taken into custody that day, a new group would sit on the vacant stools and await their own arrest. The Nashville Police filled the jail. In all, 79 were arrested in the first days, and lawyers for the NAACP went to work to secure the students' release.

Lawson was arrested in an even more dramatic fashion. On March 4, police officers went into the sanctuary of First (Negro) Baptist Church in downtown Nashville and led a non-resisting James Lawson down the front steps in hand cuffs. The news media were out in force and the photo of Lawson was flashed all around the world. In it, Jim was flanked by two officers and they were passing the church's sign which displayed Pastor Kelly Miller Smith's sermon topic for the coming Sunday: "Father, Forgive Them." Lawson was booked and stood trial that day along with the last 17 of the demonstrators. They were charged with violating a state law against conspiring to interfere with commerce and business. This was a new charge; the earlier defendants were charged with disorderly conduct, though their conduct had been anything but.

In a bizarre twist, the Vanderbilt University Board of Curators had already expelled Lawson from school for civil misconduct under a vague rule that had been adopted several years earlier to punish students involved in a panty raid. The venerable guardians of rectitude and the status quo exercised a creative use of an irrelevant rule to maintain order and preserve the Southern Way of Life. They were guilty of only one oversight: they did not consult the Dean of the Divinity School in which Lawson was enrolled, in violation of standard, established academic procedure. The dean was Dr. J. Robert Nelson, a noted scholar and well-known ecumenical leader of that era. He and the majority of the Divinity School faculty threatened to resign, which would have closed down the school.

Dean Nelson began negotiating with University Chancellor, Dr. Harvey Branscomb, who was himself a noted New Testament scholar. They agreed to an arrangement whereby Lawson could be readmitted and finish his degree. The Board of Curators, the trustees of the university, refused to accept the compromise, and in May Nelson and a dozen of the other faculty resigned and began seeking other teaching positions. The incident was big news in the seminary world. Letters of support poured in from all over the world, including some of the most prestigious theological faculties. Positions were immediately made available for Vanderbilt's very highly qualified resigning professors. They left. We students were not sure there would be classes when the fall semester began.

In response to the sit-ins Nashville's mayor appointed a committee to resolve the issue. Their recommendation to have all stores maintain separate lunch counters (separate but equal?) was rejected by both the sit-in leaders (still segregated) and the downtown merchants (too expensive). The next step was to get representatives of the two groups together to work out a solution. In preparation for the first session the downtown merchants agreed to meet under two conditions: First, that representatives of the sit-in activists be included; they had found to their surprise that the conventionally acknowledged leaders of the Black community did not really represent the students. Second, they insisted that no white person be in the delegation; as they said, "whenever whites were represented they started preaching about morality!" (Westfeldt). The negotiators met three times and came up with a plan to have a controlled number of students come to the lunch counters over several weeks' time, to be served by the stores' wait staff. It worked. The lunch counters remained open, and by June the city breathed a sigh of relief.

It is interesting and instructive that the sit-ins were not effective by themselves. There was a spontaneous boycott of downtown stores by the Black citizens of Nashville which began within days after the first arrests. No one could put their finger on how it started, but one observer had heard that it started with four African American women at their regular bridge game. Each of them agreed to call ten friends and ask them not to shop downtown until the lunch counters were desegregated. Whatever initiated it, a boycott developed rapidly, was announced in most of the African American Churches of the city and became a major force.

The two prominent downtown department stores reported substantial losses in sales over the next months, as did other downtown businesses. It was apparently a shock to the leaders and citizens of Nashville that adults in the Black community were just as frustrated and determined to change the status quo as were the students. When that fact became clear, a solution was not far behind: the downtown merchants needed their business.

The facile assumption of southern whites had long held that Black people were satisfied with their circumstances and did not support the students or any such disruptive activity. They repeatedly intoned the nostrum that it was outside agitators who misled the students. This conventional wisdom was suddenly and resoundingly shown to be false. It was also a wake-up call for southern white liberals who were all for equality in principle, but counseled gradualism through legal means. Direct action went giant steps beyond that approach.

* * * * *

At the Divinity School the impact of the social change that was taking place before our eyes was profound. In addition, the very personal crisis of the expulsion of Jim Lawson, a friend and classmate, and the reverberations throughout the seminary and the university caused many of us students to rethink our sense of vocation. I had committed myself to prepare for parish ministry in the presumably stable, middle-class environment in which I was reared. Now it was more than clear that any ministry would have an additional dimension which would call for a deeper commitment and a whole new orientation toward social justice. For me, as someone reared in the Deep South, the experience carried a clear sense of obligation to serve in the south as an advocate for racial justice and reconciliation.

Several of us had participated in later sit-ins in March and April at the bus and train station lunchrooms, and members of the faculty joined us. I still have a very vivid image of sitting with a black student from Fisk at the Union Station's segregated lunch counter, and professors Gordon Kaufman and Langdon Gilkey sitting with us. The purpose of that and other such demonstrations was to show that there were whites who not only did not object to eating with Blacks, but who also supported the movement.

Every class that semester took on a new depth of relevance and excitement. In Old Testament Theology, Prof. Everett Tillson taught the justice message of the prophets with passion, and he showed how the Ten Commandments *all* pertained to the sin of racism (use your imagination). In our class on the History of Christian Doctrine, Prof. Gilkey showed how issues of social justice in each generation tested the Church's faithfulness. It was a turning point in our understanding of our faith and of the ministry for which we were being prepared.

My closest friend, Malcolm Carnahan, had gone to a noontime demonstration on a day that I had a 1:00 class. It was a "stand-in" in front of an upscale, downtown restaurant that refused to serve African Americans. Here the tactic was for a mixed-race group to attempt to enter the restaurant to be served, and when denied entry, to stand in a tight semi-circle around the door to make it difficult for other diners to enter. As in earlier lunch counter sit-ins, there were several white teenagers who taunted, shoved and finally punched several of the demonstrators, among them, Malcolm. A graphic photo of one angry young guy punching Malcolm was taken by an Associated Press photographer, picked up by the Associated Press, and appeared in newspapers around the world. Malcolm and his assailant were both arrested and hauled off to jail.

Malcolm and I had begun attending meetings of the student group which planned the demonstrations. That group eventually took the name, "Student Non-Violent Coordinating Committee," thus identifying with the movement that spread throughout the South. The two of us were probably viewed with a mixture of suspicion and forbearance, and we did not have much to offer except that we could turn out a few of our classmates for demonstrations. That was seen as a plus. Malcolm was elected treasurer of the group, so I guess they trusted us some.

The meetings were usually held at Howard Memorial Congregational Church across the street from Fisk. It was a local church of the historic Congregational Churches that founded Fisk University and other distinguished Black colleges, though I did not understand the full significance of any of that till years later. Participants in those meetings varied from week to week, with a number of students from the two Black universities attending when they could. The Chairperson was James Bevel, and he and Diane Nash were at every meeting that Malcolm and I attended. They, of course, became well-known leaders in the movement over the next years.

We also met John Lewis. At the time he was a student at Baptist Theological Seminary and later was assaulted and beaten when he was a Freedom Rider and again as the leader of the march across the Edmund Pettus Bridge in Selma, AL. John became a key figure in the Civil Rights movement and was one of the speakers at the March on Washington where Martin Luther King's famous "I Have a Dream" speech made history. Unknowingly, I was present at events that shaped the movement, and that educated me and prepared me in ways I never imagined for challenges in my later life.

Several days after the stand-in where Malcolm was assaulted I responded to a phone call in our apartment, and a nervous young man asked if Malcolm Carnahan lived there and if he was at home. I told him that he did, and he was, and I hollered for Malcolm. When he came to the phone, he recognized the caller as the guy who had punched him earlier that week at the demonstration. I went back to my reading as the two of them talked briefly. In the paddy wagon on the way to the police station on the day of the stand-in and assault, the two had ridden in silence until his attacker mumbled that Malcolm was clearly bigger than he, could easily beat him up, and why hadn't he hit him back? Malcolm had simply replied that he believed in non-violence. That obviously had gotten to his assailant.

That encounter was a window for me into the strange, conflicted, confused internal feelings of many southerners who were suddenly wrestling with traditional assumptions and their painful conflict with new realities. In the following weeks the semi-penitent assailant called infrequently to whisper conspiratorially what his group of guys were planning to do at some presumed future demonstration. He could not finally come down on one side or the other, but the moral authority of non-violent resistance had thrown him into confusion and caused him to waver in his long-standing assumptions. Even this "tough kid," with his inherited racist attitude, could change . . . some.

My previous sense of calling to the Christian ministry had come from a very positive experience in the churches of my youth, including a love of classical, sacred music. Bach, Beethoven, Mozart, and Handel were our steady musical diet in the anthems at church and in recordings played at home, plus we sang the great hymns of Charles Wesley and Isaac Watts. Singing that music, or hearing it well performed, filled me with joy and a sense of well-being. It still does. There were also several experiences of personal inspiration, moments where I found myself in the presence of the Holy and, as John Wesley put it, "felt my heart strangely warmed." Like many in my generation, commitment services at the close of youth conferences were particularly significant as we pledged ourselves to follow the way of Christ, and some expressed the intention to go into "full time Christian service."

But now the necessity of setting things right in American society through advocacy for social and racial justice added urgency and resolve to my sense of vocation. Indeed, some of the most moving spiritual encounters happened in the solemn, joyous, spirit filled services of worship in the First (Negro) Baptist Church that prepared us for each demonstration. Even further, I came to the painful realization that I had been complicit in an insidious system of oppression that gave me privileges as it disadvantaged others.

I had an enormous debt to pay, and I was being given the tools through my seminary education, and the opportunity through the calling to ordained ministry, to pursue a life's work that was very compelling and in accordance with what I now understood as the clear will of God. And, even further, having grown up in the South, I was better able than many to understand and deal with these issues. Further, I had witnessed the fact that change was possible. So, by the beginning of the next academic year, my senior year in seminary, I had a genuine and deep sense of purpose.

I also had some other things on my mind!

6

LOVE, CRAZINESS AND MARRIAGE

anderbilt University Theatre was having tryouts in February 1960 for parts in its spring production of "Picnic," a show made famous in its movie form by William Holden and Kim Novak. I decided to audition for the male lead and stopped by the theatre to sign up. Several days later I arrived at the appointed time, watched from a seat in the darkened theatre as several other guys read for the part, then went up on stage when my turn came and my name was called, mispronounced, as usual: Rowland? Ronald? "It's Rollin, as in 'pollen,' and I'm here."

The redhead who was reading the Kim Novak role for all the would-be William Holdens, sat expressionless center stage as I took a seat angled toward her. I smiled. She made no response. We started reading the scene, the torrid love scene that, in the movie ends with a seduction as a train roars past. I read it in character, and tried to make contact: hey, it was a love scene. She read it straight, as I am sure she was told to do and, after all, I was probably the tenth guy she read it with. I tried my best to get her involved in the dialogue, unsuccessfully, and then I got tickled and started over-playing, teasing. She was not amused. She turned red with embarrassment and everyone in the theater laughed. She gave me a withering glance as I walked off the stage. I did not get the part.

I went outside and waited in front of the theatre till she emerged, having finished the last of the auditions. I said, "uh, hi. I'm sorry about . . .." She kept walking and looking straight ahead. I tagged along. She soon condescended to tell me her name, that she had been in several plays at VU Theatre and had agreed to read for the auditions; that no, she was not in "Picnic." OK. To keep the conversation going I told her I was thinking of auditioning for a part in the play that was to be done at Wesley Foundation. I was a regular customer at Wesley Foundation's noon lunches: soup and sandwich, cheap. A lot of us from Divinity School ate there regularly. I had no idea that she was a Methodist and frequented the place. I had never seen her at lunch.

I found out that the play was Christopher Frye's "The Lady's Not for Burning," and that I could still try out for a part. I went to the auditions and did get a minor role. It was at the first reading by the cast that I saw her next, and I figured that she had come and gotten a part because she knew I was going to be in the play. She liked me! I could hardly wait to take her out and see what would happen. Little did I know that she had long since been asked to audition for the female lead and was to be "the Lady" of the title.

We soon found out that the announced director, fairly well known in theater circles and a friend of the head of the Wesley Foundation, was not going to be able to do the show, and that the Wesley Foundation director had decided to direct it himself. Many were visibly disappointed since he was a total novice at directing. It did not bode well for the production.

It was, however, a topic for conversation, and I managed to get "the Lady" engaged in talking about it and offered to drive her back to her dorm. We were talking away, and it was well before her curfew, so I drove on out to Centennial Park, a popular nearby spot with an exact, full scale replica of the Athenian Parthenon. We walked and talked around that enormous, imposing structure with its twenty-four massive columns (nothing suggestive in that), and I found that she was interested in my participation in the sit-ins, unusual for a Vanderbilt co-ed, especially one from Deep South Alabama. In fact, we found that we agreed with each other on the issues of segregation, desegregation and the sit-in protests.

She had grown up in a large, progressive Methodist Church in Mobile whose pastor had participated in the desegregation of that city's public transportation and who was not bashful about addressing the issue of social justice. It "took" with Betsy. That like-mindedness on racial justice and social ethics became a bond between us from the outset.

I was so pumped that when we got back to the car I came on a little strong. Betsy was not cold to my advances but was certainly not encouraging. We got to her dorm, Tolman Hall, I walked her to the door, kissed her good night, and asked if I could meet her again soon. She was noncommittal. I learned later that she had been more than a little miffed. When she talked to her friend, Claire that night she said that she liked me alright, but I was all hands. Claire responded that she had dated a seminary student who was the same way, and she figured that all pre-ministerial types had to do that to show they were real guys. Give him another chance. She did, and I am eternally grateful to Claire.

The other chance came soon. A State Senator from South Carolina was coming to campus to give a lecture on why segregation was necessary and good for all concerned. I don't know which campus organization invited him, but Betsy and I joined a fairly large crowd in Neeley Auditorium and listened as he worked hard to make segregation sound plausible, legal and noble. There were no questions or discussion following, but Betsy and I hashed and rehashed his speech thoroughly and critically as we left. Our next outing, again not really a date, was a trip across town with Bob Stiles, my friend and fraternity brother from Transylvania College, and also a "middler" at the seminary, to hear Dr. Martin Luther King, Jr. The speech was to be at The Tennessee A. & I. Gymnasium. The three of us were not the only white people there, but nearly so. All the men present were dressed in coats and ties, the women in nice dresses. Everyone was solemn, spoke excitedly about hearing Dr. King, and was polite but not deferential to us obvious outsiders. I had some nervousness about how we would be regarded, and I am sure Betsy did too, but those seated in the bleachers reassured us with smiles and nods. I was impressed that she did not appear to be nervous in the least.

When Dr. King came in and mounted the steps to the platform there was loud applause which he immediately quieted with a gesture of both hands. He went to the podium and calmly announced that the local authorities had notified the administrators of the university that a bomb threat had been received, that we would have to vacate the gym, that we would do so in an orderly fashion and wait outside while the premises were searched and the authorities had satisfied themselves that there was no danger, and that we would *all* then return to the gym for his speech. Just as quietly and decorously as we entered, we all filed out. It was a remarkable display of mutual self-discipline. When we got outside Betsy realized that we would have to leave soon to get her back to Tolman Hall before her curfew. Hence, we never heard Martin King in person. But I bet every other person there waited patiently and then, to one person, went back in to hear the speech.

We dated frequently throughout the remainder of that semester, and that increasingly intense romantic relationship kept me doubly "pumped" as I went with seminary friends to civil rights demonstrations and planning meetings several times a week and went out with Betsy as often as we could manage it. Most weekday evenings we went together to the library to study: my grades got a whole lot better. Betsy was an academic star, later a Phi Beta Kappa, and I had to try to keep up. On weekends we partied or double dated with my seminary friends on Friday nights before the guys all left for our weekend student ministry assignments in nearby small towns.

* * * * * *

For the first two years of seminary, I was a student pastor in the Dale Hollow Larger Parish, which included six small congregations in the villages around Dale Hollow Lake in eastern Tennessee. There was a resident pastor who lived in the parsonage beside the Midway Christian Church, and I was his associate, came up on the weekends and stayed in a small trailer in the church yard. We each led worship and preached at three of the churches each Sunday morning. Services were at 9:00, 10:00, and 11:00 am, lasted forty-five minutes and we had fifteen minutes to drive to the next place, get settled and get the service started on time. We alternated Sundays, so that I could use the same sermon for two weeks and preach it six times! The poor folks at the end of the line on the second week: everything I said I felt like I had just said two minutes before. Then I went back to Nashville to study for next week's classes.

God has a special blessing, I am sure, for the members of the small congregations all over the country which are near seminaries and where generations of pastors received their initial experience. On Saturday mornings, driving the ninety miles to Dale Hollow, I would be thinking, "Now, what was it that Dr. Harrelson said about Genesis 18 and the problem of theodicy?" "Did I remember to bring my notes from that class with me? Oh, shit! What will I do if I can't find them?" Seminary professors across the nation are no doubt painfully aware of how their finest insights and scholarship got garbled in the halting sermonic efforts of their students.

Betsy went with me up to Dale Hollow one weekend near the end of the semester. It was a big deal. We had to find a place for her to stay; it certainly wouldn't do for her to stay in the trailer with me. She stayed with a family in the Love Lady Christian Church. I could not make that up: the community was named Love Lady and I never learned how it got the name. It was the third stop on my circuit for that Sunday and it was one of the larger and more lively of the congregations. They had a pianist who had been a school music teacher and played very well, and the people sang with gusto and in harmony.

In stark contrast was Hatcher Hall where only five or six people usually came and the singing was *a capella* and pretty dreary. The most unique was Bethsaida Christian Church, locally pronounced, "Bethsaydee." The singing was *a capella* there, too, but it was always done with gusto. Tasso Logan was the music director, and they had Stamps Baxter, shape note hymnals. Most had been to singing conventions where they learned to sing shape notes and, of course, bought Stamps Baxter hymnals for the church. Tasso would blow a note on his pitch pipe, sing the notes of the major chord: "do, me, so, do," then count, "one, two, three, four," and off we would go, singing in four-part harmony. *Will the Circle Be Unbroken; How Beautiful Heaven Must Be; Shall We Gather at the River;* they knew them all.

It was a new experience for Betsy. She had been baptized and confirmed in a very large Methodist Church on fashionable Dauphin Way in Mobile. She seemed to enjoy the Dale Hollow experience however, and we finished the day at Love Lady with dinner on the grounds. We were very close by the time we parted for the summer. Betsy went home to a summer job at the Mobile office of the Internal Revenue Service; she worked as a clerk in the Collections Division. I visited New Orleans briefly and then returned to Nashville to take two classes in the summer session. That was my way of lightening the anticipated load for the two semesters of my senior year. I had been elected Vice-President of the Class of '61, and the class President, one of the many married students, resigned at the end of the semester when he learned he had another baby on the way. So, I anticipated a number of extra duties in my senior year and, of course, I didn't want to work *too* hard.

I worked as a dishwasher that summer in the evenings at *The Tulip Is Black,* a coffee house across from the Vandy campus. It was run by a student and a recent graduate who thought it would be a good business and might make a little money. The name came from an old cast iron bird bath with a wrought iron tulip sticking up from the center. Larry Connatser, the artsy one, found it in a junk yard and painted it black. It was situated in the center of the coffee house with the tables arranged around it. I would have called it the Black Tulip, but that would have been too obvious. Larry was a remarkably good painter and several of his paintings were on the wall, and he would later be locally well known as an artist in Atlanta.

We served all manner of fancy coffee drinks and exotic teas. It was a sort of forerunner of Starbucks, and while not an uncommon sort of establishment in Greenwich Village or the Castro, it was very unique in Nashville in 1960. The coffee maestro was a friend of Larry's who could whip up delectable concoctions, and who read Taro cards on the side. We had live entertainment from time to time, mostly kids who were trying to make it in the Nashville music scene and wanted to be heard by somebody. I worked alone in the back room washing cups, saucers and spoons till 1:00 am.

I had resigned from my student ministry position at the Dale Hollow Larger Parish; I could make as much money washing dishes. At my last meeting of the Parish Council the Senior Minister announced that I had resigned and he asked for ideas of what the Council should do. I think he expected someone to make a motion to accept the resignation and express thanks for my two years of service. Instead, Tasso Logan said, "Well, I guess we can get us another playboy from Vanderbilt."

The fall semester of my senior year at seminary, September through early December of 1960, was laughably chaotic, though some of the chaos wasn't all that funny at the time. Half of the faculty had resigned the previous spring over the expulsion of James Lawson for leading the sit-in movement, and new faculty members were arriving and offering their first classes. We seniors had to take our comprehensive exams, the passing of which would qualify us for graduation. This practice was instituted as an alternative to the senior thesis, and it was intended to ensure that graduates were knowledgeable in all the fields of study, not just well informed on the subject of the thesis. The catch was that anyone who failed the comprehensive exam could retake it only one more time, and to fail it the second time meant no graduation, no degree and, aside from the three or more wasted years and thousands of dollars of tuition, no ordination. A student could opt to take it the second time orally before a faculty committee, but that was even more intimidating. So, it was pretty tense.

Happily, I passed, but a surprising number did not. It was such a shock to the faculty that a new approach to curriculum and course offerings was instituted in the spring semester: cross-discipline courses taught by two faculty members. But more important was the sense of near panic among the numerous classmates who did not pass. For several of the Methodists it was downright frustrating. They knew they would be required in their ordination vows to abide by the Methodist Discipline which, at that time, included a promise not to smoke or drink alcoholic beverages. Most were not drinkers, though some would have a beer with the rest of us down at Ireland's Tavern. But to quit smoking; that was asking a lot, and several had been debating for the entire three years of their seminary studies whether they could do it. Maybe they could cross their fingers when they took the vow, knowing they had no intention of quitting. It helped some that Methodist ministers that most of them knew smoked and seemingly thought nothing of it, pledge or no pledge. So, it was tense within the hallowed halls of the seminary.

* * * * * *

In the fall of 1960, I got word of what was going on in New Orleans. The city schools were under a United States District Court order to desegregate and agreed to start with the first grade and tenth, the first years of elementary and senior high school. The story of Ruby Bridges is the most lasting and one of the most dramatic of the many incidents that happened on the first day of school that year, but there were numerous other tales of heroism and of infamy to be told.

My dad was called early in the morning on the first day of school by one of the church's elders, Chuck Bennett, a good friend and supporter of dad's preaching and teaching regarding racial equality. Bennett's son, Ross, was ready to enter tenth grade at Fortier High school, my old *alma mater*. For days the news had carried stories of how white parents were going to keep their kids out of school and demonstrate their anger at the school buildings that morning. Chuck wanted dad, his pastor, to accompany him and his son when they went to school that morning. He agreed to do it, of course. Dad went to the Bennett's house and drove with them to the school where they encountered a hostile crowd around the front entrance, shouting, cursing, spitting on the three of them, the only folks taking a white student to that school that morning. The most painful part of the experience, however, was seeing members of the church in the crowd. Dad smiled; they looked embarrassed.

A few months later a road show of *South Pacific*, the musical stage adaptation of James Michener's novel, came to town. Ed Russell, in his sermon the following Sunday, reflected on the portrayal of Nellie Forbush, the female lead in the show, who was from "Little Rock A-R-K," one of the show's hit songs. She also sang the song whose lyrics rocked the South: "You have to be taught to fear and to hate, / You have to be taught before it's too late,/ Before you're six or seven or eight./ You have to be carefully taught." Dad was pointing to the truth of the lyrics and the ironic image of that song, sung by a character from the city which first barred the schoolhouse door.

Not everyone appreciated the reference! The wife of one of the church's elders, a longtime member of the congregation, stood up in the middle of the sermon, walked to the chancel and started arguing with the preacher. Just before it turned into a shouting match, and before anyone in the congregation wet their pants, the organist had the good sense to start the introduction to the closing hymn. Ruth Winston, our organist, will be eternally blessed for her inspired intervention.

There were letters to the church board asking for dad's resignation, and letters of support from the Board citing freedom of the pulpit and his long and faithful service. But the posse was gathering. My mom and dad were just as much involved in the civil rights movement as I was

* * * * * *

There was also a political campaign going on in the fall of 1960, and all of us were enthusiastic about the candidacy of John F. Kennedy. Malcolm and Mickey Miller and I were sharing a two-bedroom apartment a few blocks away from the seminary. Malcolm had been my buddy and suite mate from the Disciples House the previous year, and Micky was a Methodist seminarian who had been thoroughly disillusioned about the church and churches by his first field work experience and had spent his first year asleep in his dorm room. He was fully awake his second year, and was fun to hang out with. We had a used television set which Malcolm got for $10 at the Goodwill store, which is where we did all our shopping for household items. It was rigged up with a coat hanger for an antenna, the original having been broken off by some previous owner. We were able to get intermittent, snowy reception, enhanced by someone holding the coat hanger, enough to watch the news and delight in the Kennedy-Nixon debate.

We were looking forward to election night with great anticipation. Mickey was dating a graduate student who lived in town, so Betsy signed out for an overnight with her at her house, and four of us and our girlfriends crowded into the living room of our apartment to watch the election returns. We only had one broken down couch and a wire frame butterfly chair, so we took mattresses off the beds and lounged on the floor while we watched. We had laid in sufficient beer and soft drinks for the presumably long night until a winner was declared. About nine o'clock Micky got a phone call and left for half an hour. When he returned, he had a prospective student in tow, a friend from his college who was planning to come to the seminary the next year and was visiting the campus and his friends there. He stayed briefly then left without much notice from the rest of us.

On Thursday Malcolm, Micky and I were called into Dean Herman Norton's office. Our visitor was the son of a Methodist Bishop who thought his father ought to know what was going on at the seminary. By the time the story got to the Dean, we had been having an all-night drunken orgy with mattresses all over the floor and who knows what else! Maybe the Bishop and son were disturbed by our boisterous cheers for Kennedy, only to be further shocked by Kennedy's victory. We will never know that. Whatever the motivation was for the Bishop's call, the

Dean felt he had to do something. So, he put us on "Social Probation." Sounded severe, but the Dean informed us that there was no such punishment in the seminary or the university student code. He also revoked our scholarship assistance for that semester. That sounded serious too, but the grants had already been awarded to cover our tuition back in September, so, no harm was done. The school did not want to be embarrassed by having to discipline the senior class president, so no public statement was ever made, and life went on as though nothing had happened.

Forty-five years later Betsy and I went to our more or less annual reunion with my seminary friends, Malcolm, George, Micky, Bob Stiles and their spouses, all but two of whom had been undergraduate classmates at Vanderbilt. We gathered that year at the Evins State Park in Tennessee. We were reminiscing and laughing about that incident when Bob reminded us that he had been away that semester doing a campus ministry internship at the University of Illinois and was not involved in the festivities. But he had received a mysterious letter which had been forwarded from his Nashville address. It informed him that Dean Norton had put him on "social probation" too, assuming, I guess, that if the rest of us were at the apartment on that infamous night, Bob must have been there too. Bob had no clue until that day *forty-five years later* why he had been put on social probation. None of the rest of us had ever known that he had shared our fate *in absentia*. We all laughed so hard we had to go get another beer.

During the Christmas break in 1960, four of us, plus the women we were dating, went to New Orleans. The guys all stayed at the parsonage next to St. Charles Ave. Christian Church where my dad was the pastor, and the women stayed in the homes of hospitable church members. On New Year's Eve we wandered through the French Quarter, then ended the evening with a champagne toast and took the girls to their lodgings. The guys went back down to the Quarter. On New Year's Day we all went to the Sugar Bowl game at Tulane Stadium, just walking distance from the house. I don't remember who played, much less who won.

We drove back to Nashville the next day to resume our studies and our courting. By the end of the spring semester Betsy and I decided that we wanted to be married. There was no dramatic, kneeling proposal, just a growing sense of rightness about our being together and that our life together would be very good. We started thinking about timing and decided that December, during Christmas break, would be perfect for our wedding.

Betsy had just finished her junior year, and her parents had to be convinced that she would complete her senior year "in spite of being married." In order to make that work, I applied for and was accepted to work on a Master of Sacred Theology, a degree that could be completed in one full academic year, and which would allow us to finish together in June 1962. Betsy worked at the IRS office in Mobile again that summer, and I worked as a carpenter's helper with a construction company operated by Owen Burley, a member of the St. Charles Church.

My ordination service had long since been planned for a Sunday in June, contingent, of course, on my graduation. Betsy and her parents came over from Mobile for the auspicious occasion, and one of my professors from Vanderbilt, Ron Sleeth, had agreed to preach. I was to preach in the morning service, be questioned and examined by the pastors and elders of the other Disciples of Christ churches in the area in the afternoon and then be ordained in an evening service with Dr. Sleeth preaching.

The Sunday morning service went smoothly, and my sermon must have been OK, at least everyone greeting me on the way out said it was just fine. We had dinner with all the guests, and then went back over to the church for the examination. There were probably fifteen pastors and elders from Disciples churches in the area, and after the introductions and expressions of welcome and congratulation, we got down to business. The first questions were softballs: what did you do for your field work? What was your major and why?

Then it got interesting when one of the elders asked, what do you believe about the Virgin Birth? I responded with the standard (at that time) divinity school answer, that it was a classical and typical story of a hero, similar to several others, which indicated that Jesus was anointed by God to be God's special servant or messenger. There were nervous coughs and shuffling of feet, and the questioner asked, "Well, was Mary a virgin?" I responded that she was a young woman, and that is what the Hebrew word in Isaiah meant in the passage that was referenced by Matthew and Luke in their Greek gospels. More coughing and shuffling. A young, recently ordained pastor from a church in Baton Rouge then intervened and saved the day with a long explanation of historical and literary criticism that left everyone with glazed-over looks, and the moderator asked for other questions.

That is when it became interesting. Owen Burley, the owner of the construction company I was working for that summer, then asked what I thought about integration, and I told him about my participation in the sit-ins and in the Student Nonviolent Coordinating Committee. Everyone started getting nervous as he continued on a strange and ironic line of argument: Blacks are demanding things and pushing their way into places they have no right to be and telling us what we can and can't do; if someone draws a line and tells me I can't step across, that just makes me determined to do it.

There was a moment of silence, and it seemed to me that he had made my point and that of the Civil Rights movement, albeit in a strange, backward way. So, I said so. There was another moment of awkward silence. Then the chair of the gathering opined that it was getting late, almost time for the service, and that if I would step out of the room they would take a vote. I did, and they did, and I was invited back and told that the ordination service would proceed as planned and, "congratulations." The vote had obviously not been unanimous, and it clearly signaled the painful realities that would be the warp and woof of my ministry for the next forty years.

* * * * * *

In addition to working on the construction crew that summer, I also served as the part time supply pastor for Bethany United Church of Christ. Their pastor had resigned and left in April or May, and they were glad to have someone preach and lead worship for a lot less money. It turned out that their organist resigned too, and one of my buddies, Bob Patton, who was finishing his pre-med work at Tulane, could play the organ and was willing to fill in.

We had a good time at the church, and I made fairly good money on the construction job. Betsy and I found ways to be together almost every weekend. It was easy to meet in Biloxi. She could ride the train from Mobile and I would drive over to meet her on Fridays after work. We could eat in Biloxi, take a late swim in the gulf, then drive to New Orleans, spend the day together on Saturday and put her on the train back home that evening. She attended church several times at Bethany and went with me to the church picnic in Audubon Park, where she was referred to as "the Reverend's intended."

Everything went suddenly into fast forward, pretty much all at once. I think her mother was mortified: we were engaged, but there was no diamond ring! That is just not how things were done. So, I got a phone call to the effect that a diamond engagement ring was needed, post haste. I was less than thrilled. I was cognizant of what could be done with the money that a suitable ring would cost, and how little we would have to live on. But necessity carried the day.

A diamond ring was purchased in something of a hurry, and it served as a *quid pro quo* for the other problem Betsy was facing. How could she plan for a wedding in Mobile in December while she was studying in Nashville and living at her sorority house? She especially dreaded going through rush, not only for the time required but also because of her negative feelings about the non-inclusive aspect of Greek life. All this was anything but conducive to studying or planning a wedding. The only solution was to get married in September before we went back to school.

For me, that meant contacting all my friends to see if they could come to Mobile for a wedding in September, just before the fall semester. They all could, and with the concurrence of all Betsy's friends and relatives the date was set: September 8. That's when I learned that my folks would be leaving New Orleans in August. They had not been sleeping while the posse at St. Charles Avenue Christian was on the loose.

Dad had visited a couple of churches in Texas where there were pastoral vacancies and accepted a call to First Christian Church in McKinney. So, August was spent helping my folks get moved, settling into a spare room at Bob and Jean Bennett's, working a full week for Owen Burley Construction, courting Betsy and working on details for the wedding on weekends, plus preaching at Bethany Church on Sundays.

The wedding was to be held at Dauphin Way Methodist Church, a grand building on one of the more fashionable boulevards in Mobile. The pastor, Rev. Dr. Carl Adkins, had been Betsy's pastor her whole life and was greatly admired and beloved by her, the whole congregation and many in the community. My close friend from college, John Fryer, was to be the organist. John had been a fraternity brother at Transy, had been in Medical School at Vandy while I was in Divinity School, and we had stayed in touch on an irregular basis, plus he was a dynamite organist. My dad was to assist Dr. Adkins in the ceremony, Betsy's cousin Judy would be her Maid of Honor, and Bob Stiles, my college and seminary buddy would be my best man.

All my friends from seminary came to New Orleans early in the week of the wedding, I quit work the day they arrived and we partied for several days and nights on Bourbon Street before going to Mobile. Betsy worked right up till the day before the rehearsal and was not entirely happy that I had taken several of those days off to party with the "heretics."

When we arrived in Mobile, we found that the Howards' entire living room and dining room was set up with long tables to display our wedding gifts. Everyone was surprised at the loot, but as we looked at who sent what, it all became perfectly clear. Friends from St. Charles Ave. Christian Church sent many of them, and some were clearly guilt

gifts for having made life so miserable for my folks since the desegregation turmoil. We had more sterling silver than the British government,
and more China and crystal than we could have imagined.

The groomsmen were all staying at the Alba Club on Fowl River
where Betsy's folks were members. It was two steps down from a yacht
club and was used by fishermen and crabbers and their families for a get-
away. It had a boardwalk out into the river, which at that spot was very
wide as it neared its opening into Mobile Bay. At the end of the pier was
an octagonal gazebo, a great place for a post rehearsal dinner party.

The guys had brought several coolers well stocked with beer, wine
and sodas, and our girlfriends, by now several of them fiancés, were
there too. As the evening wore on and we joked about this being a very
delightfully weird bachelor party, someone suggested that it would be
only right to throw the groom into the river. We all laughed as they tus-
sled with me and carried me out of the gazebo and down onto the apron
below.

They had me by the arms, legs and belt as they swung me back and
forth: one, two, three . . . . Just then Betsy took off her shoe, a pump
with a four inch heal, and banged Micky on the head. She apparently
had flash visions of the groom drowning before making it to the altar; she was not laughing! Everyone did a surprised double take then resumed the frivolity and heaved me into Fowl River. They had let me
take off my shoes and remove my wallet and watch, so no harm was
done. The river is only about three feet deep, so I stood up and they
hauled me back up onto the deck.

The wedding went off without a hitch, John Fryer tried to raise the
dead with his prelude and postlude, and Dr. Adkins and my dad did
their thing. The reception was in the church's fellowship hall, complete
with punch and cookies and a tiered cake. One of our photos shows
Betsy's and my hands on the knife while cutting the cake. I had worked
outdoors all summer and was very tan; it looked almost like an interracial couple. We both went to change clothes and make our escape and
that's when the fun began.

Several of the guys had prepared well, with soap to write on our car windows, and with strings of tin cans to attach to the bumper. But we had prepared, too. They couldn't find my car. I had parked it on the upper level of a downtown parking deck operated by one of the Howards' close friends, Shaw Freeman. He pulled up on cue in his car at the rear door of the church, my buddies, in their confusion, ran for theirs to give chase. Didn't happen. Shaw knew the area so well that he lost them quickly, then calmly drove us to get our car and head west out of town for Biloxi where we checked into a motel on the beach.

The wedding was on a Friday evening, and we intended to go on Saturday to a Gulf Coast cottage that New Orleans friends were letting us use for our honeymoon. We would then drive to New Orleans on Sunday morning for me to preach at Bethany, then back to resume our tryst. But that's when Hurricane Carla started making her presence felt.

On Saturday morning it was raining hard, really hard. We got the car stuck in the mud on the way to our honeymoon cabin and had to be pulled out by an obliging farmer with his tractor. We made it to the cottage, which had been stocked with all sorts of goodies, including champagne, and enjoyed each other immensely, all the while listening to the weather reports.

When it was announced that water was coming over highway 190 and they might have to close the road and causeway to New Orleans, we decided we needed to head out that afternoon. So, we drove through the downpour and were one of the last cars through before the road was closed. We pulled up at Bennett's house to stay over Saturday night. The Bennetts had a nine-year-old daughter who kept asking, "Who is she and why is she sleeping with Rollin?" She disappeared in a hurry.

I preached at Bethany Church on Sunday morning, and the congregation surprised us with a reception following the service, so we were sent off back to our honeymoon cottage with more gifts and some much-appreciated cash. It is a measure of how I understood ministry and of how Betsy then understood the role she was marrying into, that we went through hell and high water, literally on this occasion, to keep our commitments.

When we went back to Nashville for our final year we had an apartment in the Disciples House, an apartment building sponsored by my Christian Church denomination, and I had a weekend supply job at Auburn Christian Church in Auburn, Ky. It was there that we had our first real argument. It was theological . . . sort of. The stage had been set for it on New Years' Day, 1962, just four months after our wedding. My mother was a true zealot for the Christian Church, and church friends from New Orleans had gotten tickets for all six of us, Mom and Dad, Betsy and me, and the host couple, to the Cotton Bowl game in Dallas.

They took us out to dinner before the game and our host was talking with Betsy and learned that she was baptized (as an infant) and confirmed in the Methodist Church, and he asked, "Are you going to be baptized in the Christian Church?" He meant, of course, re-baptized, as was the practice in some Christian Churches. My mom immediately answered, "Of course she is!"

I made no issue of it then, but I had no intention of re-baptizing her. I had become thoroughly convinced in my theological studies that re-baptism was an inherently sectarian act that denied the authenticity of the prior baptism and hence was an anti-ecumenical act that denied the authenticity of the church that had performed it. No way I would do that!

We argued for several weeks. She did not want to be re-baptized, but her new mother-in-law clearly expected it and, Betsy felt, required it. I argued that it did not matter what my mom thought or what Betsy wanted to do to acquiesce, it was against my principles and betrayed everything I had learned and believed about ecumenical Christianity.

However, on a cold Sunday in January, three weeks later, I told the deacons at Auburn Church that Betsy would be baptized, and they prepared the baptistery: they filled it with a garden hose and dangled three electric coil, cup-size coffee warmers in the water to kind of take the chill off. It was freezing! We went down into the frigid water, both trying to look serious and calm as our lips turned blue, and both grumbling through clenched teeth, she that she was having to be re-baptized and me for having to re-baptize her.

At least we agreed on the basic issue: it was wrong to do it. We also learned that sometimes we end up doing the wrong things for the wrong reasons, still feeling compelled to do them because of the relational dynamics. Had it been 15 years later and had the feminist movement and perspectives been on our mental radar screen, Betsy would probably not have felt so beholden to my mother. But those liberating impulses came a little later. What was so maddening and funny was that the good folks at Auburn Christian Church, while we were both grinding our teeth, thought it was so precious: the young pastor baptizing his new bride! They were elated. Apparently, some good can come from even so convoluted a mess. Welcome to parish ministry!

7

CHARLOTTESVILLE, AND A BIG CHANGE

The phone rang at about 10:30 pm. Betsy and I were still awake and up. She was grading papers from her French classes at Albemarle County High School, and I was reading and scribbling, trying to decide what I was going to say in my sermon on Sunday morning. We finished Betsy's senior year at Vanderbilt and my master's degree at the Divinity School and moved to Charlottesville, Virginia. Park Street Christian Church there was a delightful first parish for me. It was a small church, a new church start of four years before, and I was its' first full time pastor. Though the salary was meager, we were able to get by because Betsy had gotten the teaching job through our church members' connections. The phone call that night was from a woman, a member of the church, who blurted out, "Reverend Russell, please come quick, Walter is drunk and is waving his shot gun around." I said I would be there in five minutes, got in the car and headed over to their house.

Walter had managed to hold on to a job at the local train depot, though everyone was aware that he had a long-standing drinking problem. His wife was a regular at church and had a young son and teenage daughter. She was a cloying, goody-goody type that might drive any man to drink, but the daughter, Angie, was a really sweet kid and was obviously looking for help and for support she was not getting at home. The thought of those kids possibly getting hurt touched me deeply; the thought of dealing with the drunken husband and his shot gun just about made me wet my pants.

Because the rest of the family came to the church, I visited the husband at his job at the train station, we had had a fairly brief, guarded but cordial conversation. It had occurred to me to tell the wife to hang up and call the police, but I guess I thought that might make him really angry. Why he would not be angry with her calling "the preacher" did not cross my mind. I arrived at their house and all the lights were on.

I knocked on the door and was admitted by the wife who had a panicked look, her daughter a sheepish one. They motioned toward the kitchen, and I called out, "Hey, Walter, it's me, Rollin. Can we talk a minute?" No response. I went on in and noticed that the shot gun was leaning up against the wall by the fridge, a good sign. Walter was seated at the table, and I took a seat, trying to get between him and the gun. As I looked around the room, I saw that the phone had been pulled off the wall and was dangling by its wires. I asked what was going on and Walter mumbled something about an argument. It was about time to call it a night and go to bed, I suggested. No response. He looked anything but angry now, more exhausted, so I said, "How about if we put the gun away and go to bed and we can talk about it in the morning." He nodded and I quietly called his wife to come get the gun and put it away.

As she did, the phone rang. I looked at my watch and it was after midnight. It was probably Betsy calling to see if everything was alright. I tried to answer the dangling phone, but it was dead on the receiving end and just kept ringing. I helped Walter into the bedroom and got him to sit on the bed and then lie down. I told his wife that I needed to get home before Betsy called the police and that she should call me in the morning. There were many apologies, she for having to call me, and me for having to leave so abruptly, and I hurried home. When I got there Betsy was hurriedly dressing and trying to call a cab (we only had one car) to come over to the family's house, fully expecting to find a carnage. And she was seven months pregnant! We laugh about it now, but what was she thinking?

The congregation at Park Street Christian Church had been started just four years previously when the First Christian Church downtown voted to sever ties with its founding denomination. The denominational loyalists who lost that vote determined to leave and start a new church. As one friend used to say, some churches are like cats: when they fight the result is kittens. These founders of the new church viewed themselves as the "righteous remnant" that persevered through a losing conflict. What was the fight about? The denomination, the Christian Church (Disciples of Christ), had long supported overseas missions through a mission board. That was scandalous to the ones who voted to leave as they intoned the 19th Century slogan, "where the Bible speaks we speak; where the Bible is silent, we are silent." There is no mention of missionary societies in the Bible! So, they voted out. Never mind that there is also no mention of light bulbs, restrooms or Sunday schools!

The loyalists got organized, bought a beautiful property on the edge of town, engaged a young pre-ministerial student at the University of Virginia to provide part time leadership, and constructed two modest but very adequate buildings by the time Betsy and I arrived in June 1962. There were eighty members and an average worship attendance of fifty. The sanctuary was designed to be a fellowship hall after the church grew sufficiently to build a new and larger worship space. That meant that I spent a lot of time putting up and taking down folding chairs for various meetings; a family was designated for getting the buildings ready for Sunday mornings each week, but other than that there was no janitorial service. Small churches are an exercise in shared responsibility, and that is no small or insignificant thing. My salary was $400.00 per month, with no benefits. We rented the ground floor of a small ranch style house nearby, next door to one of the church's founding families: Haswell and Zada Walker.

The Walkers were a local legend. Haswell was a math teacher at Lane High School, *the* high school in Charlottesville's city school district, and had been for several decades. After his retirement the district named one of its new middle schools in his honor. Zada Walker stayed home, kept house, had "high tea" ready for her husband when he returned from school each day, and she ran the church. They had been on the search committee for a new pastor when I was "called" to serve Park Street Christian, they had arranged for our rental of the house next door, and they were wonderful neighbors and friends. But I soon learned that anything that was done at the church had first to receive their blessing. Thank heaven they were open-minded and open-hearted. That is not always the case in churches, as any pastor knows.

Our closest friends were Mary and Julian King. Betsy had secured a position teaching at Albemarle County High School, and the Kings both worked there and were active members at Park Street. Mary taught math and Julian was the head football coach. We had several kids in the church that played on his team, so we spent most Friday nights in the fall at the stadium. At least twice each week we would go together to the ice cream parlor; Julian was an ice cream freak. At the church, Mary taught a Church School class and Julian was a deacon. We could not have been closer.

Julian's untimely death at too-early an age a couple decades later hit me hard. In the intervening years Julian had left coaching and become an elementary school principal and found that that was his groove. He was beloved by his students, their parents and his faculty. Mary was kind to ask me to give the eulogy at his funeral service. The large, downtown Methodist Church where they had become members was totally packed. It was a very hard moment for me to get through. Julian was a person of genuine kindness and utter integrity, maybe the closest friend I have had.

Not all the members, however, were quite so congenial, kind or sterling, though many who were not came out of their own peculiar realities. One particular family was constantly at the church and clearly wanted to run things. One Saturday morning they were on clean and set up duty and I was in my little study working on my sermon. A tragic auto accident had taken the life of a young girl in their daughter's elementary school class on the previous day. I went out to help them set up chairs for Sunday's service and was totally astonished when the wife asked if I didn't agree that the little girl was killed because her parents are atheists. The Holy Spirit (or something) helped me bite my tongue and not respond in the anger I immediately felt. I took a deep breath and tried to give a reasonable explanation that while there were Biblical passages that indicated that God did sometimes respond with angry retribution, on the contrary, from Jonah to Jesus, God was revealed as a loving Father, not an angry, vengeful tyrant. These folks clearly preferred the vindictive version. They were not happy.

I found out that day in my gut what I had known in theory since my courses at seminary in Pastoral Ministry, a fact that every pastor soon learns. We are ordained to be "Pastor and Teacher" to our congregations and sometimes those roles are in painful and direct conflict. What I believed about God, a belief that was at the core of my faith and was a conviction I felt called to teach, would, if I pushed too hard, make it difficult to be a pastor to that family. Teaching for the kind of change in faith and values that they needed would be a long-term effort, and they needed a pastor in the meantime, and in the worst way. Their daughter was six years old, was on tranquilizers and, while I had no knowledge of what was plaguing her, I thought it was a pretty good guess that her very strict and judgmental parents played a role in it. That was just the beginning.

Skip and Martha Parker were a different sort altogether. Both were funny and a joy to be around. Plus, they had great kids: two daughters, the oldest was smart as a whip, a child who always had the right answer. The youngest was plenty smart, but in a weird kind of way, the kid with the totally unexpected answer from outer space. Martha was a stay-at-home mom, not unusual in the early '60's, and eagerly helped organize all sorts of receptions and social events; the kind of person every congregation needs and that most have. Martha had a buoyant spirit and a good sense of humor. Skip was Chairperson of the Church Board, a high energy businessman and leader. They were among my favorite folks to work with, always dependable, and as committed to the church as any of the families.

Imagine my distress, then, when one evening in a committee meeting as we were talking about the future of the fledgling congregation, Skip, in all sincerity, said he felt like the church was "like Kiwanis Club for the whole family." So much for my preaching on the "cost and joy of discipleship," not to mention my constant effort to get members engaged in ministry to and with the still segregated, impoverished neighborhoods in town. Social justice and deep commitment were not on the radar screen.

These teeth-grinding realities are not uncommon for first-parish pastors serving small, struggling churches, but there was an added dimension to this situation that finally pushed me over the edge. Park Street Church was part of the state organization of churches of our denomination, and of the local subgrouping, the Piedmont District. The twice-yearly meetings of this group would have been funny if they weren't so painful, or maybe painful if they weren't so funny. I was the only seminary graduate among the fifteen or so pastors who served these rural and small-town congregations. One other was a college graduate. The discourse at our meetings was so bereft of any meaningful theological or spiritual content that I wanted to just go home and go to bed or maybe even scream at the top of my lungs.

One fairly goofy debate was over whether or not an old campground which was owned by the district should be sold. It had not been used in years and was totally run down. It was not on a lake or in the mountains, just in a field, on a dirt road, miles from the highway. It was composed of four or five one room cabins, all dilapidated and without plumbing, two properly designated out-houses, and a pavilion that was caving in. Decades ago, it had been the scene of revivals where fire and brimstone were preached with passion, and where numerous people were "saved."

Several of those who found the Lord at those camp meetings were now the preachers of our district. They did not want to raise the money to restore and renovate it, nor could they imagine camping out there for a week of preaching. But it was the church's, it was God's, it was holy ground, though no one ever went there or intended to. "Emperors, Bishops and Kings are important people, but the children of God are more important, and we must keep it," intoned one of the preachers. What that had to do with the debate I am not sure, but weird demagoguery was not beneath the dignity of some of the leaders. Finally, the motion was tabled; the property was not sold. I decided that this was no place for me.

* * * * *

In the summer after my third year at Divinity School I had gone home to New Orleans to do construction work and earn some cash. A month before I left for home I was called by an old friend who was a leader in a small congregation of the United Church of Christ, Bethany Church on Broad St. Their pastor had resigned, and they needed a supply preacher for the summer while they sought a new one. I went to talk with Dr. Bard Thompson, my all-time favorite Church History professor who was a member of the UCC and, though I did not know it at the time, had been an important figure in its founding. He briefed me on the historical background of the Evangelical and Reformed tradition of which Bethany Church had been a part, on the merger of that German ethnic denomination with the Congregational Christian Churches to form the United Church of Christ, and on the current realities in the UCC.

I called my friend back, agreed to preach and lead worship for the summer, and had a great time at Bethany. All the families were just two or three generations away from Germany, many spoke with an accent, all loved beer, brats and kraut and served it at church fellowship events. They had a very formal liturgy which I had come to appreciate, and they appreciated the more casual and personal way that I led worship and that I preached.

One memorable incident occurred the first time I officiated a Holy Communion at Bethany. They used the liturgy from the Evangelical and Reformed Book of Worship, a very formal and poetic liturgy that I loved and studied carefully in preparation for that Sunday. Worship was at nine o'clock on Sunday morning because it was just too hot later in the morning in New Orleans, and even at that hour they had two large fans on either side of the chancel to keep the air cool. All went well until the deacons, having served the wafer thin, melt in your mouth bread of communion to those in the pews, solemnly returned to the chancel and handed the trays to me. I took the trays of wafers and turned a little too fast. The breeze from the fans caught the wafers and blew them all over the place. The deacons gasped and started hurriedly picking them off the floor. It was too solemn an observance to laugh, but too funny seeing the deacons scurrying around for some folks not to. They forgave me, and we all laughed afterward. It was a delightful summer.

So, when it was clear to me that I needed a change from Park Street church in Charlottesville, I thought immediately of the UCC and called Dr. Thompson to see how to make the change. This was more than an impulse born out of frustration. The founding of the United Church of Christ had been the big story in current church affairs for the entire time I was in seminary. It was formed by a merger of the Evangelical and Reformed Church and the Congregational Christian Churches in 1957. The former was made up of a 1930's merger of two German ethnic church bodies with strong liturgical and social service histories. The latter was the result of a 1930's merger of Congregational Churches and one branch of the Christian Church movement, groups with histories of social justice and service. These were churches and people who were committed to Christian unity, and many saw their new merger as a bold step toward the unity of all Christians, or at least all Protestants. It was the subject of many news stories and much conversation in the halls and at dining tables at the seminary.

Dr. Thompson invited me to Lancaster, PA where he was then teaching at Lancaster Theological Seminary, drove me to Harrisburg to meet the Conference Minister of the Penn Central Conference, and the two of them arranged for me to meet with two search committees in central Pennsylvania. They also instructed me in how to secure "Privilege of Call," i.e. have my credentials examined and be interviewed by the appropriate Church and Ministry Committee. That interview and review of credentials was accomplished with a committee in the Shenandoah Valley, and I passed muster. Next, a visit was scheduled for me to interview Search Committees at St. Paul UCC in Lancaster, and at Salem UCC in Harrisburg. Thank heaven Betsy, who was great with child at that time, went with me on that trip for the two interviews.

The first was at St. Paul UCC in the heart of downtown Lancaster. The position was Director of Christian Education and included running a summer camping program at a camp site the congregation owned on a small lake nearby. The visit included a trip to the camping site. It was in fair shape, needed some work, and there were lots of program possibilities. I had always wanted to run a camp, conference and retreat program, so I was very interested to that point. The Search Committee included long time Church School teachers and the Professor of Christian Education at the seminary. The interview did *not* include the presence of the senior pastor, which seemed a little odd. We met him briefly in his study and he seemed totally disinterested in this potential staff colleague, in Christian Education, in talking to me about the position, in my questions about the congregation or in anything else.

The meeting with the committee went very well, and the members were enthusiastic about the program and seemed eager to attract us to work with them. I was excited about the prospect; large church, big Church School program, a conference and retreat facility: what was not to like? Betsy, however, was skeptical. It looked to her like something was not right with the senior pastor, and she was on target. We did not find it out for several years, and then only by chance, but said pastor was, at that very time, being tailed by a private detective hired by the church. He was soon discovered to be having an illicit relationship with a woman in the church. The facts were all made public the day after the young minister who eventually took the position was installed and started work. He lived through a nightmare. It was hard to ignore Betsy's intuition and instincts after that.

The interview at the other church was a different matter entirely. Salem UCC had been founded in 1787 and was the downtown "mother church" of a dozen Reformed tradition UCC congregations in the city, and was located just blocks from the state capitol. The building was a beautiful, colonial structure standing like a sore thumb, the only building left in an eleven-acre tract that had been cleared for an urban renewal project that never got off the ground. The Salem Search Committee met at the home of its chair, Donald Royal, Esq. I had no idea what the "Esq." meant and learned that it just meant that he was an attorney.

Betsy and I both immediately liked Don and Margie Royal, and each of the committee members as they arrived. The Pastor at Salem UCC was Ed Butkofsky, a warm and gentle soul with whom we fell in love immediately. There were no topics on which all of us did not see pretty much eye to eye that evening. And then, Margie served cocktails. No one seemed the least bit surprised, and I thought I had died and gone to heaven.

This was a really laid-back group; and they wanted me to do Christian education, with an emphasis on adult education, primarily because they did not have many kids anymore. The families with children had moved to the suburbs, but their parents were very active, and the sanctuary was nearly full each week. The other emphasis was on community ministry with other churches in the capitol area and with the residents of an impoverished downtown neighborhood, just blocks away, on the banks of the Susquehanna River: "Shipoke." Betsy and I looked at each other and knew we had found a new home.

That all happened in April and May, and we agreed that I would preach my "trial sermon" on June 21. After that service and sermon, the congregation would vote on whether or not to call me as their Associate Pastor. Betsy was due to have our first child by or on June 6, so the timing of the candidate visit seemed appropriate. Wrong! Bethany was born at 9:30 pm on Saturday, June 20.

I made several calls to Don Royal to keep him up to date on the progress of this childbirth. Mary and Julian King, the only friends in Charlottesville who knew about my need to get out of town and why, sat with me at University of Virginia Hospital throughout the labor and birth. When we got the news I hugged and thanked them, went in to be with Betsy and see the baby, then hurried home to call her parents and mine, got into bed, and set two alarm clocks for three o'clock in the morning. The trip to Harrisburg was hurried but blissful. I arrived at Royals' house at about 9:00 am, washed my face, changed into a suit, grabbed my sermon notes and went downtown to Salem to preach.

It had not occurred to me amid all the hustle of getting the baby born and getting to Harrisburg, but that Sunday was Fathers' Day! Dr. Butkofsky made reference to the occasion in his announcements, and to the fact that the guest preacher was clearly the newest father in the house. That received a happy response from the attendees, and as every preacher knows, it is helpful to have the congregation in good spirits when you get up to preach. Tired as I was, I apparently did well enough on the sermon for the congregation to vote to "call" me to be their Associate Pastor. I could have floated all the way back to Charlottesville.

Instead, I called Betsy at the hospital, took a nap at Royals' and then drove back to be with my wife and new baby, Bethany. What a day. What a wonderful new opportunity. I sang all the way home: "Joyful Joyful We Adore Thee;" "Immortal, Invisible God, Only Wise;" plus my entire repertoire of Isaac Watts and John Wesley hymns. There were gut wrenching days that lay ahead, but that day was pure blessing and bliss.

8

BLESSED TRANSITION

I had never paid much attention to liturgy. An order of service was standard, and I had dutifully put one together every week at Park Street Church, selecting hymns whose themes were consistent (more or less) with my sermon topic, and the scripture passage that would be my text. At Salem United Church of Christ I was introduced to a German Reformed tradition of liturgical worship based on the lectionary.

I was vaguely familiar with the lectionary and its use from my days in seminary, though most of the preaching there was topical, especially on social justice issues during the years of the civil rights movement. In the Christian Church (Disciples of Christ) congregations of my youth, and in all the Disciples churches with which I was familiar, the lectionary texts for each Sunday of the Church Year were not utilized. There was a liturgical form to the weekly celebration of the Lord's Supper, but it was scant liturgy in comparison to the rich heritage of which I became part at Salem UCC.

Within a month of our arrival in Harrisburg, our new baby, Bethany, was baptized. Beth's birth had been several weeks later than predicted, she weighed nine pounds and two ounces, Betsy is five feet one inch tall, and prior to pregnancy weighed only one hundred pounds. It got crowded in there for Beth, and she was born with her lower legs curved inward and was extremely pigeon-toed. The doctor's remedy for that was to prescribe shoes that turned her feet outward and a rigid bar between her shoes that forced her knees together and straightened her legs.

She was so, so pretty, dressed in the baptismal dress that had been her grandmother's. But it looked to anyone who did not know the circumstances like we had her shoes on the wrong feet and had her hobbled. Betsy was painfully aware of how that would look and the consternation it could well cause (what are her parents thinking?). The dress nearly covered baby Beth's shackled feet, and we hoped no one would notice. It was, therefore, with some nervousness that we approached the service that Sunday morning.

The Service of Baptism was not a big "Aha!" moment for me. Just a small "click" as something previously only vaguely grasped fell into place. Dr. B. asked, in the words of the Baptismal Liturgy, "Into what faith is this child to be baptized?" The congregation and we, in response, recited and/or read the Apostles Creed. I knew it by heart from frequent use in chapel services at seminary. I did not intellectually affirm every clause in that creed and still don't. It is a testimony to the faith as held at the time it was written, as are all subsequent creedal statements. It is not a test of anyone's current beliefs.

We were, in the confession, placing ourselves and our daughter into continuity with a community of persons who have committed themselves to Jesus of Nazareth and his vision of God and God's will. Baptism is being grafted into a living vine, the lineage of faith and faithfulness. Then came the practical questions: would we "bring her up in the nurture and admonition of the Lord?" We would try, though we were clear that there was no guarantee of outcomes for her or ourselves. Then the prayers: for strength and faithfulness in keeping our vows, then came the baptism and the blessing.

That moment was like a polished gem, a concise and beautiful encapsulation of the meaning of Christian faith and life. Christian history has been characterized as a long journey, a continuing conversation about faith and faithfulness, where new persons join the journey and conversation every day. They learn from each other and make their contributions. People in the Reformed tradition think of it as a covenant journey where the direction is set by our covenant with God, and each true step is determined by our covenantal relationship with each other. Hence the liturgy for Baptism, the beginning of the journey, is a covenant ceremony, focused on a baby, or in many cases an adult, and confirming for all.

Regular Sunday worship at "Old Salem" was just as different and enlightening for me as was Beth's baptism. It followed the basic order of Martin Luther's German translation of the Latin mass as it had been frequently revised by Reformed Church liturgical scholars through the generations since. It included the invocation of God's presence, a hymn of praise, a unison, general confession of sin, the Kyrie (Lord, have mercy upon us) with a sung response, an assurance of pardon, followed by the singing of the Gloria In Excelsis Deo: "Glory to God in the highest and on earth peace, good will toward men . . . ." Then followed: prayers, hymns, scripture readings, sermon and offering, all appropriate to the lectionary and the seasons of the Church Year. Of course, there was an altar, pulpit and lectern hangings in the colors of the Church Year.

I came to see that each service encapsulated the dynamics of the Christian experience: praise of God, confession of our sinfulness, forgiveness, thanksgiving, instruction, and the response of generosity and sharing. And all was in the context of the annual Christian pilgrimage of the liturgical year, from Jesus nativity, through his life to Good Friday and Easter, then to Pentecost and the saga of the mission and discipleship in the Church. Through the months I began to internalize just how elegant and artful this drama of the Christian faith and life really is. I was hooked. Having been reared in a free church, a non-liturgical tradition, this rich heritage fed a hunger I never knew I had.

The sanctuary where worship was celebrated each week was remarkable in itself. It had Tiffany windows and Tiffany candelabra (of which the members were sinfully proud, though we never confessed that), numbered pews that dated from the era when families paid pew rent, and one of the better pipe organs in the region. The organist-choir director was a wonderful musician and delightful friend, Pierce Getz. He had been a missionary to Japan who returned to study music and received his PhD from the Eastman School of Music in Rochester, NY. The choir was led by four paid soloists and, under Pierce's direction, they sang the finest classical repertoire and sang it well. Sunday morning worship was a delight.

* * * * *

However, the congregation was made up of people, and people do not always agree with each other (startling new fact!). Church people can, in fact, disagree over the damndest things, and do so with vigor. Part of the urban renewal project that was going on around the church involved widening Chestnut Street to an extent that would place the sidewalk along and up against the front wall of this historic edifice. Architects and engineers had designed new entrances and steps that would prove to be very serviceable and attractive, but the church members were very apprehensive as the widening of the street began, and well they might have been.

In digging the footings for the sidewalk, a backhoe nudged one of the foundation piers of the front wall and of the tall bell tower that rose above it. Workmen on the job told of the terrifying moment when the front and side brick walls of the building cracked loudly and the bell tower shuddered. Everyone ran and then looked back to see that the tower had not collapsed. They carefully went back to inspect the damage, called in the engineers, and soon realized that the foundation of the front wall would need to be shored up. It was a huge and risky challenge.

Workmen began digging by hand in the crawl space in the basement of the church and moving dirt out in wheelbarrows. They carefully dug holes for new footings under the existing walls, shoring up as they went so as to cause no further movement or shifting in the foundation. It was a long, backbreaking and laborious task that lasted weeks. One day the foreman came to the pastor's office and handed him a bundle that had been found deep in the basement. Whatever the contents, they were wrapped in oil cloth and tied with heavy twine. When he opened it Dr. Butkofsky was astonished to find a beautiful communion set, a pewter chalice, paten and pitcher.

Dr. B convened the members of the Consistory (the elders of the church) and one of them, a historian, examined the pieces carefully, and found that they were made by a well-known Philadelphia silversmith in the late 1700's. He was also aware that pewter items of all sorts, including church communion ware, were requisitioned to make bullets during the Civil War. Apparently, our ecclesiastical forebears, though staunch Unionists, were not too keen on having their communion set used in that manner, so they hid it. They apparently forgot about it after the war, and it stayed hidden in the bowels of the church basement until discovered during the construction.

Everyone rejoiced in the totally unexpected discovery. The local newspaper carried the story. The items were polished and displayed at the church for several weeks until someone expressed the opinion that they ought to insure them against the possibility of theft. Salem was a downtown church and had, in fact, been broken into and had items stolen in the past (though none of the thieves so far had the wit to steal the Tiffany candelabra).

There ensued a mighty controversy. One side held that the set should be insured and put on display in a secure case in the church's library. Their opponents wanted to give it on loan to the State Historical Collection in the State Capitol complex, where it would be displayed for the public, and the church could have it for historical occasions.

It all came to a head at a specially called meeting of the congregation. It was the largest attendance in recent memory. One member, in righteous indignation, proclaimed that we should "render unto Caesar what is Caesar's and unto God what is God's," and keep it in the church. There were many supportive *harrumphs* and some scattered applause. Back and forth the argument went for over an hour, until Don Royal, attorney, civic leader and genuine saint, suggested, "that we wrap it back up in oil cloth and squirrel it away in the basement!" Finally, in a very close vote, it was decided to give the controversial communion ware on permanent loan to the State Archives. There it remains.

Then, of course, there was the annual Christmas standoff. The Altar Guild had a long-standing tradition of decorating Salem's historic and beautiful sanctuary with the usual garlands, bows and candles, and with two tall Christmas trees, one on either side of the altar. The trees were adorned simply with a hundred or more red balls. To them it looked elegant. To Pierce Getz, our organist and choir master, it looked garish and pagan. Each year he carefully prepared the choir to sing one of the classical Christmas cantatas, and he was incensed at the very idea of singing it against a backdrop of these pagan symbols. And each year he made his displeasure known to Dr. Butkofsky. Dr. B saw his point but did not want to insult the altar guild ladies by asking them to do something different and having to explain why.

The conflict was successfully confined to the staff and a few members of the choir until one fateful Christmas Eve. Pierce arrived early for the evening service and hastily draped strings of red, white and blue Christmas lights on the two trees and turned them on to make sure they would blink as intended. Just at that time Dr. Butkofsky arrived and nearly fainted. The blinking lights had to go. But, instead of raging at his organist and choir master, it is a measure of his pastoral maturity that he took a deep breath and said, in effect, "You have made your point. Now I will help you take them down before anyone else arrives." They did it together. The Christmas Eve service went on without a hitch. Oh, the plight and perils of the parish pastor!

Incidentally, Pierce Getz left Salem church not long after that, on good terms with Dr. B and everyone. He had a remarkable career as professor of organ and choral director at Lebanon Valley College, his *alma mater*. He was a well-known recitalist who played all over Europe and the United States, and he served until his retirement as organist and choir master at the Market Square Presbyterian Church in Harrisburg.

* * * * *

Of course, the issues of racial justice and civil rights were never far from the foreground. One night in March 1965, my dad called from my parents' home in San Jose, CA, to tell me that he and several other pastors from Northern California were planning to go to Selma, Alabama to participate in the demonstrations there. After leaving New Orleans in 1961 my parents had moved to McKinney, Texas where dad served a church for two years before moving on to the west coast. Mom had always wanted to get back to be near her family there, and the first Christian Church in San Jose was an ideal location for them. It was a university town, a strong congregation, and it was an easy drive to visit her family in and around Sacramento.

A number of the younger pastors in that area had followed the developments in Birmingham and Selma with deep concern. On March 7, after all attempts at voter registration for Black citizens were met with unconscionable red tape, insults and violence, Martin Luther King Jr. led a march toward Montgomery. As the marchers started across the now infamous Edmund Pettus Bridge, hundreds of armed police accosted them in a bloody melee. It was all carried on nationwide television. The next day King sent out a plea for pastors from all over the country to join him in a Ministers' March. These pastors in California decided that the Spirit was moving them to join the hundreds of others who were expected to respond to the call. They knew that dad had spent years in New Orleans and had some deeper grasp of the situation, so they prevailed on him to join them. He agreed.

The phone call that night created a painful situation for Betsy and me. My first impulse was to arrange to fly down and meet them in New Orleans, and drive with them to Selma. But we had a brand-new baby, and Betsy was pregnant. Betsy, being from Alabama, knew first-hand the dangers involved: several had already lost their lives and the violent response to demonstrations was shown graphically on the news each evening. She had visions of being stranded in Harrisburg with two babies and a husband imprisoned, injured or worse. So, I did not go to Selma.

Dad later told me the story of what happened. When he arrived at the San Francisco Airport to start the trip, only one other of his colleagues was there to accompany him. The others had found reasons that prevented them from going. His traveling companion was Rev. Bob Lemon who had asked him in the first place. They became life-long friends because of their shared experience in Selma.

When they arrived there, they were greeted by representatives of the Southern Christian Leadership Conference and accompanied a local member to his home for their lodging. A demonstration was planned for the next day, and Dad, Bob, their host and several others who were staying in the same house, went to the assembly point where several hundred were gathered. They listened to instructions regarding orderly conduct during the march and a speech on the purpose of the march and on the necessity for non-violence.

The leaders and those closest to them started for the Edmund Pettus Bridge, but before those farther back even got started police moved in from every side, told them they were all under arrest, and marched them off toward the outskirts of town. It doesn't take much imagination to grasp what was going through their minds and the fears that surely troubled them. As it turned out they were marched to the local high school football stadium which had an eight-foot chain link fence around it. They were herded in and told to sit in an area of the grandstand. There they waited for the entire day, not particularly uncomfortable, but still wondering and fearing what would come next. There were water fountains and restrooms, such as they were. But there was no information until late afternoon. Finally, they were lined up and processed, charged with a misdemeanor offense, admonished to leave Alabama, and released.

They went back to their host residence, gathered their belongings and headed for the New Orleans airport and home. Two days later President Lyndon Johnson made his famous speech to Congress supporting voting rights for all, and he sent the National Guard and 100 US Marshalls to Selma to protect the marchers to Montgomery. It wasn't particularly heroic as things turned out, but Dad and Bob Lemon had answered the call. I had experienced it only vicariously, and was proud of my dad. He did receive some notoriety decades later when a new library was built in San Jose, a joint project of the city and San Jose State University. There was to be a display on the civil rights era, and Rev. Dr. Edward E. Russell was to be honored as the only citizen of the town who had been at the by-then-famous March to Selma.

* * * * * *

My commitment to social justice was the result, of course, of my experience in the civil rights movement while in seminary and my understanding of Christian social ethics that was at the heart of that movement. But the beginning of protests against the war in Vietnam found me very ambivalent. My close friend from seminary, Malcolm, was an Army lieutenant in combat there. We had taken a course in the last semester of our studies on The Doctrine of Man. Today it would be called Doctrine of Humanity if it were taught at all. That's where I first read Reinhold Niebuhr's classics, The Nature and Destiny of Man, and Moral Man and Immoral Society. Malcolm and I reveled in the energetic class discussions of those great theological works and of the issues of human pride and sloth, of citizenship, social ethics and the relation of church and state.

Those studies and discussions shaped my understanding of social justice for the rest of my ministry. For Malcolm they were life changing in a much more immediate and dramatic way. He soon decided that seminarians should not be exempt from the draft and pastors should not be exempt from military service. Soon after he and Joanna Evins were married, he made good on his convictions and volunteered for the Army. Joanna's dad, a long-time United States Congressman representing the Fourth District of Tennessee and chair of the House Ways and

Means Committee, immediately pulled strings to get Malcolm assigned to the guard detail at the Tomb of the Unknown Soldier in Washington. It would have kept Malcolm safe and Joanna close to home. Malcolm promptly volunteered for Vietnam. Betsy and I drove up to Fort Devon, Massachusetts to visit with them just a few days before he shipped out.

So, Malcolm was in Vietnam in the summer of 1965 when the youngest son of one of Salem Church's and the city's leading citizens came home from college and began talking to everyone who would listen about Vietnam. He especially talked to people at Salem about the immorality and illegality of the War. Young Ted First was handsome, articulate and passionate on the subject, and he made it hard not to at least pay attention. He asked to meet with the Church Consistory where he pleaded that people needed to know the full facts about the war. He was so persuasive that they agreed to invite Harold Stassen, the former Governor of Minnesota and an outspoken opponent of the war, to speak at Salem and to open his address to the public.

Governor Stassen was much admired nationwide because he had resigned his office as governor in 1941 to be deployed with his Naval Reserve unit to the Pacific and was a decorated war hero. Upon his return he served as President of the University of Pennsylvania and had been a candidate for the Republican nomination for President in every presidential year since, including most recently, in 1964. He was, therefore very well known in Pennsylvania and especially in heavily Republican Harrisburg. But none of us was prepared for the standing room crowd that filled the church for his speech. He was eloquent and persuasive. From that night I became convinced of the folly and tragedy of the Vietnam War. That event gave Salem Church a reputation as a social action-oriented congregation, and it put me in touch with some of the anti-war leaders in the area.

I began meeting with a group of political, religious, and labor union leaders to develop educational and protest strategies in the city of Harrisburg. The two most well-known and important political figures who had come out strongly against the war were Senator William Fulbright,

Democrat from Arkansas, and Senator Wayne Morse, Democrat from Oregon. They had cast the only two votes in the Senate against the Tonkin Gulf Resolution which officially committed the United States to full involvement in the war in Vietnam. We learned that Morse was available for speaking engagements and immediately began planning for an event in Harrisburg. He committed to a date in early 1966, and we were able to secure the Memorial Auditorium at the State Capitol complex, which seated several thousand, for the event. We received contributions from several labor union state committees to handle Morse's expenses and fee. Each of these groups had resolutions and statements opposing the war. The treasurer of the International Ladies Garment Workers Union handled the funds and the accounting. I learned that the I.L.G.W.U. had been in the forefront of social justice efforts nationwide for decades.

The planning was complete, and we had a lot of publicity by the unions and anti-war groups, plus one short article in the newspaper. The auditorium was huge, and we worried that we would look like a mere handful in it. We need not have been faint of heart. The auditorium was filled, including most of the balcony. Wayne Morse did not disappoint. He was a small man with steel gray hair, combed straight back, a bushy mustache and dark, heavy eyebrows (Sam Ervin was reportedly asked by a new Congressman how he might succeed in Congress. Ervin responded, "Grow eyebrows.").

Morse carefully laid out the facts leading up to the Tonkin Gulf incident, what we knew about that attack on U.S. Navy vessels, and questions about the official account. He then meticulously built his case as to why he voted against the resolution and why he felt our involvement in that civil war was ill-advised, illegal and morally wrong. He was brilliant, and I was hooked on the anti-war movement.

When Dr. Martin Luther King, Jr., delivered his now famous sermon at Riverside Church in New York City in April 1967, everything fell into place for me. It was titled, *Beyond Vietnam: A Time to Break the Silence*. Many advisers had warned him not to speak out about the war in Vietnam, that it would overshadow and diminish his focus on Civil Rights. None-the-less, he addressed a packed house at that mammoth cathedral and made clear the connection between an ill-advised and interventionist war and the struggle for full citizenship of all Americans at home.

In his eyes it was a tragedy that the nation was squandering its resources and the lives of its young men in a vainglorious and unauthorized war while the hard work of supporting the legitimate needs and aspirations of an oppressed group of citizens languished. He saw it as a tragedy that would cause both efforts to founder. From the time I read his speech I saw the unbreakable connection between social justice and ethical integrity in domestic as well as foreign affairs. My vision of a just society was more fully shaped from that moment.

* * * * * *

In the midst of all these ethical and political struggles, on August 5, 1966, our son, Stephen, was born. Betsy's obstetrician suggested that she have the baby at Holy Spirit Hospital in Camp Hill, just across the Susquehanna River from Harrisburg. Several friends told us they had had good experiences there, especially in childbirth.

It was a Roman Catholic founded hospital and many of the nurses and staff were nuns, but that posed no problem for us. Its location did. It was a half hour drive from our house on 25th Street near Derry Avenue. Nonetheless, we decided to take their advice. We had arranged for Ms. McKelvey to come to the house when the time came for us to dash to the hospital. She was a delightful, feisty widow who lived nearby and had often been our babysitter for Beth.

That time came suddenly in the night when Betsy and I awoke, lying in a puddle of water. The baby was on the way, and it was scary. I jumped up, threw on some clothes, got Betsy out of bed and into a chair, and hustled out to go pick up Ms. McKelvey and bring her back to take care of Beth.

On the way I told her that Betsy's water had broken and flooded the bed, and we needed to hurry to the hospital. Betsy and I were both surprised when Ms. McKelvey walked in the front door in a semi-panic, waving her arms and repeating over and over, "We have to stay calm! We have to stay calm!" She had seemed so calm and confident before. But we didn't have time to worry about that. I helped Betsy down the stairs and into the car, packed towels around her and drove off toward the hospital at a barely safe speed.

We were so glad we were at Holy Spirit Hospital. I was able to go into the labor room and be with Betsy right up until she was taken into the delivery room. At University of Virginia Hospital when Beth was born, I didn't see Betsy for the entire time of her labor. The nuns/nurses at Holy Spirit were great, considerate, and apparently delighted that a Protestant Pastor's wife was having a baby at their hospital.

But when I got home mid-morning the next day, I found two-year-old Beth all but traumatized. Her eyes were big as saucers, and she clutched me around the neck and would not let go. I went upstairs and found that Ms. McKelvey, in her zeal to do something, had dismantled our bed, leaned the box springs against one wall, thoroughly cleaned the mattress and leaned it against another. When Beth had awakened, she had gone into our bedroom and found both her parents gone and the bed taken apart, and she started screaming and didn't stop till I got home.

She still clung to me as I drove Ms. McKelvey home and thanked her profusely for helping us. I am not sure Beth ever recovered. She would not go to sleep for naps or at night. For years I rocked her and sang "Row, row, row your boat gently down the stream . . .." over and over again until she finally conked out.

We brought Stephen home three days later. We half expected Beth to show some resentment, especially after the trauma to her when he was born. Maybe she didn't make the connection of that shock with his arrival and, mercifully, they bonded. As it turned out in later years, they bonded big time. For the time being, however, I sang a lot of, "Row,

row, row your boat." Stephen was, like his older sister, a beautiful baby. He too was baptized by Dr. Butkofsky at Salem Church, in that same elegant liturgy. We were very, very happy.

But, in the midst of all our family, church and community involvements a painful reality was becoming obvious to Betsy and me. Dr. B was, by that time, 67 years old and church members began hinting, subtly at first, that he should think about retiring. I later found out that several members of the Search Committee that interviewed me had in mind that I would succeed him as pastor.

They began to suggest in Consistory meetings that instead of preaching once a month I should preach more frequently. I could tell that he was hurt by the very idea, and I knew that he had no intention of retiring any time soon. He and his wife, Mary Alice, had one child in high school, one in middle school, and one in grade school. And the salary they paid him and had over the years was not enough to retire and send those kids to college. Plus, the treasurer was so lax that he would often be several days late with our paychecks. It was an awkward and painful situation.

Dr. Butkofsky and Mary Alice had been very kind and supportive of us and sweet to our children. We spent Christmases together at their parsonage, complete with her delightful *pfeffernüsse* and *springerle* cookies, dinners after church on Sundays, and family outings to the parks where Dr. B loved to hike. We could not stand to see him pushed out to make room for me. We decided to seek another parish and, once I started the process, received a number of inquiries from churches that were vacant and interested. Several were in Pennsylvania, and we visited them in Reading and Allentown. Then one night I received a long-distance call, and the voice at the other end was pure Texas.

9

LEARNING TO SPEAK "TEXAN"

The phone rang one evening in November 1966. It was Ben Reid, the chairperson of the Search Committee for Bethel UCC in Houston, Texas. It had never occurred to Betsy and me to want to go to Texas, but Ben was congenial and persuasive over the phone, and Houston was closer to Betsy's folks in Mobile and to mine in Phoenix. So, we talked.

They had received my professional profile, and they sent us a profile of the church. It was intriguing: they had a good record of mission support, had good worship attendance and a fairly large Church School. So, we talked some more, and we agreed to visit Houston, meet the committee, preach as a candidate for the pastoral position, and be voted on by the congregation. It was the routine process in the United Church of Christ.

The only hitch was that they would only pay my expenses, and I would not go without Betsy; she needed to see the situation as much as I did. That seemed to be a surprise to the committee, though Ben understood and convinced us that it could be worked out. In addition, we had two little kids to take care of in the process. Beth was two years old and Stephen four months old when we agreed to make the visit.

We decided to drive to Mobile, leave the children with Betsy's folks, and fly to Houston. We would pay for Betsy's flight. The trip was planned for early March, and if we liked the situation and the church liked us, we could move to Houston in May. We did and they did, but it was like entering a different world: Texas!

Ben and his wife Marilyn met us at the airport on a Saturday afternoon and took us to their home in Southwest Houston to change clothes before meeting the Search Committee. They lived a full thirty minutes from the church, a factor that was to become a major reality in our lives.

Houston is a huge sprawl, and the members lived all over the place. Marilyn Reid had been baptized and grown up in Bethel Church and Ben had joined the church when they married, so they drove across town and thought nothing of it. Nor did anyone else. Betsy and I both spent a major portion of our time in the next years driving on Houston's freeways.

The Reids took us to see the parsonage on the way to the meeting. It was a really great house, a lot nicer than anything we had lived in Charlottesville or Harrisburg. It was in a nice neighborhood, a block from the lush oaks and lawns of Memorial Park, and fairly close to the church. We were impressed. We then had our first look at Bethel Church. It is a brick structure, with a sanctuary, a fellowship Hall, connected by a classroom building, with a cloistered walkway between. It was well designed and attractive. The sanctuary was nice; not elaborate or elegant, but a center aisle nave with an adequate choir, divided chancel, above which was a very lovely stained-glass window of Christ. So far, so good.

We had a simple supper with the committee, and we got to talk informally with most of the members. It was a good mix of young and senior adults, all long-time members and leaders. They were working class folks, third generation German immigrants and those who had married into their families. Then we got down to business: my questions for them and their questions for me. They responded to my questions with candor and humor and I was well satisfied.

But I had a strange feeling of ambivalence: they all, especially the men, had a kind of raw-boned look about them like, well, ranch hands. It turned out that a number of them had been farmers and small ranchers in South Texas before Houston grew so fast and so big and sucked them into its oil, shipping and industrial orbit. I felt a kind of cultural disconnect at first. It was their humor and obvious joy at being with each other that helped me relax.

Their questions were friendly until they got to one in particular. I could see some nervous looks as I was asked how I felt about "social drinking." I was surprised and amused by the question but replied with candor of my own: I enjoy a beer now and then and have no problem with moderate consumption of alcohol. I could have quoted Martin Luther's advice to take a glass of wine before bed, or cited the beer making of our Puritan founding parents, but I refrained. It seemed to be the right answer, however. There was an audible sigh of relief and smiles all around.

It turned out that it was customary at Bethel Church, as part of the dinner celebrating a new confirmation class each year, to enjoy a keg of beer. They did not want a pastor who would give them grief about it. Many of the families were also members of the *Saengerbund*, a German singing society that had a small auditorium and beer garden just a few blocks away. It was a brat-and-beer culture.

Bethel United Church of Christ had been founded as Bethel Evangelical Lutheran Church in 1909, a congregation of the Evangelical Synod of North America. The founders had immigrated from Prussia beginning in the 1840's, settled mainly in the Missouri River Valley and in the heartland states of Mid America. In 1934 that Synod body merged with the German Reformed Church in the United States to form the Evangelical and Reformed Church: Bethel became Bethel E. and R. Then in 1957 the Evangelical and Reformed Church merged with the Congregational Christian Churches to establish the United Church of Christ: Bethel became U. C. C. But they were ethnic Germans, just three or four generations removed from Prussia, and they were very *gemütlich*.

Their worship was, however, very formal. I had appreciated my introduction to liturgical worship at Salem in Harrisburg but was not prepared for the service the next morning when I was to preach and be voted on. The pastor of a nearby UCC church had preached for Bethel during the interim since their previous pastor left, and he led the opening liturgy. In person he was very relaxed and casual, but when he put on the clerical robes, he morphed into Pastor Pious Q. Sanctimonious.

It was High Church South Texas German all the way. The sanctuary was packed, everyone eager to hear the potential new preacher. They all had their most serious and solemn faces on, awaiting a profound word from on high, no doubt, or maybe they were just bored catatonic. The supply guy left after the offering and went on to his own congregation. We sang a hymn, and I was on. I was ready, and they seemed receptive. Worship ended with a hymn, lustily sung, and the benediction.

The President of the Consistory then came to the chancel, called a Congregational Meeting to order, and told the people that the Search Committee was recommending that I be called as pastor. Then the whole congregation got to ask questions. That too seemed to go well, and I was impressed that some of the questions were asked by teenagers. Whoa: bright and confident kids! Then Betsy and I were ushered into another room to wait while they took a vote. We waited and waited; it seemed to take longer than was comfortable. A woman from the Search Committee who sat with us seemed nervous that the wait was taking longer than anticipated. But then we found out why.

Ben and the members of the Consistory came in smiling and walking on air. It had been a positive vote, and it was unanimous. That had never happened before at Bethel. What had taken so long was that they had taken an offering to pay for Betsy's air fare. The treasurer, with great relish, dumped two offering plates full of bills and coins in her lap. She had to open her legs and hold on to her skirt to catch it. We had visions of her having to walk out to Ben's car holding it like that, but several people helped gather it up, and we eventually received a check.

They made a salary offer and we talked about dates for a possible move. I looked at Betsy, and she at me, and I said we would let them know after we had a chance to talk. They seemed disappointed, so we assured them that we had had a wonderful time and were very impressed, but it had all happened so fast that we needed time to think it through.

On the flight back to Mobile and on the drive home to Harrisburg, we talked, and talked, and talked. I was acutely aware of the cultural difference and was not comfortable with the move. Betsy was acutely aware of the need to move and of the welcoming atmosphere. We had met previously with two search committees in Pennsylvania, and neither was nearly so warm or positive. So, when we got home, I called Ben and told him we were ready to move to Houston. We agreed to get there and start work in early May. I felt confirmed in the decision when, on May 5, 1967, we finished loading the car and left Harrisburg, PA *in snow flurries*! When we got to Houston it was 90 degrees.

* * * * *

Pentecost Sunday occurred just a week after our arrival in Houston. It was my first opportunity to celebrate Holy Communion at Bethel Church. I was familiar with the liturgy; the place was packed and all went well. That afternoon I began the task of taking home Communion to the shut-ins. It is a tradition in the former E and R churches of the UCC that all shut-ins should receive the Lord's Supper following each Communion Sunday.

I had a fairly short list from the church's elders, and began getting to know the aging members, several of them having been the founders of the congregation. In each case our conversation went well, and the brief Order for Communion for the Sick was ordinary until we got to the Lord's Prayer. We would start together, "Our Father who art in Heaven . . . ." But, by the end, the communicant would be praying in German: ". . . dein ist das Reich und die Kraft und die Herrlichkeit in Ewigkeit. Amen."

They had learned it in German as children and, when praying, went to their default mode. From the church's founding in 1909 till World War I, catechism was conducted in German. They switched to English abruptly in 1917 because people of German background were suspect in South Texas, as elsewhere during WWI. I had studied German for a year in college to fulfill the language requirement, though I had not re-tained much vocabulary. I could understand a good bit of liturgical Ger-man; parts of the UCC liturgy were derived from it. But these people had grown up speaking it in their homes and had church school and confirmation classes taught in German. The folks back in Harrisburg were of German descent, but they were several generations farther re-moved from the saga of immigration to America. The older members of Bethel still had it in their bones.

My next bump on the learning curve happened the first time I bap-tized a baby in worship at Bethel. I had visited with the family several times, a young couple having their first baby baptized in the church where the baby's father and his brothers and sister had been reared. I had discussed it with the Elders of the church, and they said all would be ready. At the appointed time in the service, I invited the young family to join me in the chancel as we sang a baptismal hymn. I removed the cover from the baptismal font and panicked when I saw that *there was no water!*

My mind raced: the hymn has three short verses; could I run out the side door, get a glass of water from the kitchen and run back before it ended? How idiotic would that look? The new pastor forgot to put wa-ter in the baptismal font! Could I fake it, go through the motions and pretend I was using water? The parents and anyone else who was paying attention would think I was nuts.

Just then I noticed that J. D. Nelius, one of the Elders, was walking down the center aisle with great solemnity and with white gloves on. He went straight to the altar, picked up a tall, golden pitcher, and walked ceremoniously to the baptismal font and poured water into it. That, it turns out, was the tradition at Bethel. But no one told me! I guess they assumed that I knew the drill . . . what do they teach them in seminary anyway? Don't they do that everywhere? Well, no! All else went as in-tended, and good old J. D. Nelius will always have a warm spot in my heart.

* * * * *

Texas Southern University in Houston is one of several historic state universities for African Americans in Texas. Just three weeks after we arrived in Houston and at Bethel Church, a riot took place on campus. The newspapers and TV news journalists called it a student riot. It was the last week of school, and a lot of partying was going on, some students got rowdy, and the police, always attentive and close by, stepped in. There was scuffling and some male students ran into a dormitory. Shots rang out. The students said that the police fired first in an effort to calm the situation; police claimed that the first shots were fired from the men's dorm. Gunfire was directed at the dorm. A general melee ensued with numerous injuries and arrests.

I received a call the next day from the pastor of another UCC church in town indicating that a meeting of some Black and White clergy had been scheduled to discuss and try to defuse the situation. That meeting was my introduction to the social activist community in the city. I learned that day of the vast gulf of perception and of the resentment that existed between the White and Black communities in Houston, as it did elsewhere.

The students and faculty at T.S.U. referred to the incident not as a student riot, but as a police riot. Black people were under a constant, high pressure blanket of suspicion in the city, and there was persistent intimidation by the police. The Mayor and Chief of Police were on record as committed to suppressing any suspicious or unruly activity, especially around the university, and the public media hewed to the official versions of all such events.

From that day through the next several years an interracial, interfaith group of clergy met regularly at the Episcopal Student Center at Rice University to discuss how our ministries could bring about change toward justice and reconciliation in Houston. Some of the friends I met through that effort stayed connected throughout the fifteen years we were in Texas. But the most immediate result of that incident and of my initial meeting with social justice-oriented clergy in Houston was my sermon the next Sunday at Bethel.

It was clear to me that our members did not have a very informed understanding of what happened at T.S.U., of why it happened, and what it meant in minority communities. I have no recollection of the biblical text I chose, or of how I framed the sermon, but there are plenty of passages in both Testaments that admonish Christians to do justice and embrace all their neighbors.

The response was a sort of stunned silence. No previous pastor had ever addressed the issue of race relations in quite so direct a way. Every preacher knows that the greetings of parishioners as they leave worship are a good gauge of what they thought of the message. Contrary to the warmth of greetings on previous Sundays, some would not make eye contact, others hemmed and hawed, and a blessed few expressed gratitude. The rest of my tenure at Bethel Church was tense, exciting and exhilarating. Then, a touchstone event happened at the local barbershop.

One piece of conventional wisdom for pastors and community organizers was, get your haircut at the local barbershop and pay attention to what is being discussed. I found Sam Seahorn's Barber Shop just two blocks away from the church on the downtown side of Shepherd Drive, in a part of the neighborhood that was mostly Black. Sam was cordial and funny and, after several visits, haircuts and conversations, let me in on what was happening just down the street at Shepherd Gardens. It was an apartment complex which was owned by a real estate tycoon in another city, managed by a local Black businessman, and housed around 200 Black families. It was a mess.

Several men from The Gardens got their hair cut by Sam, and they were full of talk about a young mother who was trying to get the manager to clean the place up. Hulen Hill had asked the manager repeatedly to fix the torn screens, paint and clean up the worst looking of the buildings, fix the plumbing, etc. He blew her off. So, she organized children and teenagers to do it themselves. He objected and ordered her to stop. She got so angry that she started talking about withholding rent until those needs were met. Nobody wanted trouble. It was hard enough for low income people to find an affordable place to live as it was; they sure did not need to get evicted for causing trouble.

I called Ms. Hill and introduced myself as pastor of the church on Shepherd Drive. She sounded skeptical but invited me to a residents' meeting later in the week. When I showed up at the apartment, she was obviously surprised, and everyone else looked at me like, "what is that white guy doing here?" They were all clearly hesitant to talk, but Hulen went ahead with the discussion and proposed a rent strike. They would pay their rent into an escrow fund which she set up at the local bank, and not turn it over to the manager till he had begun the repairs that they demanded.

They agreed to hold a rally on a Sunday afternoon ten days later to get as many residents as possible to sign a petition demanding that the needed repairs be done and encouraging them to pay their rent into the escrow account. I hung around after the meeting adjourned to talk to Hulen. I did not have much to offer, but the church had a mimeograph machine, and I could produce fliers announcing the rally.

The fliers were delivered door to door in Shepherd Gardens, and a large crowd gathered on the appointed Sunday. Someone had given the fliers to friends outside the Gardens, and one of them made it to the Houston Post. So, the crowd was unexpectedly large and included a couple reporters and photographers. Hulen and other supporters stood in the bed of a pickup truck to make their speeches, and the petitions were passed around and signed by some, not many.

On Monday I got a call from Sam Seahorn telling me that Hulen and her family had been evicted, and their furniture had been moved out onto the street. I went over to see what was going on, and Hulen was sitting on her couch, out at the curb, looking like she intended to stay there through the next hurricane. Neighbors came by and expressed sympathy but were clearly discouraged. Hulen and her husband Andrew and their three boys moved in with relatives temporarily, and their belongings were moved to a friend's garage. That was the beginning of my long and delightful friendship with Hulen, one of the most remarkable persons I have ever had the privilege to know.

Not satisfied with the family's eviction, the manager hauled Hulen into court to collect his back rent. The judge was Woodrow Seals, a bear of a man who had a reputation for fairness. She was defended by an attorney who had been recruited by a Vista Volunteer that worked in our neighborhood, and the attorney represented her *pro bono.*

When all the testimony was heard Judge Seals ruled against Hulen, then cleared the court and told her to stay behind. She nearly died, imagining that she might be carried off to the county jail. Instead, he told her, in effect, "Young lady, I had to rule against you because the city ordinance gives no rights to tenants at all. But you are right in protesting the conditions at Shepherd Gardens, and I hope you will appeal and take this all the way to the State Supreme Court if necessary."

Hulen took it to St. Louis instead. Our Vista Volunteers knew of an upcoming meeting of the National Tenant Organization, and we raised the money so she could go. Hulen was elected National Vice President. One of the organizing groups for that conference was the American Friends Service Committee, the social justice agency of the Quakers. When she returned to Houston Hulen was offered a job as a staff member of the Houston office of American Friends Service Committee. She impressed the people in that organization so much that when the AFSC was designated to organize the first trip of Americans to China after travel restrictions were lifted, they named Hulen to the delegation. She figured they needed someone Black, and she was the best they had. What a woman! What a story! And it will be continued.

* * * * *

In the first several years I learned to understand and even speak a little "Texan," but I never learned to think it. While the United Church of Christ was a perfect fit for me with its firm convictions regarding racial equality, global justice, Christian and interfaith unity and peace, that was a strange perspective for many in Bethel Church. When the General Synod of the UCC was to consider a resolution on gun control the national office sent out copies of it in advance to all the churches and asked for feedback.

I eagerly called a meeting of the congregation to discuss the resolution following worship one Sunday in 1969. Nearly everyone stayed for the discussion, we distributed copies of the resolution, and I reviewed the contents. It was a good discussion and people spoke, both for and against, with those against emphasizing the need to be able to defend ourselves and their homes. Neither Betsy nor I had grown up in homes where there was a gun, and I had never shot one, so the resolution seemed good to me. *Not so much*, to many of my parishioners.

Eventually, one of the respected elders of the church stood and said, "Well, in Switzerland they give every boy a gun when he is six years old and teach him how to shoot it. And did you ever hear of anyone ever invading Switzerland?" Many in the room went, "Oooh, wow, yeah." At that point Betsy, who was then pregnant with our third child, decided she was sick and made a hasty exit through the women's rest room. Women in the room thought, "Oh, poor dear."

I could tell that Betsy was thinking, "We've got to get out of here." There was another door on the other side of the women's restroom and Betsy went out that way and drove home. I had to walk. That was the beginning of the end of my pastoral service at Bethel.

It was also the beginning of our life with our third child. Amy was born at Herman Hospital in the massive Houston Medical Center in June 1969, just two months later. She was a delight, and with an older sister and brother, just smiled, paid attention, learned what would and would not be appreciated, and behaved accordingly. That wisdom apparently carried over into her school years and she was a really good student.

That same respected leader who thought six-year-olds should be armed, taught one of the adult church school classes. Worship was at 9:00 am since the sanctuary was not air conditioned, and church school was at 10:00. This revered teacher took the opportunity, when he disagreed with something I said in the sermon, which was frequently, to critique it. On one particular Sunday morning he opined, "the reason the early church did not grow was that they had all those folks like Amos and Hosea always talking about social justice." Abysmal ignorance of the scriptures and of biblical history is not confined to Bethel Church, but it was evident there, at least in that one Church School teacher.

I worked hard at adult education and developed and taught evening sessions on the Synoptic Problem, a comparative study of Matthew, Mark and Luke, and on the various traditions that were edited and combined in the Old Testament: the Documentary Hypothesis. It was what I learned in first year Bible courses in Seminary in the '60's. That particular teacher of the adult class never attended. But unexpectedly large numbers did, and they seemed to get it, and they liked it.

In that German Evangelical tradition, there was a high level of respect for "Herr Pastor," and if the pastor taught it, they believed they ought to at least think about it. The most frequent comment I heard was, "Why hasn't anyone told us this before?" The answers to that are fairly obvious: 1) Most Christians get what they do of Biblical knowledge from Sunday worship, and there they hear only brief passages out of context, unless the preacher supplies it. 2) Many pastors are reluctant to share anything they know or believe that might cause trouble in what may be a congregation with enough trouble as it is. So, basic knowledge of the Bible is shallow and does not include its historical and contextual background. I found, even at tradition-bound Bethel, that when church folks were given this basic information, they felt liberated.

* * * * *

One of the most remarkable experiences of our time in Houston and at Bethel Church grew out of a decision I made the first summer we were there. I convinced the Education Committee to agree to invite children from Allen Parkway Village, a nearby public housing project, to come to Vacation Church School. We ran off fliers and distributed them in the Village and got volunteers to drive there to pick up the kids on the first day. There were 16 or 18 children the first day, most of them Black or Latino.

The number fell off each day until there were a handful that finished the week, but we all felt good about the experience. Three brothers asked if they could come to Church School the following Sunday, and of course we said "yes," and arranged for their transportation. They were 13, 12, and 9 years old and it turned out that they had a six-year-old little brother. The Belvin boys were the only Anglo kids in Allen Parkway Village, and they were all good looking and cheerful. Church members arranged to pick them up every Sunday morning, and that lasted throughout the fall.

I went to check on them frequently at Allen Parkway Village and learned that their mom, Shirley, was from Virginia and had moved to Houston with her second husband who was the father of the youngest boy. They also had a daughter, J. J., who had serious, debilitating birth defects. Shirley told that me her husband had been a heavy equipment operator, found a good job in Houston, and they had located a house to rent. But they had gone swimming at one of the nearby lakes and the husband drowned. Without income they had to give up the rental house and move into public housing.

Shirley had previously worked as a telephone operator, but could not seek a job because the daughter, J. J., could not be placed in daycare: besides being severely mentally disabled, her skull failed to grow as she did and a portion of her brain was covered only by her scalp. I spent many days taking Shirley and J. J. to see doctors, waiting in their waiting rooms, and finally getting what looked like a tiny football helmet fitted for her. Care centers, public and private, still would not take on the liability of caring for her. So, Shirley stayed home.

And Shirley drank. She covered it up at first and the boys covered for her. An elderly African American woman, Ms. White, lived upstairs from them in their Allen Parkway apartment, and she cared for J. J., and did the best she could for the boys. Joe, the oldest, tried to take care of the younger boys, and Mike, the next oldest, became an expert beggar. He was baby-faced and winsome, and he hung around outside the downtown movie theatres after the shows closed and did well begging from the patrons. The family received commodities from the Harris County Welfare Department: Agriculture Department surplus food, including lard, corn meal, peanut butter and powdered milk. The boys foraged, and Shirley wasted away. As they became more desperate, they stopped calling and coming to church.

Bethel families had made several efforts to clean up the apartment, to bring in food staples and had even gotten a fairly good used car for Shirley to drive to work if she could ever get J. J. cared for. I made a pest of myself at the Social Security Commission, trying to get benefits for the family, only to find that J. J.'s father, Shirley's second husband, had never worked a steady job and had never received a Social Security number, nor had payments been made by any employer. He did day work for cash. There would be no additional financial support for Shirley and the kids.

Late one night I got a desperate phone call from Ms. White. She said, come as quick as you can. Shirley had told her and Joe that if anything ever happened to her, they were to "call Rev. Russell." I arrived at Allen Parkway and found Shirley unconscious, barely breathing, on the floor of the kitchen. Ms. White called the EMS, and they arrived quickly, took Shirley's vital signs, and remained stone faced as they loaded her into the van and took her to the hospital.

I went back inside and found the three youngest boys and J. J. sitting stunned and frightened on the floor where their mom had been. But where was Joe? He had been there when the EMS arrived. Ms. White told me that while they were putting Shirley in the van and I was outside with them, Joe had run away into the night crying.

Ms. White watched the younger children while Mike and I did a hurried and futile search for Joe. Then I asked Ms. White to call Betsy to tell her what had happened, and I took Mike and drove to Ben Taub

Hospital, Houston's public and charity hospital in the medical center. We were directed to the emergency room, saw Shirley briefly, still unconscious, as they took her into a curtained area. In a very short time, a doctor came out and told us that she had died.

I was stunned. Oh, God, what was I to do? Mike was in shock. I hugged him and he was almost limp. I half supported, half carried him to my car, and he fell asleep on the way back to the Village. I roused him and got him into his bed. Ms. White had gotten the others to sleep. Joe had not returned. I told Ms. White that I would come back in the morning and we would figure out what to do. In seminary they told us, when in doubt, pray. I prayed hard that night.

The next day I went again to the village and Ms. White and I decided that she would take J. J. up to her rooms and I would take the boys with me. All four piled into my old Fiat station wagon, and we went home. I called the church families who had helped with the boys and were fond of them, told them what had happened and asked them to meet me at the church. In the meantime, I called the Harris County Welfare Department and learned, to my astonishment, that all the social workers, including the Belvins' case worker, were on strike. No one was available. We were on our own.

If you don't believe that church people have compassionate hearts, just ask them for help in this sort of situation. Everyone I called came. We met with four families at the church one afternoon and began to ponder together what we could do for and with the boys and J. J. in the short run and, with some trepidation, in the long run. Of course, we had to contact Shirley's relatives who lived in Virginia. I would work on that with Betsy's help, and would also contact a friend who was an attorney to clarify the children's legal status. While we were waiting for information from those contacts, one of the young mothers in the church agreed to take the two younger boys, John and Richard, and Betsy and I would take care of the older boys, Joe and Mike.

Amy, our third child, had been born just months before and slept in a bassinette in our bedroom. Joe and Mike slept on bunk beds that I, in-

ept carpenter though I am, had built the previous summer in anticipation of the new baby. We planned to eventually put the new child, if it
was a boy, in with Stephen on the bunks and, if it was a girl, she and Beth
would get the bunk beds. So much for planning. But we had the bunk
beds. I drove Joe and Mike to and from their inner-city school every day,
thinking it was best to keep them there with kids they knew rather than
move them to the one near our house.

Joe and Mike fit in well with our family, and Joe especially bonded
with baby Amy. He actually caught her in midair one day when she
rolled off the changing table as Betsy turned to get the diaper pins (remember diaper pins?). He still reminds her of that. Our only problem
was that we could not keep food in the fridge. They had to forage for
food and beat their brothers to any that was in their apartment at Allen
Parkway for so long that they had a hard time breaking that urge. When
I brought them home from school each day I would return to my office
at the church, and they would dash for the fridge. It didn't take Betsy
long to figure out why the food was disappearing, but it took weeks to
change the pattern.

After our meeting with the Bethel Church families Betsy started the
process of making contact with Shirley's Virginia family and I called
Thatcher Adams, our attorney friend. Then I called Mrs. White to see
how she and J. J. were doing, and I got my second shock. Staff from the
Welfare Department, when they got the message that Shirley had died,
had come first thing the next morning and taken J. J. away. Mrs. White
could not remember where they said they were taking her or if she had
even been told. So, I began trying to get in touch with the social workers again, and with the same result; they were on strike and no one was
available.

Thatcher and Mary Adams lived just around the corner and he and
I played tennis together fairly regularly. The Adams' kids were the same
ages as ours, and we were together a lot. Thatcher gave us the legal implications of the situation, including the need to contact Shirley's family,
the boys' next of kin. He came over to the house and met the boys and

his mental wheels started turning. These were nice kids, good looking kids. We should have no trouble finding guardians or adoptive parents for them. But there were four! Who could afford to take care of them? How could an adoptive family or families ever educate them? He suggested calling the newspaper to get them to do a story, and also to set up a foundation for the boys' long-term support. I agreed, and he called the Houston Post. That's when things really started getting hectic.

A reporter and photographer came to the house on a Friday afternoon and talked with the four boys, then had them photographed on the swing set and slide in our back yard. Joe had mentioned to the reporter that his mom would want them to stay together. That was the headline on the front page of the Saturday morning edition of the Houston Post, complete with a large photo of the four boys looking angelic. The appeal for funds for a foundation was buried near the end of the article on page ten. Our phone started ringing at 6:00 am on Saturday morning as people in Houston opened their morning paper. It rang all day.

Between calls, Betsy phoned a friend and asked her to get some others from the church and come to the parsonage to help answer the phone and take notes. There were over 40 calls from people who wanted or were willing to take all four boys. Friends took turns answering the phone and taking notes, promising each other that we would be back in touch. One man had looked up our address and drove up to the house in his pickup truck and wanted to take all four boys right then. I took his name and phone number and promised to contact him soon. One thing became very obvious: we needed help!

One of our church families knew a social worker who had recently retired from working in a nearby orphanage, and one of her jobs had been interviewing families that were applying for adoptions. Thankfully, she was free and willing to help us sort through the deluge of requests and follow up with the appropriate sort of inquiries. She was officious, much impressed with her special status, but she was efficient. We had phone interviews with a number of the most likely seeming families, and narrowed our list down to three whom we called for interviews.

We finally chose the Hilliards, a family with three daughters who were by then young adults and away from home, and they had adopted and reared two orphaned teenage girls. They at least had some idea of what they might have to deal with. Mr. and Ms. Hilliard met the boys at our house, and a week later joined us for Thanksgiving dinner and took Joe, Mike, John and Richard to their new home. By then we had received the necessary legal release from Shirley's family, and I even managed to track down the father of the older boys who was eager to have someone else take them. Little sister J. J. was finally located in a state run home for invalid children 200 miles away in North Texas. They couldn't help Shirley find placement or assistance, but when she died, they whisked the child away in a heartbeat!

Joe stayed in touch for the next decades and has joined us for Christmas and other family celebrations. Betsy and I regard him as a foster son and our kids as a brother, and he still has a special affection for Amy. His story could be a whole additional chapter, or even a book.

* * * * *

Pastoral duties at Bethel were somewhat unique, though every pastor can tell similar anecdotes from his/her own experience. One of the most bizarre started as a phone call from Beverly in which she told me that her husband had left the house waving a gun and shouting, and had just called from a strip mall near their home, and asked if I would go calm him down. Lloyd was her third husband, and they were both still in their twenties and children of Bethel Church families. I drove over to the strip mall, located Lloyd's truck, parked next to it, opened the passenger door and said something like, "uh, hey Lloyd, it's me, Rollin. Can we talk?" He nodded.

I got in and there on the seat between us was a pistol. I was able to talk him down, but did not want to reach for the gun. So, I asked if I opened the glove box, would he put the gun in. He said, OK, so I did, and he did. We talked some more, and I asked him to drive home; I would follow. He said, no, but he would drive to his momma's. He did, and I went home.

That was the craziest incident, but not the only unusual one. My tenure at Bethel occurred at a time when M. D. Anderson Hospital was regarded as one of the premier cancer hospitals in the nation. St. Luke's Hospital boasted of Dr. Michael Debakey, an early and successful heart transplant surgeon, while next door at Methodist Hospital, Dr. Denton Cooley was quickly gaining heart transplant notoriety. Almost weekly I would get a call from a UCC pastor in another part of the country who had a parishioner in one of those famous hospitals. There were and are a dozen UCC churches in Houston, but Bethel was listed first in the UCC Yearbook. Some of my colleagues got these calls, but none as frequently as I did. So, I made regular visits to the Houston Medical Center to visit patients and families from around the country as well as with my own parishioners.

The physicians there were among the best at the diagnosis and treatment of diseases, but a number of them were obviously ill equipped, and therefore reluctant to deal with fear and grief in their patients and families. Not that I was any kind of expert, but I did sit and talk and pray with them. I heard their stories, tried to help them deal with the news they may just have received, and prayed with them, for them and for the doctors and nurses who attended to them.

I tried to call up their own resources of memory and faith, the support they knew they had from family, friends and church. It's not easy being a stranger in a strange city, there to care for someone who, by virtue of the fact that had traveled far to seek the care of the finest physicians, were in dire straits. The presence of someone who had a connection to home and to a familiar religious tradition and who knew the area seemed to bring some relief.

I was and am very uncomfortable with the conventional comments made to folks in such situations: "He's in a better place now," or "God wanted her with Him," or "It's all part of God's plan." I could always think of a dozen theological and practical reasons why such comments were both trite and, in most cases, less than comforting. "So, what's God's plan for me to raise these three kids alone and with no income?" "What's God's plan for the drunk that hit my wife's car?"

There are, of course, stock "religious" answers, but they are precious little consolation or comfort. Sometimes words are woefully inadequate to articulate the unspeakable pain, fear, confusion and even anger that people feel. And they are equally inadequate to express the support and empathy we would like to give.

We all stumble in our attempts to be of comfort in tough circumstances. So we pray, in faith that "the Spirit intercedes with our spirit in sighs too deep for words." And I would pray and sigh, with and for them and all the way back to my office at the church. Pastoral ministry is an emotionally demanding and draining vocation, which is why a strong sense of calling is required to sustain it, and why, even so, there is so much "burn out."

One of the blessings of ministry, however, is the collegiality with and among other pastors who know and experience the cost and joy of this particular form of discipleship. I cherish the friendship of those ministry colleagues with whom I have shared late night conversations, laughter and the raucous singing of the bloodiest of Gospel Hymns. Art always brought his guitar and David his banjo to clergy retreats and to after-hours sessions at annual meetings. Those are the times when kindred spirits find each other, and we did. We shared a lively sense that our churches needed to change, become more open to new ideas, to racial and social justice, to new forms of worship, to the ecumenical unity which was a hallmark of the UCC. We were all engaged in our own communities in various activities that these commitments inspired. So, we had a lot to talk and laugh and sing about.

It was at a Pastors' Retreat that I first met Clarence Baldwin, then the pastor at First Congregational UCC in Fort Worth. He had been a friend of my father when they both served churches in Indianapolis in the 1940's. We talked and laughed about memories of Indiana and about the challenges of pastoral ministry. He was planning to retire soon, and he later gave my name to the Search Committee that would seek his successor. Events moved very quickly from there.

10

FORT WORTH

It was two weeks before Thanksgiving in 1971, my first year as pastor at First Congregational United Church of Christ in Fort Worth (pronounced, Fo't Wu'th). The family had moved there during the summer from Houston, we had a very nice parsonage fairly near the church and the welcome was warm and good natured. These were our kind of folks. I wanted to do everything well, so I wanted to start planning early for their special Thanksgiving Day Service.

I asked Polly Webb, the longtime church secretary, to come into the study so we could sketch out the service. Polly had been the secretary there through the previous two pastorates and was efficient, congenial and full of information. She knew where all the bodies were buried and who buried them.

"How do we get started planning for Thanksgiving," I asked. She replied, "We don't," then grinned and walked into her office which was next to mine. She came back in a few seconds with a small box, from which she took a small, white piece of cloth, held it up for me to see a 20 inch strip, an inch and a half wide, with two strips hanging from the middle. It was a set of clergy tabs, the clerical emblem worn by Puritan preachers in the 17th Century, and still worn by many Reformed and Lutheran pastors in Europe. She then said, "All you do is prepare a sermon, wear your robe and put these on. The Deacons take care of everything else."

Whoa! How great is that: a church where the Deacons and lay leaders actually take primary leadership? I was delighted. But how would it all work? Would I need to prepare a printed program, pick out hymns, an article in the newsletter? Not that I have control needs or anything like that, but, well, I like to see how it all fits together. Polly began to explain that Thanksgiving morning was an annual big event, and the congregation took great pride in it and pulled it off every year with zeal and good humor.

She then took me up to the choir room where there was a separate wardrobe next to the one where the choir robes were kept. In it were racks of gray "good wife," ankle length dresses with white aprons, collars and caps. The women all wore these to breakfast and the service. Next to them was a rack of simple black jackets, pantaloons and white knee sox and collars for the men. There were children's versions of both, and I was assured that Betsy and my daughters would be properly outfitted. That evening, I called Joe Henry, who had been on the Search Committee that recommended me, and he explained the whole set up.

On Thanksgiving morning, we all got up early, Betsy and the girls put on their pilgrim outfits, Stephen, now five, rolled his eyes in a combination of envy and disdain, and we all arrived at the church a little before 8:00 am. Members were gathering outside the main entrance and in the parking lot, most of the women and some of the men and children were in costume as custom required.

One of the Deacons stepped ceremoniously through the front door and blew several loud blasts on a conch shell, and we all trooped into the fellowship hall for a huge breakfast prepared by one of the women's groups. There were additional blasts from the conch shell during the meal by the irrepressible Deacon, much to everyone's delight.

Promptly at 8:50 Bill Skokan, the Sergeant at Arms for the day, banged his long staff on the floor, led the procession into worship, and divided the flock: women into the pews on the left, men on the right. I followed in my black robe with the heavily starched clerical tabs properly displayed at my throat. The singing was *a capella*, with the choir director leading the traditional hymns: "We Gather Together to Ask the Lord's Blessing," and "Come, Ye Thankful People, Come."

Bill Skokan prowled up and down the aisles brandishing his staff. It had a feather attached to one end and a knob to the other. If anyone dozed off during the sermon he would tickle the ladies and rap the men on the head. Of course, many made a show of doing just that, with the desired result.

Appropriate scriptures were read, prayers of thanksgiving were offered, and I preached, though not for an hour or more as would have been the case in Plymouth in the 1620's. The day's levity faded as the service progressed, and the ended in heart-felt, if light-hearted, gratitude and praise, with the singing of the Doxology.

As I reflected on that odd, happy experience I recognized that it offered these folks a celebration of their own social and cultural history that was a shade unique in Fort Worth, Texas. Most of them were transplants from New England and the upper Midwest. The men had served in the military, gone to school on the GI Bill and came to Texas to work in the booming aeronautic industry. They were self-conscious, died-in-the-wool Congregationalists, and this was their day.

* * * * *

The congregation was founded in the early 20th Century by a group of New England Congregationalists when Fort Worth was a center of the beef industry, and the Stock Yards were the commercial hub of the city. The original church building was on the south side of town a short distance from downtown and the stock yards beyond. Members recalled that the C. W. Post family had been members, Yankees who had a grain business at the stock yards and later founded their cereal company after C. W. Post spent time in Battle Creek Michigan. Hey, he already had a corner on the grain market! Later, with Post family support, the congregation rebuilt on its site a small, elegant church building. There it remained, serving northern Congregationalists and their kinfolk and friends, until after World War II when Bill Burton became their pastor.

Rev. Bill Burton was a real piece of work: energetic, visionary, affable, persuasive; exactly what was needed at the time. He saw the town expanding in every direction but especially toward the Southwest, around Texas Christian University and beyond. He was a member of the World War I Fliers Club and of every civic club that would let him in, and he got to know everybody who was anybody in Fort Worth.

One of those buddies was the developer of a new, up-scale housing tract on Trail Lake Drive. Bill convinced his friend that it was good business and good for the community to give to the congregation a choice parcel of land on which it would build a beautiful, eye-catching church. The land was deeded to the church and the building was erected.

It was every bit as attractive and picturesque as Bill promised. Built of blonde stone in a gothic style, it had a tower at the junction of its sanctuary and education buildings and stained-glass windows with scenes of Jesus' life and ministry. The sanctuary had a long nave with center aisle, perfect for weddings, and a rose window above the chancel. It was on the brow of a hill overlooking Trail Lake Drive, surrounded by acres of lawn that, obviously, had to be mowed regularly, a perpetual crisis.

Unfortunately, when the building was completed, the money had run out. There were no funds for furnishings, or even painting. Did that slow Bill Burton down? Are you kidding? He went to first one civic club and then another and convinced each of them to furnish a room in the new church. Then he would ask, "Do you want to do the primary classroom or the men's room." Of course, each chose a classroom or an assembly room. Bill Burton, laughing all the way, then painted the walls and laid the flooring in the men's room himself. It was, sort of, Bill Burton's church, and as he got older that became a bone of contention.

Younger members felt they were expected to do everything Bill's way, and it got to be more than tedious. So, they started meeting in the Scout Hut on the property until a new pastor was called. They kept giving, but to a separate account, promised to come back, with their money and participation, and let the loyalists choose the new pastor.

So, Bill Burton resigned, moved to a retirement community in Florida and, at age 70, started a new church--a rapidly growing new church! The remnant called Rev. Clarence Baldwin to be their new pastor, and the dissidents came back as promised. Clarence Baldwin was my predecessor, and it was he who recommended me to the Search Committee when he retired eight years later.

* * * * *

Pastors sometimes refer to their choirs as the War Department. Not so at First Congregational in Fort Worth. What a delightful bunch of relocated Yankees. And they could really sing. Much of the credit goes to Chuck Miller, our choir director: happy, positive, cooperative, gifted Minnesotan, for whom choir members would jump off a cliff.

It was their custom at Sunday Worship, following the prelude and before the Processional Hymn, to sing, *a capella*, an introit from the Narthex. They produced a sound, in perfect harmony and balance, that was hauntingly beautiful. Then Edith, our organist, would start the Opening Hymn of Praise and the choir would process down the center aisle with Chuck in the lead and me bringing up the rear. Joy and praise were palpable, and worship felt deep and true. Usually.

The choir members, however, had one fixation that became somewhat problematic. They were Dallas Cowboys fanatics. Roger Staubach was the quarterback, and the team was winning nearly every game, and was expected to win them all. There was a sign in the choir room, a teeth-grinding abuse of scripture: "With Roger, All Things Are Possible."

The problem arose on Sundays when the game was in the Eastern time zone and televised starting at noon. It was made very clear to me that the service, which began at 11:00, dare not run overtime. The sermon was the last thing before the Closing Hymn, and Chuck would give me a sign at 11:50. I was sort of afraid that Edith might start the hymn at 11:55 whether I was finished or not. The congregation really appreciated the brevity.

The choir had a seasonal social calendar. In the summer there was always a pool party and luau at one member's home. In the fall there was a roasting ear feast. Chuck would make a trip home to Minnesota just as the corn was being harvested, and when he returned the choir and families would gather to roast and eat corn-on-the-cob, with maybe a salad for variety. I concluded that the farther folks were from home and family, the more closely they bonded and the more important to them was their shared life, especially in the church where they sang, laughed, ate and prayed together. Blessed, indeed, is the pastor or member who finds or helps create such a mutually supportive community.

It was the teenaged kids of the choir families that made up most of the youth group. This was the early 1970's, the Vietnam war was raging, and many of the dads were working on defense contracts at General Dynamics making fighter planes, at Bell Helicopter making Hueys and combat choppers, or at Carswell Air Force Base servicing or flying B-52's, the Magic Dragons of the USAF. The kids were not anti-war demonstrators . . . yet, but they sure did not want to go to Vietnam. They adopted the sloppy dress, long hair and counter-culture music that drove their parents nuts. I was 34 years old at the time I began serving there, and I think there was an ulterior motive to the congregation calling me at an unusually young age for a fairly large church: they hoped I could communicate with and "straighten out" their kids. Not that they were mean or angry about them, just perplexed and concerned about where they might be headed.

It turned out that many of them were headed to college and some to graduate school, but that was anything but apparent at the time. We took carloads at every opportunity to our church camp, Slumber Falls, on the Guadalupe River near New Braunfels, Texas. There was always a full camp of kids from UCC churches around Texas and Louisiana. At camp we ran the schedule in accordance with their body clocks: breakfast at 9:30 am and lights out at midnight.

We enjoyed lots of tubing down the river and the gentle rapids at our site, lots of singing and guitar accompaniment around evening campfires, and lots of talking, with biblical themes, spirituality and ethics at the center. It was bonding time for kids, and since there were twenty African American congregations in our Conference, their teenagers were always part of the group. Everyone got an education they could not, at that time, have gotten in many other places in Texas or Louisiana.

One special feature of the camp site was an old mule whose coat turned gray then white over the years. He belonged to the farmer who owned the property next to the camp and who helped our camp manager care for the grounds. One of the Black kids started calling him Honky the Donkey and the name stuck. Every veteran camper would head for the barbed wire fence on the day they arrived and whistle for Honky the Donkey.

The second unique feature of Slumber Falls Camp was Old Man River, invented by one of our lifeguards who came to camp every year and told hair raising tales around the campfire at night. Old Man River lived in the cedar brakes down by the river and was never seen in daylight, but often at night would silently come up the bank and hang around the cabins closest to the river, which, of course were the girls' cabins. There was much scary rolling of eyes and nervous laughter, but a good many girls looked cautiously both ways when they left their cabins in the morning. And, of course, there were always guys who were willing to hang out with the girls after dark, uh, just in case.

Having directed one or more youth camps each summer and seen some of our annual campers mature over those years, it is gratifying to note how many continued in leadership roles. Some became camp directors, others counselors, some eventually served on the camp board of directors. It is particularly satisfying that a number of young men and women became pastors, some in our Conference, and brought their youth groups to Slumber Falls. Be still, my heart.

On the Sunday before Christmas in 1973, the sanctuary was packed, and spirits were high. The chancel and the nave were decorated with greens and candles, and a large Christmas tree had been placed in front of the chancel next to the lectern. The choir sang the introit and processed down the center aisle with Chuck Miller in the lead, singing "O, Come All Ye Faithful." I followed the choir, as usual, and as we went up the steps into the chancel, I noticed that the lights on the tree were blinking. Then, when I stood behind the lectern, I noticed that they were blinking in time with the music.

I could see various people in the pews starting to notice the lights, looking concerned, then confused, as they recognized the rhythm. Then I looked up to the balcony where the teenagers always sat, and they were holding their sides laughing. They had conspired to place a sound activated circuit breaker from the microphone on the lectern to the Christmas tree lights.

In the meantime, one of the ushers saw the blinking, thought it might be a short in the wiring and, trying to be unobtrusive, came crawling up the side aisle to unplug the tree. Just as he reached for the plug it dawned on him that it was blinking in time with the hymn. After the service we all had a good laugh: the kids were somewhat disappointed in that they intended for the blinking to take place when I spoke from the lectern. Blessed kids. A very memorable Christmas.

* * * * * *

The church's four-bedroom parsonage was in a suburban development about a mile south of the church. Beth was in the second grade and Stephen in kindergarten when we moved to Fort Worth, and Amy was two years old and at home with Betsy. School desegregation was on the horizon and the Fort Worth Public Schools chose a somewhat peculiar, though not totally unique approach to satisfying the federal courts. Students in the second grade from all Fort Worth's predominantly white schools were to be bussed every morning to a "Second Grade Center" in what had been a Black school. All the third, fourth and fifth graders from schools in African American neighborhoods would be sent on the return busses to various schools in white neighborhoods. So, all children, from the second to the sixth grade would be bussed back and forth across town. There was much questioning and some protest, but the city largely cooperated with the plan.

The parents of second graders at our neighborhood school decided that one mother each day would ride with the children to their east side school. Then another mother would follow the bus in her car and bring the 'chaperone' back. Betsy dutifully volunteered to be the bus monitor/chaperone and, when told of the arrangement for the return trip, said: 'that's OK, I'll just ride the bus back. She was puzzled by the puzzled look she got from the return ride volunteer. Apparently, none of the other mothers had been interested in riding back with the Black kids.

The ride over with the second graders was uneventful, though a little noisy. The trip back was also uneventful and was made in total silence. After the children had all gotten off the bus Betsy asked the driver why the ride back with the Black children was so quiet, and she was told that they were afraid that the 'white lady' had been sent to 'keep an eye on them.' Those early days of desegregation in Fort Worth were reluctant and cautious.

Back on our side of town, at the school where the Black kids were bussed, our daughter Bethany was a fourth grader. We were somewhat concerned about her because she was not getting good report cards and had comments like, "she doesn't seem to be paying attention" or "she doesn't seem to understand what I'm saying." Betsy had her tested at the Easter Seals learning lab and found that she was plenty intelligent, but had a problem with auditory discrimination: she could not focus on what she needed to if there was background noise... It was suggested that she be moved to the front of the classroom and that her teachers be made aware of the issue.

So, Betsy went in to see the principle to deliver the news and introduced herself as Bethany Russell's mother. The principal grinned and said, "Oh, I know Bethany." Betsy looked confused and he told her that just a few days earlier Beth had come into his office and informed him that some of the kids on the playground were saying things that their mothers would not want them to say. He had asked, like what? And Beth proceeded to tell him: "one two, fuck you, three four, do it some more." The principal kept his cool and asked if she knew what that meant, "and she gave me a look, like, do I have to explain this to you?" Beth was our irrepressible child.

* * * * * *

The Black community in Fort Worth was fairly small at that time, but the Latino community was growing and was facing resistance and exploitation. Illegal Mexican workers were routinely hired by small manufacturers and fired without notice on Thursdays if the employer couldn't meet payroll on Friday. One of the members of the congregation shame-facedly mentioned that illegals provided a ready supply of workers at his car wash. He asked no questions and was legally safe because they all came with Social Security cards, fake, of course, and he withheld FICA deductions from their wages. He figured that the never-to-be-collected Social Security taxes paid on behalf of illegal workers is what kept the system afloat.

At one point in my tenure at the church we needed a janitor. I would like to think it was providential, though it may just have been dumb luck, but one day, Isidro Mendoza walked into the church and asked if we had any odd jobs he could do. His English was pretty good, and I had half-heartedly studied Spanish in high school ("El burro es un animal. El burro es un animal importante," etc.). We were able to communicate and had fun with it, each laughing at the other's stumbling attempts. I offered him a job on the spot. What a relief: no advertising, no interviewing. Hey, I interviewed him. Isidro was a gift. In the ensuing months I learned that he was undocumented, had made his way across the border and north by riding the rails, and jumped off near the church to try his luck in Fort Worth.

The luck was all ours. He was tall and hefty, a happy, joking person who could and would do anything that was asked, and church people sometimes ask a lot. He worked mornings, kept the church spotless and the grounds in good shape. In retrospect, the church could be seen as exploiting him, but the wages were fair for part time work, and at the time it seemed like a mutually satisfactory relationship.

It was at about that time that I met Jose Garcia. He had been one of the first Mexican American students at TCU and he was trying to organize the Latino community to protest and alleviate some of the gross injustices and indignities that they suffered. He was looking for Anglo church folks who would support his efforts and I was a ready ally. One of the most egregious affronts was The Frito Bandito. The Frito-Lay company ran its ads for Fritos every day on all three of the then available TV channels. The "Bandito" was a caricatured cartoon Mexican, complete with sombrero, serape and blazing six guns. The image was deeply offensive to Latinos. It seemed like a good place to start.

We organized a group and called it Free Flow of Information. The issue was the media and the ways in which it ignored the Latino Community and the issues that plagued it, as well as the mindlessly aired offensive stereotypes, including the Bandito. Free Flow of Information was never a non-profit organization and never attempted to raise money; just a group of five or six folks who wanted the community to recognize and respect its neighbors. We began at the top: local managers of the three major TV networks, all in Dallas. We wrote letters and made phone calls and finally got an appointment with the station manager of one of the stations.

By that time, I had been elected President of the Fort Worth Area Council of Churches, so it was Jose and I who were tagged to keep the appointment. We prepared our presentation, drove to Dallas, waited patiently in the lobby and finally met with an assistant manager. He was cordial, asked a few questions, assured us of his full understanding of the situation, and that he would speak to his superiors. He was otherwise non-committal. We felt shafted. The ride back to Fort Worth was spent in puzzled, discouraged conversation as we tried to decide if our interview had accomplished anything at all. The Frito Bandito did not disappear from the ads, not right away. Our group and others continued to call and write, and it disappeared in a year or so. Latino communities grew, their scorn for Frito Lay products and their informal boycott became apparent. It was a sort of a slow, quiet victory and I have no idea if our effort had any impact, but it put me in touch with the issue of immigration and the issues facing the marginalized immigrant communities.

* * * * *

Fort Worth in the early '70's, like many other cities, was alive with controversy over the influx of teenage runaways. Interstate 20 ran through the town and most of the kids, "wanna be hippies," were headed to California. Many were from the northeast and had some harrowing and some garden-variety tales of why they left home. They showed up on church doorsteps and hung out around the shops near Texas Christian University. Some had credit cards, but most looked for odd jobs and hung out with the credit card holders.

I had gotten to know two young Lutheran ministers who were renting a large old house near the downtown area where these kids could stay and be safe. I proposed that our church folks get involved and they were eager to do so. Members from various local churches were volunteering to help with cooking one meal each day and making sure there was at least one adult staying overnight.

The churches involved also contributed to the monthly rent, and expenses, and Steve and Piet, my Lutheran ministry friends, coordinated and oversaw the effort. Their number one rule was that for a kid to stay there, they had to contact his/her parents to let them know where they were and that they were in a safe place.

It became clear that several of the kids were sexually active and threw precautions to the wind. Abortion was illegal in Texas, as it was elsewhere. Like most pastors, I had counseled families who faced the nightmare of a daughter with an unintended pregnancy, or a son who was co-responsible, but I never thought of suggesting an abortion.

I had been a delegate to the UCC General Synod meeting in 1971 and voted for the "Pronouncement on Freedom of Choice Concerning Abortion." So, I was receptive when my colleagues gathered a group of pastors together to discuss the need for pastoral counselors to screen women and girls who were seeking an abortion. A doctor in Dallas was willing to perform safe, therapeutic abortions in a clinic, but wanted to make sure potential patients were screened and counseled before being referred there. I nervously accepted the responsibility and the risk.

I only saw five or six women and made several referrals before *Roe v. Wade* was adopted by the Supreme Court in 1972, much to my relief. Most of the women I saw were married and had children, or were recently divorced, had children, and were pregnant by the former husband. Several were co-eds from the university. All were mortified and desperate. Those were difficult, sometimes painful, tearful interviews, but I felt that I had been appropriately helpful.

There is a question to the candidate in the ordination vows of the UCC: "Will you seek to regard all people with equal love and concern and undertake to minister impartially to the needs of all?" I had affirmed that vow. Another question was: "Will you keep silent all confidences shared with you?" I had also affirmed that vow. There is a statement in the denominational Manual on Ministry: "The pastor will minister to all persons without fear or favor." Most churches have that or similar standards for their pastors. I can't say I had no fear, but I felt authorized by the General Synod pronouncement and bound by those commitments

.

* * * * *

Rearing children in a parsonage is a unique challenge. I should know, having been the "Preacher's Kid" in our church and neighborhood during my tender years. So, I was determined to try to shield our kids from that hazard. But relating to church members and leaders involves some unanticipated surprises.

The Church Moderator and Chair of the Church Council and his family lived only a couple blocks from the parsonage and his daughter had been our babysitter on numerous occasions. We left our kids with that family for a weekend while we attended the Conference Annual Meeting.

When we got home, the teenage daughter could not wait to see us, and she was bursting with laughter when she recounted the scene at an evening meal. Out of the blue, and as though she had been contemplating it for some time, our by then three year old, Amy, happily pointed to each person in turn around the table saying, "you have a vagina, you have a penis, you have a vagina . . . ." There was a long silence. The mother and father turned red, then purple, coughed, stared at the ceiling, while the daughter and her older brother nearly exploded trying not to laugh. Beth and Stephen did not seem surprised at all, and Amy smiled sweetly. Neither of those words had ever, ever been uttered aloud in that household.

The unfunny sequel to that anecdote and in relation to that family sent chills down my spine. There was a controversy over the fact that "the pastor had met with the youth in the Ladies' Parlor which had just been redecorated." Gasp! Within days, the wife of the moderator took eight-year-old Beth aside and cajoled her into telling her daddy that he should not have done that. Being kind to the pastor's children: good. Manipulating them and using them to manipulate the pastor: not good! I could not abide by that.

All parish pastors have favorite stories of their experience in pastoral visitation and counseling, some strange, even weird, and some downright funny. Several of my "unforgetables" happened in Fort Worth. I got a call late one night from the parents of one of the girls in the youth group. She had run away from home earlier in the day with her boyfriend, and they had just heard from the police in Wichita Falls: they had the two kids in custody. The parents asked if I would ride with them to Wichita Falls to pick her up. Of course, I went. The 110 mile drive up featured much speculation about where they had been headed and why, plus comments on the boyfriend and their dislike of him.

We arrived at the police station in the early morning hours and found the daughter waiting, sullen and silent. The paperwork was finished and as we walked back out to the car the father suggested that I ride in back with the girl. Oh boy... They expected me to do a heavy duty counseling session on the ride home with her, and them listening in the front seat. I liked the kid. She was lively and funny in the youth group and at camp, but tonight she was not having any!

I started with, "Uh, where were you going?" The answer she gave almost made me laugh out loud: they were headed to Woodstock. The famous/infamous Woodstock Festival in upstate New York had happened in 1969, three years before. It was over. And they were headed in the wrong direction! At that point she yawned and went to sleep.

That trip to Wichita Falls was the weirdest and biggest flop of my pastoral counseling efforts, but not the funniest. I kept a list of shut-ins who I visited once or twice each month, and I had been visiting with Elsie for nearly a year. She lived alone in her home near the church and had been a deacon when I first arrived. The conversation was always pleasant, and she loved to tell stories about her kids and grandkids. One day in early November I was visiting Elsie and she told me that I should really go to the Thanksgiving Day service at her church. They all dressed up in Pilgrim outfits, had a big breakfast then went into the sanctuary for a worship service. I was confused at first: had she been going to another church that had a similar observance? Then she added: you would really like our pastor. I said, "Elsie, you don't know who I am, do you?" She responded, "Of course. You're the Fuller Brush Man."

The joys, sorrows and challenges of pastoral ministry always amaze me. God bless all parish pastors and the lay folks who appreciate and support them. The First Congregational Church was a gift and a blessing, and during my time there I also became deeply involved in the life of the South Central Conference and that was a gift, too. It is one of the smaller conferences in the United Church of Christ, only 87 congregations scattered through all of Texas and Louisiana.

In addition to leading youth camps and conferences at Slumber Falls, I had been a Conference delegate to the UCC General Synod, its national assembly of 2,000+ delegates held every second year to set denominational policy. I was also a member of the Conference Board of Directors and felt blessed to be part of such a dynamic and historic church tradition, so committed to the ethical and spiritual values that were dear to my heart. Hence, the next change in our family life and in my pilgrimage was no real surprise.

11

NOTHIN' COULD BE FINA' THAN
TO BE IN CAROLINA

James H. Lightbourne, Jr., was the revered and beloved Conference Minister of the Southern Conference since its founding in 1965. It was a shock when he died unexpectedly at the age of 59 from a heart attack. He was the picture of good health, an avid golfer and tennis player, he died on the tennis court. He was playing with a long-time friend and tennis buddy when he collapsed after the first set. At Jimmy's funeral that friend expressed the shock and pain that the large congregation of friends and admirers felt, then said, "He beat me in the first set then died so I wouldn't be able to even the score." It was a fitting testimony to Jimmy's famous sense of humor.

The first time I attended a gathering of the Council of Conference Ministers, 39 leaders from each of the UCC Conferences, it was to represent Jim Tomasek during his recovery from surgery. A portion of a session one day was set aside to hear a story from Jimmy Lightbourne; it was a regular and highly anticipated part of every agenda. He would regale the group with humorous tales of the crazy things church folk do, always elaborately embellished, and his colleagues would laugh uproariously. Unfortunately, it was Jimmy's last meeting with the CCM.

I received a phone call the next November to let me know that my name had been submitted to the Southern Conference Search Committee and to see if I would be willing to have my ministerial profile submitted for their consideration. I was surprised, pleased and a little frightened. Those would be some big shoes to fill, a hard act to follow.

I was told later that four people had suggested my name, two from the national UCC offices in New York: Dr. Purcell Alston and Rev. Yvonne Delk, both African American staff persons of the Division of Education who knew of my commitment to racial justice and to Christian education. The other two were from leaders in the Southern Conference: Cally Rogers-Witte and Ken Clapp, who knew me through regional leadership development sessions. They were both on the Search Committee.

The meeting with the Search Committee took place in January, and it was a straight-talking, good-natured group that truly represented the strange and complicated mix of churches in the Southern Conference. There were about 300 congregations spread across North Carolina and Southern Virginia. 80+/- were from the German Reformed tradition, 120+/- from the Afro-Christian tradition, and 100+/- from the Southern Christian tradition. More on that later: it's complicated. It was clear from the start that these folks were committed to building this unique conglomerate of churches into a vibrant Conference, focused on mutual understanding, unity, and spiritual growth. The discussions were lively and good-humored.

I was excited when I left the interview and things moved quickly from there. Dale Bennett, the committee chairperson, called two days later and told me that the committee wanted to submit my name as their candidate for Conference Minister. He invited me to meet with the Conference Board of Directors in February and, if all went well and the board concurred, to be voted on at a Called Meeting of the Conference in March.

Betsy and I had been talking about the prospects of this move ever since the committee asked for my profile. If we moved, she would want to find a new teaching job there, and while the Search Committee folks were sure that would be no problem, it was still an issue for us. Now we told the kids about a possible move to North Carolina. It would mean new schools for them, and they were okay with that. Beth was to graduate from Liberty Hill High School in late May, so if the move happened it would have to be scheduled around that, and it would mean a big decision for her on where to go to college. Plus, we had two cats and a dog to take with us and those logistics were daunting. There were lots of questions to be worked out, but everyone was on board.

Betsy, Beth, and I went to Burlington, NC for the meeting with the Southern Conference Board of Directors. Stephen and Amy stayed next door with the Galles. Beth was along to visit the two colleges that had been founded by Southern Conference churches, Elon College, near Burlington, and Catawba College in Salisbury. She intended to apply to a college in Georgetown, TX so we hoped it would go well at one of the two in NC and she would be closer to us. The plan was to see Elon on Friday evening, meet with the Board on Saturday, and then visit Catawba on Sunday before heading home.

We arrived on a Friday, were lodged in a motel, and taken to dinner that evening at the faculty dining room at Elon College. It was a formal dinner with linen, candles, China, silver, flowers, etc. We were hosted by the academic dean who was a UCC minister and by the former Associate Conference Minister of the Eastern NC Association, a colleague whom I had known for years through regional meetings. He was a very fine gentleman and respected leader, and he clearly was pleased with my nomination and with meeting Betsy and Beth.

The dean had invited a handsome young man from the admissions office, and he was seated strategically next to Beth. She rolled her eyes. Plus, Beth learned that the college's athletic teams were called the Fighting Christians. That dated from the days of its founding at the turn of the century when Wake Forest's teams were the Demon Deacons (it was a Baptist-related school) and Duke's teams were the Blue Devils (Methodist-related). But Fighting Christians? Are you kidding? More eye rolls.

To our surprise and no one else's, dinner was served by an African American woman dressed in a maid's black dress with a white apron, cuffs, and collar. Halfway through the meal, we were told with some degree of pride, that Mrs. Leath, the waitress, was a member of a UCC church and that her daughter had graduated from Elon. Mrs. Leath, without missing a beat said, "Yes, she was on the Dean's list and is now working on her master's degree at Johns-Hopkins." I managed to keep a straight face and so did Betsy; Beth, not so much. It was my graphic introduction to the strange dynamics of race and racism in the South in a "tryin'-to-be-liberal" church and college. I was to learn much more.

The meeting with the Conference Board of Directors on Saturday went well. Dale Bennett introduced me, described the Search Committee's procedures and read the recommendation that I be elected as Conference Minister. There was a period of questions which were thoughtful, some probing with regard to my personal faith and my experience as a pastor and as an Associate Conference Minister in Texas. The answers and my perspectives were apparently sufficiently acceptable, and they voted to join the Search Committee in recommending my name for election as Conference Minister.

The President of the Board was a high school principal in Portsmouth, VA., the VP was a professor at A&T University in Greensboro, NC, and the Secretary was a pastor in Fayetteville, NC. I had studied the Conference Constitution and knew that one was from each of the three Associations of the Conference and the positions rotated every second year. I was to learn how important it was that these three regions be equally represented on every board and commission and that the racial and gender mix was carefully attended to as well.

All that had been painstakingly negotiated and determined in the several years that it took to hammer out a constitution that could be accepted by all the diverse parties. Racial, theological, geographic, and organizational diversity is all good, but takes time to get it right, and careful attention to adhere to it. That is my idea of a good time! I was especially attracted to the challenge of working with all these folks so that we could enjoy their remarkable variety of gifts and perspectives and thrive together.

The drive down to Salisbury on Sunday to visit Catawba College went through Greensboro, High Point, Thomasville and Lexington and I was aware that we had several Southern Conference churches in each city, as well as in the smaller communities nearby. We were met at the college by its president, Steve Worster, who was fairly new to that position himself. I am sure he was glad to meet Beth and encourage her to apply to Catawba, but also to meet me since as Conference Minister I would be an ex officio member of the college's Board of Trustees. The visit went well, Beth was favorably impressed and later decided to enroll there, much to our relief.

The Called Meeting of the Conference took place at First Christian UCC in downtown Burlington a month later. The church had a large sanctuary that could accommodate the anticipated crowd. Stephen and Amy accompanied Betsy and me on this visit; they had a stake in this decision, too. Carolyn Lightbourne, Jimmy's widow, invited us to stay at their home for this visit. She was a gracious and funny woman who, with that one gesture, placed a tacit stamp of approval on my selection. More than that, she was just fun to be with and we learned a lot that evening about Jimmy and about the Conference, some of the down-and-dirty realities.

The Called Meeting for the election began with worship and the place was packed. The host pastor led the service with Conference officers reading the scriptures and leading prayers. The music and singing were spirited, I was introduced by Dale Bennett, and then I preached. I reflected on the United Church of Christ motto from St. John's gospel, "That they all may be one," and the intimate inter-relatedness of the rest of that passage, "I in you, you in me, they in me . . ." I ended with a quote that characterized the Church as "God's intensive care unit," and hoped that together we could learn as churches and as a conference to be just that.

After the benediction the Conference President, Woodrow Piland, called the Special Meeting to order and the floor was opened for questions. One question was particularly good, "In what situations do you feel you are most effective as a leader?" I had not been asked nor had I asked myself that question before. The answer came quickly in my head: "I feel I am best in small to medium-sized group settings where there can be open discussion and exchange of perspectives; we all learn that way." That seemed to resonate. Other questions were similar to those I had responded to in the Search Committee and the Board of Directors meetings.

Mr. Piland then asked me to retire to another room while the vote was taken. Betsy knew the cue and led Stephen and Amy as they went with me to a comfortable library room out of earshot from the sanctuary. Betsy told me later that Amy, then eleven years old, asked incredulously, "They're going to vote on my daddy?" They did and it went as hoped. We would be moving to North Carolina and the Southern Conference. We were delighted: "Nothin' could be fina' than to be in Carolina. . ."

* * * * * *

The movers finished loading the van on Saturday morning and left midday for North Carolina. I drove one car with Stephen and the orneriest cat. Betsy followed in the other with the girls and Amy's docile kitty. Ernie, our dog had been run over by a car a month earlier and buried in our yard. We stopped overnight at Betsy's parents' home in Mobile, got some rest, then went on to Burlington.

We had put our Liberty Hill house on the market as soon as we knew we would be moving. By the time we left there had been no real progress in selling it so we had looked for a four-bedroom house to rent in Burlington with no success. With the help of a realtor, the wife of the pastor at First Christian UCC, we were able to rent a large 1920s house in Union Ridge, ten miles north of town. The house had been built by a doctor who raised his family and had his practice there.

We were talking about the move at church in Austin earlier and showing a photo of the house that had been sent to us when an African

American woman, a member of our church there, exclaimed, "I was born in that house." She grew up on a tenant farm in the Union Ridge area and Dr. Scott was the only doctor nearby. He had seen all patients from the 20s on, received them in a single waiting room, and seen them in the order that they came in. He was admired by one and all for that policy, unusual in the South at the time.

I was installed at the Conference Annual Meeting in early June. It was held on the campus of Catawba College, in its beautiful Omwake-Dearborn Chapel. The preacher was Dr. Robert Paul, my friend and mentor from our time in Austin. Rev. Yvonne Delk, a dear and long-standing friend, a member of the UCC Christian Education staff and the first African American woman to have been ordained in the UCC also spoke. Rev. James Tomasek, whose Associate Minister I had been for eight years, presented the Conference Ministers Medalion and welcomed me to that group. My parents were there from their retirement home in Phoenix, AZ, and it was a glorious and happy time for our family.

* * * * * * *

The Conference Office was located in half of a one-story building in downtown Burlington that we shared with a physician. The office staff included a secretary, Lucinda Graves, who was a great help and support for me over the years, a registrar, whose job it was to keep all the records of our 307 congregations and our 400+ pastors in order, as well as those of our conference and committee meetings. Our financial secretary handled receipts and disbursements and kept track of the invested funds.

I settled into the study at the Conference Office, put my books in the bookcases, arranged my stuff in the desk, looked at some back mail that needed attention, and then got to what was really on my mind. I asked Edna, our financial secretary, to bring me the financial reports, fully expecting the most recent report to the board. I had seen the previous year's audit earlier. A few minutes later she came in and placed on my desk a corner torn from a legal pad with three figures on it and quietly left. I looked at the figures, pondered the strangeness of the situation, then went into her office and learned that they were the current totals for Checking, savings and invested funds. So, I thanked her and asked for the most recent treasurer's report; she said she would get it.

I later learned that in the carefully regulated rotation of conference officers under the merger of the three previous bodies, a person from the Southern Synod, E&R, became treasurer. He wanted to see all the financial records, as well he should, and found it was like pulling teeth. The Southern Convention had a Mission Fund that was carefully guarded by former trustees to prevent the new merged partners from using its proceeds. I was beginning to grasp the underlying mistrust of some of our leaders for each other, and probably with regard to me.

Part of the problem was that in the fifteen years since the merged conference was formed the Board of Directors had not developed a financial management policy; they had a lot of other issues to worry about. So, I started working on policy guidelines for everything from financial management to staff evaluations. We began discussing each issue in staff meetings and in most cases the answer to "What's our policy on . . ?" received several differing answers. We worked on that project for several years, consulting the committees involved and having each approved by the Board of Directors.

One of my first invitations to preach came from a Black pastor who had been on the Search Committee. He had called when we were still in Burlington for the first visit and asked me to preach at Ebeneezer UCC at my first opportunity. I contacted him soon after we moved, and we set a date. Rev. Charles Thompson was a "senior statesman" of the Afro-Christian churches and had been instrumental in the work of forming the conference. Ebeneezer Church was packed on the appointed Sunday and Dr. Thompson prayed for the visiting preacher before I got up to speak. He prayed, "Lord, prop him up on every leaning side." I had never heard that phrase before, but I knew I needed it, and knew that he knew it, too.

The first really dicey issue presented itself in the first month I was there. A large company that manufactured batteries had to dispose of the PCB waste that was generated in the process. The company hired a trucking firm to transport the waste out of NC, but to save money they sent their tank trucks at night out to remote areas, opened the spigots and let the toxic chemicals drain out onto the roads and into the ditches. The Federal Environmental Protection Agency was alerted and demanded that the company and the state of North Carolina remedy the situation. The solution was almost as bad as the crime.

Road graders scraped the toxic soil from the roadsides and planned to dump it in a huge, special landfill that was lined with plastic that supposedly would prevent leakage. That landfill, to no one's surprise, was in an African American community. Rev. Leon White, pastor of the UCC church in that community organized the residents and, along with several environmental activists, stood and laid down in the road to block the trucks. 523 people were arrested over several weeks. The controversy dominated the news for several days, and I received a call that Rev. White had been arrested and was in jail. So, my first pastoral call as Conference Minister was to see Rev. White in the Warren County jail.

It was not many months, of course, until soil samples near the landfill showed traces of PCB, and not many more months before they started showing up in the well water of those homes nearby. The United Church of Christ Commission for Racial Justice was notified, and the issue was soon on the agenda of the national church. The staff member of the Commission who responded was Rev. Benjamin Chavis for whom Rev. White had been a long-time mentor.

Rev. Chavis and the Commission began to do research on toxic waste disposal procedures nationwide and found, to no one's surprise, that toxic waste was routinely disposed of in minority communities, particularly, in African American communities. The study was published, citing numerous such situations, and an Environmental Racism movement began. Ben traveled the country holding consultations with academic, church and governmental representatives to advocate for enforceable regulations on the disposal of toxic waste.

Rev. White was released from the county jail and continued his ministry at Oak Level UCC and his advocacy for racial justice. He seemed a threat to many white people, including in our churches, and they were not shy in their criticism of him. They saw him as a radical who wanted to move too fast toward social change.

At the next Annual Meeting, a year after my installation, Betsy came in the back of the church, out of breath, smiling and waving a document: our house in Liberty Hill had been sold at last, after standing vacant for a year. She found a seat in a pew near the rear of the sanctuary. I was speaking and expressing thanks for the kindness of one and all and asking people to stand and be recognized. I called on Rev. Leon White, he stood, nodded, and then took his seat – and it was next to my wife. She later told me that she was surprised that she was seated next to Rev. White. She had heard all the derogatory comments and was not expecting the reserved, pleasant, and kind person that he was.

I deeply regret not having sought Rev. White's wisdom, experience, and advice early in my tenure. I clearly would have understood the racial dynamics of the Conference and North Carolina sooner and better than I did. In retrospect, it is clear that I was so determined to gain the confidence of all the leaders and churches that I was hesitant to be seen as too sympathetic to him. I was so anxious to be a bridge over those troubled waters, that I was slow to learn just how deep and turbulent those waters were.

The saving grace for me and my ministry in regard to racial realities and their expression in the Southern Conference was my relationship with Rev. Ervin Milton, my African American colleague and office mate, and the Associate Conference Minister for Eastern North Carolina. The ENCA was our largest Association and had the majority of our African American congregations. Ervin gradually and thoroughly introduced me to the unique realities and issues he and those churches were dealing with.

For the 130 Black congregations, there were 15 African American college and seminary-trained pastors. They served our largest congregations, and those who served the others mostly had high school educations, some with a year or so of college, worked secular jobs full time, and many traveled some distance from home to serve their churches.

Those who had been serving churches at the time the Conference was formed in 1965 were "grandfathered in" as ministers in full standing, though their educational backgrounds did not meet UCC standards. Those who were called by churches later were "Licensed to Preach" and most, to serve the sacraments at their churches. It was called "Licensed with Privilege," an ecclesiastical title that occurred nowhere in the UCC standards for authorization for ministry.

Ervin Milton ran a six-hour session once each year to provide educational resources for the "Licensed with Privilege" pastors, a requirement that had been made mandatory for renewal of their authorization. It was burdensome, and many felt it was demeaning, and they let us know it. Plus, most had friends and colleagues from other churches whose denominations had no such requirements and whose standards for ordination were not as stringent as those of the UCC, namely, an undergraduate degree and a degree from an ATS-recognized seminary. It was a big problem.

We began working toward a solution. Our national UCC partners recognized the inequity of the situation: white-dominated church bodies with traditional educational expectations imposing those pre-requisites on African American candidates who for generations had not had access to those educational opportunities. Today it might be called ecclesiastical colonialism.

With assistance from leaders in our national UCC and from Lancaster Theological Seminary in PA, we devised a three-year curriculum that included studies of biblical literature, church history, theology, and pastoral ministry. Classes would be held on Saturdays with pastors doing the teaching. Plus, there was an annual summer trip to Lancaster Seminary and sessions with its faculty. The curriculum was accepted by all three of our Associations that are the examining and ordaining bodies, and they agreed to consider for ordination and full ministerial standing those who completed the classes.

There was push-back from some ordained clergy who had finished college and seminary, particularly from those who had completed their education at considerable personal and family sacrifice. However, they recognized the necessity of providing training for these candidates, who were their colleagues. The program was called SCOPE: Southern Conference Ordination Preparation Education. A substantial number of pastors were ordained through the program and have served their churches faithfully.

(I am aware that referring to "Black churches" and "White churches" is awkward, but that is how they refer to themselves in the Southern Conference, and I have been unable to concoct a more satisfactory terminology.)

One ironic and memorable incident happened a few years after I became the Conference Minister. Ervin and I were on our way to a meeting in Virginia when we drove past a large, rural UCC Anglo congregation. Ervin had tried unsuccessfully for months to help them find a new pastor to fill their vacancy. But, every time he sent a group of pastoral profiles of candidates, the search committee sent them back, sometimes by return mail.

A retired pastor was serving them part-time and, as in other cases, the church was happy to have a retired pastor and pay less. His name was on the sign in front of the church, and it indicated him as Pastor. Ervin shook his head, and I ground my teeth. The next week I called the interim pastor, reminded him that he was the interim pastor, not the pastor, and told him about the frustration of trying to get the church to consider potential candidates who were interested in becoming their settled pastor. I knew him well and it was a cordial conversation.

Two weeks later that pastor was on the golf course playing with other retired UCC clergy, as they did each week, when he collapsed and died of a heart attack before he arrived at the hospital. It was a shock to the many ministers and church members who knew him over the years, and his memorial service was crowded and mournful. I visited with his widow, participated in the service, and eulogized him for his long years of faithful service in ministry.

Several weeks later, Ervin came into my office with a funny grin on his face and informed me that news of the incident had traveled fast among the Black churches and some of their pastors had spread the word, "Don't mess around with Dr. Russell."

The enormous chasm in understanding and perception between the long-divided cultural and religious perspectives of the races in North Carolina, even in the same denomination and after years of interchange, still blows my mind. In some ways, I was still clueless. One of my deep regrets, a cluelessness that I did not understand until years later, was just how much jeopardy I and the Conference had placed my friend and co-worker, Ervin Milton in.

He had to drive the backroads of North Carolina in all sorts of weather, and sometimes late at night, to serve the needs of Black and Anglo churches in small towns and rural crossroads. It was still a time of racial tensions, and I deeply regret not having the common sense to recognize the risk involved, especially with racist law officers. Ervin was faithful, steady, resourceful, and good-humored through it all. God bless him!

* * * * * *

Hulen Hill, whom I had known through the rent strike at Shepherd Gardens in Houston years before, called one day from Americus, GA. She had, since those earlier days, remarried and was now Hulen Brown, and she and her husband, Wil, were working on the staff of Habitat for Humanity. Both had been deeply religious and wanted to find a ministry they could become involved in.

Hulen had seen a news article about Habitat for Humanity, found a phone number and called to see if they could get involved. The staff member at Habitat who answered recognized from her accent that she was African American and invited them to come to Americus for an interview; they had no one on the staff at that time who was Black.

Hulen and Wil moved to Americus, GA a few weeks later, worked with the program there briefly, then were assigned to direct a new Habitat project in Gulu, Uganda. They worked with Ugandan volunteers in building homes there, with assistance from Habitat, until the civil war erupted there, and they were forced to leave.

When they got back to Americus, they were assigned to try to get African American churches involved in the program in their local communities. Many of the homes Habitat built were for Black folks, with the future residents putting in hours of their own labor, but very few Black churches were involved in local organizations and projects.

Hulen knew that I was Conference Minister for churches in North Carolina and Virginia and had contact with the pastors and lay leaders of a number of Black churches. So, I got a call from her, and within weeks she and Will arrived at our home in Burlington, NC. Our kids were in college and graduate school by then, so we had plenty of space, and they lived with us for three weeks.

I contacted the pastors of some of our larger Black churches and arranged for them to visit and tell their story and the Habitat story. It was a moderately successful trip and a number of those churches began to get members involved in their local chapters.

When Wil and Hulen returned to our house and started getting ready to go back to Georgia, Wil told me he would like to become a pastor in the UCC. They had both been so impressed by the people and pastors, by the worship and spirit of those congregations, that they felt called to make that step. Wil had grown up in Black Baptist churches in Texas and had been locally ordained in one of them long before he met and married Hulen. I was delighted, of course, but began to explain that the standards for ordained ministry in the UCC required a college and seminary education; Wil had only finished high school, and they were both grandparents. They both said, in unison, "No problem."

First Reformed UCC, where our family were members, owned and rented out a small bungalow adjacent to its property, and it was vacant at the moment. Wil and Hulen moved in, joined our entirely Anglo church, both enrolled in Elon College, started in the fall, and graduated in three years. While there they worked with the campus chaplain to found a Habitat for Humanity campus chapter, and they led several building projects. And their joyous, infectious warmth made them the unofficial aunt and uncle for many students, and friends with the faculty and staff.

Wil then enrolled at Duke Divinity School and was one of my students in the UCC History and Polity course. I taught it every time there were UCC students there that needed it to fulfill their denominational requirement for ordination. Hulen enrolled at North Carolina Central University and received her Master's degree in sociology. Over those years they were frequent visitors at our home and got to know our family, then later, Wil officiated at my mother's Memorial service. Their remarkable story could fill a book. I hope they write it.

I had been contacted by the dean of Duke Divinity School soon after my arrival in the Southern Conference and asked to teach UCC History and Polity to the UCC students there. There were not a lot of UCC students at Duke in any given year to warrant offering the class, so it happened about every second year. I loved doing it and I taught a number of students who later became pastors in the conference, as well as others that I saw later at national and regional gatherings.

Among those I taught in the first year was Raymond Hargrove. He had begun his college experience with an appointment to the US Military Academy at West Point. His freshman year was the first year that the Academy admitted women, and he described the chaos in delightful detail: Hey, there were no women's restrooms, no separate dormitories. They had to figure it out on the fly and it was chaos.

Raymond transferred to East Carolina University for his sophomore year through graduation. After serving small congregations on weekends, he knew he needed to attend seminary, and he enrolled at Duke.

He was a gifted pastor and preacher and a delightful student and friend. He later served as an Associate Conference Minister in Church Development, and we had years of working together on our staff. He later became an Associate Conference Minister in the Florida Conference, a position from which he retired.

I had so many gifted and committed staff members through the years: Rev. Ed Alcorn, Rev. Bill Simmons, Rev. Dick Rinker, Rev. Richard Cheek, Rev. Bill Everhart, Rev. Yvonne Beasley, Rev. Alan Miller, Rev. Walter Snowa, and the afore-mentioned Ervin Milton and Raymond Hargrove. All of them were a blessing to me and our churches.

* * * * * *

The UCC General Synod was held in Pittsburg in the summer of 1983, and it was historic for our Church and our churches. The delegates voted by a large majority to recommend that Association Church and Ministry Committees authorize for ordained ministry gay and lesbian candidates who were recommended by their home churches, who met all the criteria for ordination, and were fully qualified. The Synod also recommended that congregations study the issue and declare themselves to be Open and Affirming Churches and that they would receive members and choose leaders without regard to their sexual orientation.

I had been the Conference Minister for only a year, and suddenly my schedule was full of visits to churches, of all backgrounds, who fell on a scale somewhere between puzzled and furious. The first clause in the Conference By-laws indicated that I was to be "pastor to pastors and pastor at large to the churches." The second clause stated that I was to be the "representative of the churches to the UCC and of the UCC to the churches." All 39 Conference Ministers had those or similarly defined duties, and life suddenly got complicated for many of us. I made numerous trips to meet with Boards of Deacons, Church Councils, and a few full-house gatherings of a congregation.

Several churches, particularly in cities and in university towns, were already functionally Open and Affirming, though they did not have or use the label. Some others were reconciled with the Synod action and made no issue of it but did not want to "advertise it." In many cases, church members were open about having relatives and friends who were gay or lesbian, but they were not interested in having their church seen in the community as "a gay church." There were others where leaders and members were angry and vociferous.

I would always frame the discussion and the issue as a pastoral concern. Every local pastor knew of families in their churches that had relatives or friends who were gay or lesbian, and they were concerned over the treatment those people received in their everyday lives, and frequently in churches. The resolution that was adopted had been brought before the Synod by congregations and pastors who wanted to stop that discrimination, and by some who wanted to support members who were gay in their effort to seek ordination to ministry.

The General Synod, in actions taken previously, had decried the discrimination against gay persons in housing, employment, and other areas of public life that placed extreme burdens on their "life, liberty, and pursuit of happiness." This present action was a logical extension of that pastoral concern. Some of these burdens and prejudices were codified in state and local laws, and it was a pastoral concern for churches with an open and loving heart to work toward lifting that burden. One obvious step was to give equal consideration to gay candidates for ordination if they were in every way qualified and exhibited the commitment and gifts for faithful ministry.

Our conference staff and a number of pastors took this crisis as a teachable moment. On one hand, we talked about the passages in scripture that condemned homosexuality or were understood to do so. The verses in Leviticus are part of a purity code of the Hebrew people centuries before Christ. None of our churches or people took the other restrictions in that code seriously. The similarly condemnatory passages in Paul's letters to first-century churches reflect his Pharisaic attitude more than they do the love and unity of Jesus' life and message. St. Paul had a conversion on the road to Damascus, but there was still a lot of Saul of Tarsus in his thinking and writing. It was his default mode on some issues.

This controversy also required an explanation of the polity of the United Church of Christ. Most members of our churches were and are blissfully unaware of the history and organizational standards of the denomination. They had come from other churches with a range of organizational structures, traditions, and procedures. So, we clarified: neither the General Synod nor the Conference can require a church to do anything.

When a church has a pastoral vacancy, it can receive the professional profile of any minister its' officers may want to consider. If a pastor is gay or lesbian, it will probably be clear on the profile, or you are free to ask; we believe in full disclosure and total honesty in this and all other regards. No painful surprises later. As to the principle of the UCC policy, we hope you will prayerfully consider its merits, and we could provide study materials to help you in that process.

Some of these visits and discussions were open, honest, and helpful. Others, not so much. In several cases, the conversation was dominated by persons with a literalist understanding of scripture, and sometimes there was anger. Some churches left our fellowship but most did not. Often, after a discussion was over, a member would pull me aside and tell me that the person who was most upset had a child who was gay and had been put out of the house; a painful pastoral concern, for sure.

* * * * * *

It was during this ongoing set of responsibilities that our son, Stephen, came out as a gay man. He had finished his PhD in sociology at Duke University and was doing post-doctoral research at the University of North Carolina. Betsy's mother had died recently, and he and I were clearing out her cottage at a retirement center near our home and taking some items to a thrift store. On the way back to our house I asked some innocuous question like, "How are you doing?" His response was, "Dad, I'm dating guys." I thought a moment and then said, "You will have to tell that to your mother when we get home." He did, and we had a long conversation. The biggest concern, of course, was the AIDS epidemic which was at its height. That part was frightening.

I knew that Betsy had expected that that might be the case from the time Stephen was a child. My response to her was always, let him figure it out for himself, and hoping it would not turn out to be true. I will forever be grateful to the UCC for its difficult years of discussion and debate at successive General Synods and in national church meetings in which I was involved. I had dealt with the matter academically, ethically and ecclesiastically, but now it was personal. I thank God that I was able to be accepting and supportive of him, I knew that Betsy would be, and I pray that I would have been anyway.

However, this posed a problem as I continued to meet with churches and pastors with regard to all the issues surrounding homosexuality and explaining the UCC perspective. We were open with our family and friends, and with people at our church in Burlington. To a person, they were understanding and supportive. I also shared the information with my friends and with my Conference ministry colleagues and the office staff.

When I shared the situation with my Associate Conference Ministers in a staff meeting, they each and all said that I should not share it broadly in the Conference lest members begin to think that this is the reason that I had been supportive of the Open and Affirming stance of our Church. I accepted their advice, especially because that sort of response would make their ministries more difficult. Again, thank Heaven for the UCC and its careful and long process of wrestling with this crucial issue, and that I have been involved in that journey of growth. And thank Heaven for caring and supportive family, colleagues and friends who understood, or tried to.

* * * * * *

The office of Conference Minister required that I serve ex officio as a member of the board of directors of Elon and Catawba Colleges, of United Church Retirement Homes, with its three Continuing Care Retirement Centers, two children's homes, two conference centers, and two outdoor ministry camps. Those institutions had been founded by the churches of Southern Conference, most of them decades earlier. I tried to attend all of the board meetings that I could and convinced the Conference Board of Directors to create a special committee to solicit support for them from our churches and members.

In addition, I was an ex officio board member of the North Carolina Council of churches. Having been reared in the Christian Church (Disciples of Christ), I had the words of one of its founders, Alexander Campbell, tattooed on my brain: "Unity is our polar star." I was, and am, an "ecumaniac." It was surprising and delightful to learn that the NCCC was founded in 1937, and its founding leader, Dr. Sheldon Smith was a member of the Christian Church in the South, one of the church bodies that forty years later formed the UCC. Smith was a professor of theology at Duke Divinity School where, 65 years later, I was an adjunct professor.

Dr. Smith and some of his faculty colleagues, along with heads of denominational judicatories in NC saw that it was imperative to bring Christian leaders together across racial lines to "stand in the breach" in common cause and begin to try to heal the long- standing racial divisions in NC. Strange fact: the National Council of Churches was not founded until 1952! The NCCC was a forerunner, and several of the leaders of Black and Anglo churches of the Southern Conference already knew each other and worked together when the Conference was formed in 1965.

As a member of that Board of Directors I was in regular contact with the Episcopal and Methodist Bishops, Black and White, the Executive Presbyters of NC's then five Presbyteries, the Disciples Regional

Minister, the Lutheran Bishop, Roman Catholic ecumenical delegates, and the "naughty seven" ecumenically oriented Baptist churches which were members of the NCCC and had been for decades. Our long suit was social justice ministries and support of farm workers.

I served one term as Chair of the Board of Directors, and we dealt with two thorny issues. The first was a threatened strike by contract seasonal farm workers who raised and harvested pickles for Mt. Olive Pickle Co. and who lived in terrible conditions in their housing, health care, and education for their children. A solution was complicated by the fact that their contract was not with Mt. Olive, but with the farmers who grew and supplied their produce to the company.

Sister Evelyn Mattern, a Catholic nun who worked with the NCCC, managed to get the farm workers, the farm owners, and the company executives together and worked out a solution, including some long-term agreements about improving the living conditions of the workers. The strike was averted, and for the next decade, the Council office in Raleigh received a large carton of pickles and relishes at Christmas time from Mt. Olive. A small victory for sanity and cooperation, but one to be celebrated.

The other issue was not so easily solved and continues to be a thorn in the flesh of the Body of Christ. The Metropolitan Community Church, a fledgling denomination that welcomed and served gay and lesbian members and leaders, had a state organization of congregations and it applied for membership in the NCCC. The Board discussed the matter, clear that our Constitution required that we accept all Christian church bodies into our fellowship, and we voted to receive the MCC. Of course, by then the UCC and the Episcopal Church had openly gay members and pastors, so the question of homosexuality was not, in itself, an issue.

It was, however, an issue of principle for some churches. The NC Conference of the United Methodist Church debated the matter based on sections of their statement of Social Principles. They did not vote to leave the Council but did vote to withhold funds. That, however, led to a very positive new reality: UMC pastors and lay leaders who were committed to ecumenism, to acceptance of gay and lesbian persons, and who supported the Council, raised and gave as much, and in some years more money to support the Council than their Conference had been giving. We all learned from the discussions and debates, and that Methodist Conference soon resumed its support.

One of the other happy tasks as Conference Minister was to serve as an ex officio member of the Board of Directors of Lancaster Theological Seminary in Lancaster, PA. I had been re-elected to my position as Conference Minister for the fourth time in 1998, and I could happily stay there to fulfill that term. But that would make twenty years, and that seemed weird somehow. During the ensuing year, the seminary received a grant from the Lilly Endowment. I inquired about it and was asked to apply to become the director of that program.

I loved the seminary and its distinguished history and tradition, and I admired its very gifted faculty and president. Plus, I could continue an ecumenical responsibility in which I was deeply involved and to which I was fully committed. So, when I was offered the position, Betsy and I decided to accept the challenge, and we moved to Lancaster in the summer of 1999 after 17 eventful and challenging years as Conference Minister of the Southern Conference.

In those years I was engaged in many situations that were similar to what other leaders of regional church bodies deal with. But there were two protracted pastoral issues that came to my desk and exercised my mind and heart off and on for most of those years.

12

RIDING THE RANGE

O n New Years Eve, December 31, 1973, Jim and Mary Tomasek and their kids, Mark and Dorcus, spent the night with us in the parsonage in Fort Worth. Jim and Mary were going to the Cotton Bowl game in Dallas on New Year's Day while we kept the kids. The Nebraska Cornhuskers were playing the Texas Longhorns, and both Jim and Mary were graduates of the University of Nebraska. Jim was the newly elected Conference Minister of the South-Central Conference and I had been on the Conference Board of Directors that nominated him for election to the job. We had talked frequently, and seen each other at subsequent committee meetings, and I found him to be energetic, visionary and good humored.

That New Year's Eve, after all the kids had gone to bed, Jim asked if I would consider joining him on the Conference staff as Associate Conference Minister. Whoa! Things were going well at First Congregational, and we could have remained there indefinitely, but I was pleased to be asked, and was ready for a change. Plus, Betsy and I were excited about the possibility of moving to Austin where the Conference Office was located.

It was a little scary because we would be leaving a very nice parsonage and would need to buy a house . . . and we had no equity. Jim assured us that it could be worked out, and by the next evening when Jim and Mary returned from the ball game, we were prepared to accept the offer. Nebraska lost the game, but Jim was somewhat consoled that I agreed to take the job.

My selection to the position of Associate Conference Minister was announced at a meeting of the Conference Board of directors and I was delighted that the members clapped and voted unanimously to approve the appointment. Folks at First Congo seemed pleased for me, though some may have been happy to see me go. They did a grand reception and send-off, more of a roast, and even Betsy got roasted. The women who were friends all knew that she kept the ironing board and a basket of clothes to be ironed near the telephone. Whenever someone called for the pastor and I was not home they would unload their issues on her – and she would do the ironing.

We planned to move in July and for me to start work in August. We found a house in a racially integrated neighborhood near the airport in East Austin. It had four bedrooms, a nice stone fireplace and a big mesquite tree in the front yard. Plus, there was a school nearby for Beth and Stephen and a kindergarten for Amy. Betsy's parents loaned us the money for the down payment, thus making the whole thing possible. Every Christmas they gave us a note forgiving the payments on that loan for the coming year. God bless them!

The South Central Conference of the UCC was one of the smallest of the conferences and the churches were spread over the largest geographical area. While the conferences of New England and the upper Midwest each had hundreds of congregations, South Central had 87 congregations in all of Texas and Louisiana, with one in Mississippi. As Jim Tomasek would say, "I know how St. Paul felt; our Conference is bigger than the entire Mediterranean world."

We decided to share a single office in Austin rather than try to maintain two offices and divide the conference geographically in order to save travel time. The ease of communication and the importance of the mutual support provided by our sharing the office proved to be very important, but it meant that we both traveled a lot. We took turns going to New Orleans and Biloxi, to San Antonio and South Texas, and to Dallas, Fort Worth and North Texas. I started riding the range.

A lot of the work was in Search and Call, helping churches find new pastors when the previous one had left to accept another position. We kept a more or less equal number of vacant churches on our lists. A big part of the challenge was luring pastors from other regions who saw Texas and Louisiana as too far from home, geographically and/or culturally. But many were lured by the warmer weather, and by the prevailing attitude in the conference of, "what a neat idea, let's try it."

Most of the congregations were rooted in the German Evangelical tradition and their members were from German ethnic families. I visited a small church in Lockhart, TX, to get them started on a search process after their pastor of many years retired. The Search Committee members introduced themselves: Mr. Schroeder, Mr. Schneider, Mr. Schmidt, Mr. Scharschmidt and Ms. Harris. When I looked quizzical I was told that Ms. Harris had been a Schultz before she married. They were very nice people who loved their church and wanted a new Herr Pastor.

Two very different pastoral search consultations happened with churches in Dallas. One was located in the upscale area near Southern Methodist University. Its pastor of 35 years, who had built up the congregation and its imposing facilities, had retired and the search committee faced a daunting task. It is always difficult to be the pastor who succeeds a long tenured and beloved predecessor, but this was a special case.

Rev. Dr. W. B. J. Martin was a well-known preacher and writer who taught classes on preaching at Perkins School of Theology at SMU and whose articles were regularly published in major professional journals. Other pastors joked that he had been heard to proclaim: "I will go a thousand miles to preach the gospel but wouldn't walk across the street to hear anyone else." He had devoted followers, to say the least.

The search committee worked efficiently and soon had selected and interviewed several candidates whose profiles I provided. The final candidate was invited to Dallas to meet with the committee, and I joined them for a portion of the weekend. The Committee chair was prepared to announce who that candidate was, share his impressive credentials and have the congregation vote on him. That is when the committee learned that devotees of the retired pastor had hired a private detective to investigate his background. The candidate learned of this and withdrew his name. Rather than create an uproar, the committee contacted the next, also highly qualified candidate, who accepted the call and had a long and successful tenure there.

Another Dallas pastoral search committee was at a small church in Oak Cliff, just south of downtown, in a neighborhood that had become almost entirely an African American community. The church had an attractive, small sanctuary and educational building, and an all-white, older membership. As with nearly every church, they wanted to attract new members- especially young families and wondered why no one came. I pointed out that they might want to consider changing their name. They looked confused. "Why would their African American neighbors want to attend a white congregation named Church of the Master?" I asked. I was not invited back, and the committee secured the part-time leadership of a minister from another denomination.

Part of the challenge in every situation was convincing Pastoral Search Committees to give serious and equal consideration to women candidates. The UCC had been ordaining women to the ministry since 1853, though women clergy were still relatively few. Each year, however, there were more and more women in seminary graduating classes, and most were very gifted, had a deep sense of calling and many personal gifts. They did not, however, fit the traditional image of "what a pastor should be." Jim and I always included profiles of female candidates and slowly women were called, served well and eventually became a normal part of the pastoral reality.

That issue paled in light of the one that soon followed. The UCC Northern California Conference, in 1977, ordained an openly gay minister and it created issues that some church bodies are still dealing with. Bill Johnson was a graduate of an accredited seminary, had served effectively as a student minister and was recommended for ordination by that church. The Ministry Committee followed all procedures and found him qualified in every regard and the Association of churches voted to ordain him.

The issue of gay ordination was suddenly front and center in all the conferences. It also had interesting implications for our meetings with Pastoral Search Committees. They frequently wanted to know of unmarried men, "how can we know if he is gay?" The answer we gave was, "Ask, and even if you don't choose this candidate, you may learn something."

There was, of course, a lot of "crisis intervention" regarding pastoral relations: holding churches to their obligations and/or negotiating graceful exits for a pastor or holding a pastor accountable to the UCC ethical standards for ministry. And there were crises of our own making: explaining the actions of General Synod regarding gay and lesbian rights and equality, boycotts of companies and products in support of South Africa, or of textile companies for unfair labor practices, or in support of farm workers. These were exercises in applied ethics and ecclesiology. We were constantly explaining the nature, Biblical basis, mission, and policies of the UCC – not always successfully.

* * * * * *

South Central Conference was an area of rapid population growth, and we partnered with the UCC Board for Homeland Ministries to start a number of new churches. During my eight years on the conference staff, we started five new congregations. I did the research and developed the proposals for the first three which were started simultaneously. Ed Mehlhaff joined our staff to support these new churches and plant others. All this was with financial aid and advice from the BHM staff. We were building and growing, and those were heady times.

I had additional responsibility for Christian education and Youth Ministry and for the oversight of our Slumber Falls Camp on the Guadalupe River near New Braunfels, Texas. Slumber Falls was our only Conference owned facility. It was rustic but ruggedly beautiful, and we held a lot of events there: Board of Directors meetings, Conference committee meetings, pastors' retreats and, of course, a full schedule of youth camps and conferences through the summer. The camp had a resident manager and was (barely) self-sustaining financially.

It was an almost magic place because the leaders of the conference became so close to each other there; I think that closeness was a result of so few churches spread over so large a territory, but sharing a common and somewhat unique ethos, one that emphasized liberal perspectives on faith and commitment to social justice. Everyone was so glad when we could be together, most after traveling several hours to get there.

A lot of what we did, and how we understood ourselves, was in counter distinction from the conservative, fundamentalist spirit that was pervasive in many other protestant churches and in that culture. Most of our pastors and many lay leaders knew why we were UCC and were proud of it. One member gave the conference $25,000 to create publicity that would try to clarify who we were and what we were all about. A Communications Task Force was convened and began exploring the possibilities.

One problem that was often encountered in Texas was the confusing character of our name, the United Church of Christ. There were and are hundreds of Churches of Christ in Texas, and we were sometimes confused with them. The Churches of Christ are fundamentalist in their theology and took seriously one of their mottoes, "Where the Bible speaks, we speak, and where the Bible is silent, we are silent." Hence, they had no instrumental music in their worship, just a pitch pipe and *a capella* singing (though they did not seem to have a problem with electric lights and air conditioning). UCC congregations tended to be more liberal theologically and did have organs, pianos or other instruments providing and accompanying music in worship.

The first product of the Communications Task Force was intended to clarify that distinction. Our first radio ad started with beautiful organ music, followed by a short statement of our faith, and ended with the punch line: "UNITED Churches of Christ; we are the ones with organs." The Board of Directors saw that as way too confrontational and sent us back to the drawing board.

The next effort was much better and was embraced enthusiastically. It began with the sound of sheep bleating, followed by the voice over: "You don't have to follow the herd to follow the Lamb of God." It continued with a very brief description of our faith and emphasis on social justice and ended with, "We march to the beat of a different hymn." We ran it in a test market in Houston with, sadly, no appreciable results.

* * * * *

While we were living in Austin we got back in touch with Bob Keck, a classmate from seminary. I had a meeting of Christian Education leaders in Columbus, Ohio, knew that Bob was an associate pastor of a large church there, and I arranged to stay with him overnight prior to the meeting. That's when I learned of Bob's remarkable journey following seminary. I knew that he had been an all-star athlete in college, but did not know that it was in spite of a back injury that he sustained while playing ball in junior high school. He had screws holding his spine together. He should not have been playing any sport at all, much less football.

As he got into his thirties his back pain became more and more debilitating. All his physicians could do was to prescribe stronger and stronger medications, and he could see himself becoming increasingly disabled. Through much research he learned of a doctor in Salt Lake City who taught pain control through self-hypnosis. Bob went to Salt Lake City and spent a month there learning that technique and the result was remarkable. He was able to control his pain through regular meditation and resume an active ministry and became a state champion in handball.

More important, he began pondering and studying the vast material on the body-mind connection, including eastern forms of meditation and non-traditional medicine. This led Bob to found the New Wine-skins Institute, housed at First Community Church in Columbus where he was one of the pastors. Betsy and I began attending annual conferences and learned the techniques of Meditative Prayer, a Christian approach to mediation using the stories and imagery of scripture. Bob later invited me to be trained to lead Meditative Prayer workshops which I did for congregations and groups who contacted him and the Institute.

That relationship and the experiences related to Meditative Prayer provided a new dimension for my life and deeper perspective in ministry. Our friendship was renewed and enjoyed frequently over several decades as we both traveled a lot and were able to meet fairly often. Bob's insights are expanded in his several published books: Sacred Eyes, Sacred Quest, Healing as A Sacred Path, all by Crysalsis Press, and Spirit of Synergy, by Abingdon Press. I still mourn Bob's struggle with cancer and the untimely death of this remarkable friend and leader.

* * * * * *

One of the blessings of our time in South Central Conference was our experience as members of the Congregational Church of Austin. The church had been founded in the first decade of the 20th Century when the Methodist Church Conference defrocked the pastor of a congregation in Austin because he did not believe in a literal hell. A group of lay members joined him in organizing a new congregation and buying land near the University of Texas. The only group that would lend them money to build a building was the General Council of the Congregational Churches, so they became Congregationalists! Theological arguments can sometimes result in good outcomes for some folks.

Though founded by refugee Methodists, many of the later members were Yankees who had Congregational or UCC backgrounds, and what a delightful group it was. Our pastor, John Towery, was a Yale Divinity School graduate and a certifiable liberal. The church was well known locally and throughout the Southern Conference for its involvement and leadership in community ministry efforts. Most notably, it hosted a free medical clinic which was staffed by volunteer doctors and nurses and served hundreds of folks every year.

One quirk of John's preaching was clearly an artifact of his Yale education: unlike most preachers (who don't), he cited everything that he quoted. It was a weekly sermon with verbal footnotes. One year on Youth Sunday our teenager, Amy, gave the pastoral prayer, prefaced by an assurance that "this prayer was not written by W. B. J. Martin" (one of John's favorite writers).

There were two major crises at Congregational Church of Austin in the 1970's; versions of which were probably experienced in some other "liberal" churches. The first was difficult to say the least. There was much publicity about the dangers of secondhand smoke and our pastor's wife was a heavy smoker. Ellie was loved by one and all, a very gracious hostess, cheerful, always ready with a joke and a deep gravelly laugh. The custom was to have coffee and conversation in the fellowship hall following worship, to which everyone looked forward. One of the members suggested that we place a No Smoking sign in the hall, there was much discussion, and much trepidation and Ellie was clearly offended. Eventually, all were relieved when Ellie started going out on the patio to smoke and no sign was needed.

The second crisis was funny but caused much *sturm und drang*. The congregation had long been welcoming gay and lesbian members and participants with no controversy at all. The UCC denomination had voted to encourage churches to be "Open and Affirming," and we already were. So, when a delegation from a fledgling Metropolitan Community Church group asked if they could use our sanctuary for worship on Sunday afternoons, our leaders were eager to accommodate them. The MCC was founded in the 60's as a church home for gay and lesbian Christians who had been made uncomfortable in other churches.

There was one hitch: Congregational Church of Austin had a string trio for musical accompaniment in worship: piano, violin and cello; no organ. No problem, said the MCC folks, we will bring our electronic organ. Oh, yes: that's a problem! The classical music devotees in the church said, "An electric organ in our church? No way!" The congregation had discussed securing a pipe organ on several occasions, but the cost was high, and they would rather give the money, if they had it, to missions. Besides, everyone was happy with the string trio. Even funnier, a compromise was reached: the MCC folks could bring their electric organ in if they kept it in the back, out of sight, and had it covered. Being "liberal" can get weird and funny.

Christmas at the Congregational Church of Austin was a delight. Nearly every evening for the week before Christmas there was an open house with goodies and libations at the pastor's home, complete with animated conversation and raucous laughter. The Christmas Eve candlelight service was a full house. Carols were sung, accompanied by our string trio and The Joyful Noise Band. Anyone who played (or tried to play) an instrument was invited to join, and Stephen played his French horn, Amy played her clarinet, and I got out my old trumpet and tried not to embarrass anyone. After the service we all reconvened at Mel and Pat Oakes' home for the Christmas Eve party. Those warm, happy times are deeply cherished, and many lasting friendships still thrive despite time and distance.

* * * * *

One of those significant friendships was with the Galle family. The Galles began attending Congregational Church of Austin about the same time we did. Omer was a new professor in the sociology department at the University of Texas, and he eventually was chair of the Population Study Center. Zona had been a social worker until they started having children, and the two youngest kids were the same ages as Beth and Amy. The Galles were Mennonites and pacifists, and Zona's late father had been a Congregational Church minister. When they were in a town where there was no Mennonite Church, they found the Congregationalists.

We soon learned that Omer had previously taught at Betsy's and my *alma mater*, Vanderbilt, and had lived for a while in Nashville, then bought a farm nearby with close friends. They reveled in the simple, rural lifestyle that both had enjoyed growing up in Kansas. They were living in a rented house in Austin, but conversation soon turned to their hopes of finding rural property to buy. We occasionally went to dinner after church and fellowship hour at one of the many good and affordable cafes in downtown Austin and we frequently visited each other's homes for dinner and conversation.

Omer and Zona soon found a ten-acre lot in Liberty Hill, 40 miles northwest of Austin and began looking for an older house to move to that property and remodel. It was a challenging but exciting prospect. Betsy and I were fascinated by their plans: such a thing would never have occurred to us. But we were ready to help, and once a suitable farm house was found, purchased and moved we began to help with the project. I was still travelling to churches in towns all over Texas, with periodic trips to the dozen churches in New Orleans, but we frequently drove up to Liberty Hill to help scrape off old paint while our kids and the Galles' kids explored the surrounding properties, including a small "tank" (Texas-speak for pond) farther back on the tract.

We were bitten and soon began talking about buying the ten-acre plot next door in Liberty Hill and building a house there. That decision coincided with another, namely that it was time for Betsy to go back to teaching and she was eager to get on with it. Amy would be going into the fourth grade the next school year and Betsy was eager to pursue her love of teaching. She applied for and got a job teaching French at a new high school in the rapidly growing Round Rock Independent School District.

Westwood HS was being built in the Cedar Park area, between Austin and Liberty Hill, and the school year would begin in late August. Therein lay the rub. We needed to move into our new house by or before then or life would be very difficult. But construction on the new house was moving at a snail's pace. Our contractor, Charlie, was a local business man and he used his friends as subcontractors. He cut his commission in half if I would do the bookkeeping and pay the subs. That gave me some form of quality control. Some of the subs were great, but there were problems. The framing carpenter was awesome; a big guy who worked alone. He would carry an armload of 2x4s onto the foundation, lay them out cut them to size, put together the framing and raise it himself. He started every day at sunrise, his wife would bring lunch at 11:00 am, and a two gallon, home cranked freezer of ice cream at 4:00 and he would leave at sunset. The framing went up in a hurry. So far, so good.

But getting materials delivered to our place, 40 miles outside of Austin, was a crap shoot. The sheathing, siding, windows, sheet rock and stonework were all late, but went well when delivered. One day we went out to look things over and have dinner with the Galles in their by-then-completed house. The roofer, Willie, was putting the metal roofing on with the help of his mother-in-law and his visibly pregnant wife. All were on the roof of our second-story house! My heart nearly stopped. Were they bonded? What if one of them fell? But I was not about to stop work to find out. We might never get the roof finished.

Betsy contemplated writing a book on our experience. All she had was a title: "Maybe Tuesday." Every time we asked Charlie, our contractor, when the next sub would arrive to do that part of the construction the answer was usually, "maybe Tuesday." Apparently, nobody started a new job on Monday, so we better hope that they arrived on Tuesday or, at the latest, Wednesday, because no one would start a new job on Thursday, much less on Friday. Maybe Tuesday. We finally got moved in with help from friends, and Betsy started her new job on time. I used vacation time to finish building the deck, the front steps, and a shed over the well head.

Willie reentered our life several times over the four years we lived there. He dug our well and installed the submersible pump on the end of a dozen lengths of pipe. It seemed like every time there was a strong thunder storm the pump was fried. We had to call Willie to come pull the pipe and fix or replace the pump. To get to Willie we had to call the Buckboard Tavern in Cedar Park, and they would get him to call back. You can't make this stuff up.

Betsy drove to Westwood High with another teacher who lived nearby, and I drove into the office in Austin after the kids caught the bus to the Liberty Hill schools. Living there was fun in a lot of ways. Zona's mother and step-father built a house on another adjoining ten-acre plot and we enjoyed getting to know them. Selma had grown up in a Mennonite family and was a pacifist through and through and Herman was a retired Congregational Church pastor. He had been Zona's father's close friend when both were in seminary, and they married decades after both had been widowed. We all saw eye to eye on issues of social justice, peace and living simply.

We sometimes spent long evenings with this little group of friends. Dinner together: Omer loved to cook, and he played a mean guitar so we often sang on the porch till sundown. I loved it; Betsy endured it, and I'm sure our kids thought we were nuts. The Galle's daughter, Kristen was Beth's age and she sang along. Their son, Karl, was Amy's age and when their house was completed and we had moved into ours I helped Omer build a hen house, with laying nests and all. They bought hens and Karl gathered the eggs every morning. Zona had a big and productive garden and I borrowed Omer's Gravely garden tractor to try to make a garden in the much rockier ground up the hill at our place. All we produced were scrawny squash and loads of squash bugs. It was rough, but it seemed idyllic.

* * * * *

But that's when Jim Tomasek, my boss, mentor and close friend, got very sick. He was diagnosed with a malignant tumor in his abdomen and was hospitalized off and on for weeks. Suddenly I was in charge of the office and of the administrative and pastoral duties that we had shared. I visited him often in the hospital and the Tomaseks' daughter, Dorcus stayed with us for several of the most critical days. It was a scary time for her and her mom, and distressing for our family as well.

My travel schedule increased dramatically. It fell to me to lead all the Conference committee meetings and work with all the churches seeking pastors, plus attending to local church crises. I also represented the South Central Conference at national and regional meetings on Christian education, as usual, but now I added representing Jim at the Council of Conference Ministers and at various national meetings of UCC leaders. Jim recovered and served successive terms in office till his retirement, though he battled recurrences of cancer throughout the rest of his days.

It was during that time period that I met and got to know most of the key leaders of our denomination and learned of the scope and style of their ministries and admired their ability and their spirit. Several of these new colleagues apparently thought I might be a good candidate for some of the conference and national positions that came open over the next few years. We were happy in Liberty Hill, but I was pleased and honored to be encouraged to apply for several of those job openings. One Conference Minister position came open in 1982 that seemed perfect for me and good for the family.

13

WHEN PASTORAL EVENTS
BECOME NATIONAL NEWS

Twice during my tenure as Conference Minister of the Southern Conference situations fell in my lap that became national news. The first would not have been at all remarkable, but as events unfolded over several years it became big news in North Carolina and was turned into a TV movie. The second made news in several major city media outlets over several years. Here is how each unfolded.

* * * * * *

At our first staff meeting following my installation, and after all the pleasantries were exchanged, the Associate Conference Minister of one of our Associations, Bill Simmons, related that one of his pastors got caught with his pants down . . . literally. He confessed that he had been engaged in a romantic relationship outside his and her marriages. He was very remorseful, resigned from the church and moved to his family home.

The Association Committee on Ministry saw no need to take action at that time, so he technically still retained his Ministerial Standing. The pastor was much admired and loved in the congregation and the community, so Bill spent a lot of time helping the church deal with its shock and begin to seek a path forward. A retired Army chaplain was available to serve them, did a good job pastorally and eventually, got the church back on track.

Some months later the pastor, Dwight, sought me out at a Conference gathering to see if he could return to ministry. He had separated from his wife and had no further contact with the other woman. He said he had prayerfully pondered the needs and emotions that clouded his commitment to pastoral and family ethics and responsibilities. He wanted the chance to redeem himself and his reputation by serving another church.

I responded that he needed to make his request to the Ministry Committee in his Association, and if they authorized a return to pastoral service, he could follow the usual pastoral placement procedures. Further, he needed to be totally honest with that committee, with any church with which he interviewed, and with the Ministry Committee of that Association: standard procedure.

Dwight jumped through those hoops and several months later he was invited to interview with a congregation in another Association, was called to serve it and was installed. That was no surprise. He was known by many of our churches through years of service in the Conference, was friendly, articulate, and well regarded. The congregation was one of a few churches in a mill town in central North Carolina.

An attractive woman in her 40's visited that church for an Easter Sunrise service two years later, the pastor visited her, she began to attend worship regularly, and they eventually became romantically involved. They were soon married to the delight of the members and of his many friends.

Dwight started getting sick. His doctor prescribed the obvious remedies, but he only got sicker and was soon hospitalized in the county general hospital. He recovered and went home only to have a recurrence of the illness within weeks and was readmitted. I visited him there, as did several church members, and his wife, Blanche, who was very attentive. Again, he was released, still with no clear diagnosis, but having recovered sufficiently to go home.

When he was readmitted again in several weeks all who knew him were deeply concerned, and his doctors, still without a clear diagnosis, had transferred him to Duke University Hospital. At Duke the same pattern continued, with repeated recoveries and relapses. As the situation seemed dire, I visited more often and at one visit a nurse was in the room and sat quietly the entire time I was there. Unusual.

On my next visit I was not allowed in the room and was told that agents from the State Bureau of Investigation were interviewing him. His wife, Blanche, was there in the waiting room as usual, and was very concerned. She talked about his having worked in the garden and sprayed a lot of insecticide on the plants. Maybe that was the cause.

Since they were fairly recently married, she was concerned about his health insurance and his pension policies because they had never discussed any of those details. I explained the provisions in our UCC insurance plans briefly and told her I would bring her the materials that described them in detail.

When I got home that evening, Betsy asked, "how's Dwight?" When I describe the visit, her eyes got big, then narrowed, and she said that all the women at the church where we attended knew Blanche and had said, "I wouldn't trust her as far as I could throw her!" Then Betsy added, "take the information to her, but don't you dare take her to lunch or have coffee with her." Her intuition was on target.

I visited Dwight again several days later and he was distressed that the SBI agents were suspicious of his wife, and knew she would never do anything to harm him. As it turned out, the doctors at Duke had no more success in treating Dwight than had the others. So, they ran a blood screen test for arsenic, a test they rarely do, and found a remarkable amount in his system. They posted a nurse in his room, 24/7. By law, they reported that to the SBI, whose agents began looking into Blanche's background.

What they found became news almost immediately. She had been in a long-term relationship with an earlier employer who died under similar circumstances to Dwight's several years earlier. The lover had been repeatedly hospitalized locally, then transferred to the acute care hospital in Winston-Salem where he died. When interviewed, his by-then-adult children said they had always been suspicious regarding their father's death. In their telling, their father would begin to improve, and Blanche would bring him "his favorite milk shake," and he would soon relapse.

The SBI exhumed the corpse of the ill-fated lover and found substantial traces of arsenic. Other people came forward and remembered the puzzling death of her former husband. It had been officially attributed to a heart attack. They dug up his long dead corpse and found traces of arsenic. Then they exhumed the bodies of her father; arsenic there, too. Blanche was indicted for murder in Forsythe County, where that crime occurred.

It was suddenly in every newspaper in North Carolina, and a segment on every local TV news broadcast. Blanche protested her innocence. Dwight was astounded and vowed that she would not have done that. The trial was broadcast live and was sensational. One of the assistant prosecutors, in the closing argument went ballistic: crying, she said, "I hear (your lover) calling from the grave: Blanche, Blanche, why did you do it?" Blanche Taylor Moore was convicted of murder and is now in the State Penitentiary.

To everyone's surprise, Dwight recovered and is sort of proud of that: he figured he was remarkably strong or deeply blessed. He was incapacitated for over a year, and to my surprise, later came to my office to let me know that he was ready to serve as pastor again. He had some disabilities that he could manage, and he wanted to get back in the pulpit. We had the same conversation that we had had years previously, he followed the procedure and was called to and served a small country church. I wish that was the end of the story.

Dwight came into my office a year later and he was glowing. "They are making a movie about me. Do you want to see the pre-cut version?" Of course, I said yes as he handed me a video cassette. He was obviously delighted, though he said the actor who portrayed him was not nearly as good looking as he. I slid it into our video player at home that night and watched a Miramax, made for TV, thriller titled, "Black Widow."

The story initially matched fairly closely what I had known, and the news had reported. It added a segment that indicated that she had been sexually abused by her father and by her husband, matters that were not presented by her defense at the trial. If true, they might partially explain her motives. Perhaps the scriptwriters interviewed her in prison.

When the TV story progressed to Dwight's pastoral call after Blanche came to the sunrise service, it showed him knocking on her door and, receiving no response, leaving his calling card wedged in the screen door. The camera then zoomed in on the card and focused on the UCC logo, complete with dramatic music in crescendo. Alarm bells went off in my head. I knew that the denominational logo was a registered trade mark that could not legally be used without permission. I sincerely doubted that Miramax had secured permission to use it in that manner.

The next morning, I called our UCC attorney in New York and described the situation. He confirmed my understanding of the law and said he would get back to me. In his return call I was told that when he insisted that the studio remove that portion of the film, he was told it could not be done. Our attorney then threatened to sue if they put the film on national TV without removing the dramatic moment where the UCC logo was shown.

Two days later I got a call from a representative of Miramax in which he explained that the music was already part of the finished film, and that brief segment could not be removed without stopping the music in an awkward mid-phrase. I suggested that he explain that to our attorney. Months later the "Black Widow" was shown on TV with considerable promotion locally by the network affiliate. The offending scene ended when (actor) Dwight put a card in the door and turned to leave. There was no shot of the card. Lawsuit averted: the illegal shot of the UCC logo on the cutting room floor.

* * * * * *

The second incident was not nearly as bizarre but was at least equally convoluted. I have mentioned in the previous chapter Rev. Benjamin Chavis's remarkable work in racial justice and reconciliation and his unique role in calling the nation's attention to environmental racism. Those efforts and his notoriety led the UCC to name him as Executive Director of our national Commission for Racial Justice.

In numerous meetings over the following years, we were together in national leadership gatherings, and we worked together on developing a "Pastoral Letter on Contemporary Racism." That document became a discussion guide for all our churches and a policy statement for the denomination's ongoing work for racial justice.

No one was surprised and all were pleased several years later when Ben was elected Executive Director of the NAACP. His tenure there was shortened by policy and personnel conflicts, of which I have no knowledge, but all the while he maintained his Ministerial Standing in the Southern Conference. During the next months, Ben preached at many of our churches, attended Conference meetings and was regarded as a kind of "favorite son," especially among our Black churches.

Always an activist and organizer, in the ensuing years Ben founded the National African American Leadership Summit. In that capacity he got to know Louis Farrakhan, the leader of the Nation of Islam. In 1995 Farrakhan announced that he was convening a Million Man March in Washington DC. Ben Chavis was named as National Director for the event.

It was a natural step for Ben. His work with the Commission for Racial Justice and for the NAACP brought him in contact with pastors and African American leaders across the nation and they responded. The crowd size was debated, but the most reliable estimates were that 870,000 African American men participated on the National Mall on that October day. It was just weeks after that event that Ben announced, to the astonishment of one and all, especially in the UCC, that he was converting to Islam.

At the next meeting of the Board of Directors of the Association where Ben held his ministerial standing, the Board voted to officially remove his standing. Ben was notified of that action, as our policies require. By that time Ben had been installed as the Minister of Mosque #1 in Harlem, the site where Malcolm X had been assassinated. I was somewhat astonished then, some months later, when I received a phone call from Ben. He wanted to appeal the removal of his standing and be reinstated as an authorized minister of the UCC.

It was a hard conversation in which I first heard his appeal: "Everything I know and do in racial justice and unity I learned in the UCC." Ben wanted to continue to share those principles in the Nation of Islam. I told him he had the right to appeal the Association's ruling, and we agreed to find a date for him to meet with the Ministry Committee of the Association to do that.

An agreeable date was set, and we were to meet at Mt. Calvary UCC in Durham. It was one of our strongest Black congregations, and its pastor, Rev. J. Cecil Cheek, J.C., was the chairperson of the Association Committee on Ministry. I had visited his wife during her losing struggle with cancer and spoke at her funeral. Many months later I officiated at his marriage to his second wife. I visited Mt. Calvary on numerous occasions for church and social gatherings. Ben Chavis had preached at Mt. Calvary numerous times and was much admired, though folks were perplexed by his conversion to Islam.

It was a dicey situation. I prepared as best I could and arrived at the church early, compulsive person that I am. To my surprise, there were vans from the local media stations parked in front. Neither I nor the leaders of the Association had announced the event publicly, so presumably Ben had informed the press. I knew the matter was of interest to the public, but I had no idea. When I went into the sanctuary, I found three TV camera crews and stringers for the Cleveland, New York and Baltimore newspapers. Ben had been a prominent leader in all three cities. The local press was there as well. Rev. Cheek welcomed everyone, thanked them for their interest and concern, and then introduced me. I reviewed the situation, the standards for ministry in the UCC, the procedures for conducting the meeting, and emphasized that it would be a closed-door session. J.C. then invited the committee members to convene in the Fellowship Room downstairs and made it clear that everyone else should remain in the sanctuary, and that we would return following the meeting to report the results.

When we went to the Fellowship room, to everyone's surprise, there were a dozen or so African American young men, all wearing black suits and black bow ties, looking through all of the rooms, the kitchen, the stage, the closets, etc. J.C. shouted, "Stop. What do you think you are doing?" One solemn young man responded that they were the Fruit of Islam, and they were providing security for Minister Benjamin X. It was understandable since their former controversial minister had been assassinated.

I will never forget J.C.'s response. "The deacons are responsible for security in this church. You can wait outside. And, by the way, I am the biggest, blackest, meanest Ni--er in Durham, and you will leave now!" They left.

The committee members were somewhat shaken as we took seats round the conference table, and within a few minutes Ben came in followed, two paces behind, by his wife, Martha, who was beautifully dressed in flowing robes. I had met Martha on numerous occasions over the years, but it was a surprise to see her walking the prescribed distance behind Ben, taking a seat behind him and never speak a word.

J.C. called the meeting to order and offered a prayer for guidance, amid many heartfelt "Amens," followed by an emphatic, "in the name of Jesus Christ our Savior." Then we got down to business. I was asked to state the basis for the removal of Ben's ministerial standing, and I quoted from the Manual on Ministry, page 18, section C, paragraph 3 (I will never forget that, though I can no longer quote the passage, and the manual has long since been revised). It stated that a minister in standing in the UCC who changes to another denomination will have his or her UCC ministerial standing removed. That makes sense.

Ben's response was that he was not moving to another Christian denomination, but to the Nation of Islam. It was obvious that the committee was not buying that. Then he stated his core rationale, "Everything I know and do in racial justice and unity I learned in the UCC. I want to continue to follow that path in my ministry in Islam." A series of questions were discussed, and I could see the committee members mentally struggling; Black and white alike, those were the values that endeared the UCC to them and made our unity as a Conference and in the UCC possible.

Then the Holy Spirit intervened and nudged me. I reminded Ben that in his ordination vows he promised to "Preach and teach the Word of God, to administer the sacraments of Baptism and Holy Communion, and exercise pastoral leadership in accordance with the faith and order of the United Church of Christ." I then asked Ben, "are you baptizing children and adults in the name of the Father, Son and Holy Spirit; and are you celebrating the Lord's Supper regularly at Mosque #1?"

Ben's response, after a short pause, was, "Everything I know and do in racial justice and unity I learned . . ." The unstated answer was clearly, no, and no. There was a moment of silence, then J.C. indicated that if there was no further discussion, Ben could leave and would be called back to learn of the Committee's decision. Ben and Martha left and the discussion began. There was pained and heart felt back and forth, calm but intense.

Finally, having been nudged again, I suggested that we might consider a motion thanking Ben for his long, effective and faithful service in the UCC and his witness for justice in our society, then citing the basis for the removal of his standing in our manual of standards and procedures. And, further, we regretfully deny his appeal and remove his standing without prejudice. A member of the committee said, "I move what he said." Further discussion ensued.

One member asked, "how can we kick Ben out of the church and say it is without prejudice?" I responded that Ben had committed no offense personally or professionally that would require a reprimand or disciplinary action, and he could reapply if he had a change of heart and returned to faith in Christ. At that point, one of the African American members said, "Well, I don't want anyone coming to my church and talking about Mohammed." That seemed to settle it, all my careful suggestions not-withstanding. The motion carried.

Ben was invited back in, followed by his wife, and the secretary read the motion. Ben thanked us for our consideration and left, along with his entourage. J.C. and I went back upstairs to "meet the press."

They were all still there, and clearly impatient. J.C. said that the committee had reached a decision and that "Dr. Russell will explain it." I read out the motion and as soon as I reached the phrase that indicated that Ben's standing had been removed, the room began to clear out. No one stayed to ask further questions. It was one instance where a long meeting and boring wait turned out to be a plus.

May God richly bless those who work daily to ensure integrity and good order in the life and ministry of thousands of churches around the world. It is often a gut-wrenching task, and usually a thankless one. What it involves is scarcely known, but it is crucial. I am thankful for my opportunity to have been among them.

14

EXPANDING OUR HORIZON

It was clear to me after a few months as Conference Minister of the Southern Conference that life and relationships among the churches, pastors and leaders of the Conference had been so tightly focused on race that we needed some sort of reset. The long and difficult work of writing Constitution and Bylaws by the officers of three judicatories representing two racial groups and then discussing and debating the results of their work in each, had been all-consuming for years. We needed to deal directly and creatively with those racial and ecclesial dynamics, but we also needed to widen the scope of our focus.

At my first meeting with the UCC Council of Conference Ministers in 1983, Rev. Fred Trost, Conference Minister of the Wisconsin Conference, asked me if I thought the Southern Conference would be interested in a partnership with one of the regional church conferences in the Evangelical Church of Germany. I nearly hugged him! It was the church of Martin Niemoller, Dietrich Bonhoeffer, and other heroes and martyrs of the resistance to National Socialism during Hitler's reign of terror. It was the church of Karl Barth and Paul Tillich whose theology we studied in seminary. Of course, I said yes.

The Evangelische Kirche Rheinland was particularly interested in a relationship with the Southern Conference because its leaders wanted to learn about the spiritual dynamism of the Afro-Christian churches in the South, and we had 130 of those congregations. These were the ecclesiastical descendants of Dietrich Bonhoeffer who, during his year at Union Seminary in New York became entranced by Black worship at Abyssinian Baptist Church in Harlem and even taught classes there.

This relationship with a long-standing partnership in Europe was exactly the sort of growth experience we needed to broaden the focus of our Conference. Our pastors and churches could begin to grasp the diversity and breadth of world Christianity and the beauty of our ecumenical vocation. Whether it was providential or not, I had studied German in college, and that helped.

The UCC and its predecessor denominations had maintained the relationship with the German churches from which our thousands of immigrants had come to America in the 18th and 19th Centuries. A Full Communion partnership, Kierkengemeinschaft had been established that committed our national church bodies to establish official visits back and forth, to receive each other's pastors as fully qualified to minister in the churches of either, and to sponsor a variety of exchanges. Numerous reciprocal visits of leaders and delegations had followed for theological colloquies and special occasions, mostly between UCC Conferences and EKU Provincial Churches.

Our first such experience took place in 1984 when we welcomed a delegation from the Rheinland, and in 1985 I led a group from the Southern Conference to Dusseldorf and the Rhenish churches. Visits by official delegations took place in alternating years, many of our pastors and people were involved, and a number of lasting relationships were established. We arranged for every German delegation to visit our Afro-Christian churches and our Anglo churches of different traditions. At the Germans' urging, we included Black pastors and members in each of our visiting groups.

That was no easy task. Why would any North Carolina or Virginia Black folks want to visit, of all places, Germany? As it turned out, it was easy. The first group that came to Southern Conference met, among a lot of folks, my friend and colleague, Rev. Ervin Milton, and he was invited to be our first visitor. Ervin was the Associate Conference Minister for our Eastern NC Association and was well known among the eighty

Black churches in that Association. He was accompanied by his wife, Louise, and all arrangements were made by the Rheinland Church.

When he shared the warm hospitality with which they had been received, and the challenging conversations about race, racism, the cold war, and a divided Germany, our Black leaders began to see the point. We had little trouble recruiting after that. One funny moment during his trip happened when he was visiting the home of one of the German pastors. The host had gone to extraordinary lengths to make the Miltons feel at home by securing, probably from Spain or Southern France, a watermelon. Ervin does not like watermelon, but he ate, smiled, and thanked his host.

On my first trip, one host pastor took several folks to the awesome cathedral of Koln/Cologne. After enjoying the beauty and grandeur of that famous church we went down the street to a bier stube, and engaged in animated conversation, with me speaking in my awful German when I thought it appropriate. We were talking about our Kirchengemeinschaft and I was rather proud of myself for using the word frequently. On the way back to our cars, one of the Germans, a schoolteacher whose English was very good, said, "It was a very interesting conversation, but what is this 'chicken in a mine shaft?'" From that moment I bridled my enthusiasm for trying to communicate in German.

We attended a meeting of a Pastors' Conference where tensions were high. Younger pastors had introduced a resolution for the coming EKR Annual Meeting that would demand that the United States remove its recently installed Cruise missiles from western Germany. They had been placed there as a deterrent to Russian aggression. Older pastors were adamant that the missiles needed to remain, and that the Russian threat was real; many of them had fled to the west as Russians occupied East Germany.

The President of the EKR was there and tried to moderate the discussion, assuring that all voices would be heard and changes to the resolution were possible. The debate was just short of totally cordial, and the anti-war, anti-militarization advocates remained adamant. Cold War tensions were as high there as in the US.

At a break in the meeting, I was introduced to the President and began, in my terrible German, to explain that I was from North Carolina on the east coast of the US . . . . He interrupted and in perfect English said, "Ah, yes. I was a prisoner of war in North Carolina for three years and made cigarettes for Reynolds Tobacco Company." He had been an officer in General Rommel's Africa Corps in World War II and, along with many other officers, lived in an internment camp near Winston-Salem. They were not repatriated to Germany until months after the war ended.

All our hosts were deeply grateful to America for turning the tide in that war and delivering them from the hell of Naziism. That was coupled with a deep sense of guilt by the older leaders for their elders and, in some cases themselves having thoughtlessly acquiesced. One of the leaders of the EKR committee on the partnership with the UCC, Edzard Roland, became a friend through many visits, including Betsy and me being guests in his home on several occasions, and he in ours.

As a teenager he had been a leader in his local chapter of Hitler Youth. It was a dreadful memory for him, one that drove him later to study theology and become a pastor. He shared that pain with us after several years of our working and being together. His commitment to ecumenical Christianity and specifically to the UCC partnership was a sort of penance.

A decade or more later, when Betsy and I were living in Lancaster, PA, Edzard visited again as part of a delegation. Before leaving Germany, another colleague suggested that he might want to look up a particular UCC retired pastor who lived there; Edzard had no idea why. The name he gave me was of a retired UCC pastor with whom I was acquainted and who happened to live nearby. We arranged for Edzard to have dinner at that neighbor's home.

When he returned after the dinner-time visit, Edzard was in a state of near shock. His father had been present at the Nuremburg trials, not as a prisoner, but as a witness. Afterward, Edzard's father told him about that experience, and mentioned that the only person who treated him and others with humane respect was a US Army Chaplain named Hunsicker. The host that evening was that chaplain's son, Rev. Bob Hunsicker. They spent hours talking about their strange connection and the remarkable bonds of our faith, including our commitment to accept the stranger, even a recent enemy.

On another trip, our hosts arranged a trip to East Berlin to meet Evangelical Church leaders there and to have a formal meeting with the East German Commissioner for Church Affairs. The East German government maintained that it allowed freedom of religion, and that religion would soon die of its own irrelevance. Hence, they allowed West Germans to visit their Eastern counterparts and even bring American official guests.

The meeting with the Commissar was formal and stiff, and at one point he stated that his government was more committed to freedom of religion than was the American government; why, we did not even have a government office of church affairs. For once in my life, I said the right thing on the spur of the moment: "Quite the contrary, religion thrives in the US precisely because there is no government church affairs agency, and may it always be so."

Later in that trip we shared a long conversation with our East German pastoral colleagues and discussed the many restrictions, difficulties, and indignities they suffered under the East German government. Rev. Joseph Copland, one of our distinguished African American pastors, began telling them of some of his experiences during the years of segregation, and he referenced and spoke about Maya Angelous' book, "I Know Why the Caged Bird Sings." There was silence for a moment, then our hosts began singing the Doxology. It was deeply moving.

I visited for several days in Gorlitz, a small city on the Polish border. In a meeting with the church's leaders, we talked more politics than theology. They were fascinated with American democracy, how it worked and how it didn't. They were amazed that Americans do not have to have permission to travel outside their home province: "How will the government know where you are?" I responded that our government does not need or care to know where we might travel or anything else. "Then who checks your identity papers?"

I explained that we do not have identity papers except for a driver's license, and that is only checked if we are stopped for speeding or are in an accident. Then I explained that I have a passport but only need it when traveling abroad. One German exclaimed: "Now I get it. You have ten percent unemployment, and we have ten percent checking everyone's ID papers."

The church in Germany at that time was facing an impending crisis. Their funding was primarily through a "Church Tax." The federal government collected income taxes and, for church members, added on a nine percent church tax which was then remitted to the provincial church offices which forwarded funds to the churches. National and provincial leaders foresaw that this system might not long endure. Whenever a member had enough income to need a tax preparer, they would be told: "You can save nine percent off the top." It was happening and funds were decreasing.

In addition, there was declining participation by tax-paying church members. The pastors called them the "four-wheel Christians," they are brought to church in a carriage for baptism, in a limousine for marriage, and in a hearse for their funeral. Oddly to me, if a person has not paid their church tax, they could not receive any of those services. What?! A fee for service organization? Many American pastors receive, discreetly, of course, an envelope with cash or a check following a wedding, so I guess we are not so different.

So, not only did the German Church want to learn about the spirituality of our Black churches, but they also wanted to learn how we raise money voluntarily and how we attract new members and retain their participation. To that end, they proposed that they send graduates from their theological studies to serve as interns in our congregations for a year. They would see how our churches raise funds, do programming, and work in the communities. In my mind, it would enable our churches to get to know these young pastors and it would add to their understanding of global Christianity. The program was a wonderful success in every regard.

One young woman pastor is etched in my memory. I always visited the intern and host pastor after a few weeks and, in this case, I asked the intern if there were any surprises so far. She beamed and said, "Oh, yes! When I got off the plane there were twenty people with a large sign welcoming me. Then on Sunday, the sanctuary was full, 200 people." The pastor smiled with pleasure. Then she added, "But they did not say the Apostles Creed, and they did not sing the Gloria Patri." The pastor turned beet red. I later learned that the Creed and Gloria became a regular part of their worship.

On one of my visits, I spent several days in Dessau, a city in Saxony, and was the guest of Pastor Alfred Radeloff. He was warm and outgoing, his English was excellent, and we stayed in touch over the next months. On November 9, 1989, as the East German government crumbled, the Berlin Wall was opened, and East Germans could travel to the West, I called Alfred that very evening, and to my surprise was put through to him immediately. I invited him to come to the US as soon as possible and to stay with us in Burlington.

He was able to arrange his travel in March and was with us for a whirlwind week of visiting our churches that were involved in the partnership. He was with us over Palm Sunday weekend and was invited to bring greetings at our home church, First Reformed UCC. In his remarks, he pointed out how strangely ironic it was that on Palm Sunday in 1944, he was a teenager fleeing with his family westward to escape the advancing Russian army.

They were passing the recently firebombed city of Dresden and could see the immense column of smoke and fire billowing from that beautiful, demolished city in the distance. He continued: "It is amazing that on Palm Sunday in 1990, I am standing among friends in a church in America." At the end of the service, as he was greeting worshippers, one man told him, "I was a bombardier in a B-29 over Dresden in that bombing." They looked at each other for a moment in silent acknowledgment of the horror of that war, the blessing of peace and unity, and the bittersweet irony of the moment.

Many delightful and strong relationships were established through our Kierkengemeinschaft. Visits by pastors and church friends traveled to the German churches of their former interns. Several of those interns became pastors and leaders in the EKR and continued the enthusiasm for our partnership. The unity of Christians across these national borders has been a gift to the Southern Conference, and the relationship continues to the time of this writing in 2024.

One of the highlights for me, personally, was an invitation that came after Betsy, and I moved to Pennsylvania, and I started work on the faculty of Lancaster Theological Seminary in 1999. The Berlin-Brandenburg provincial church of our German partner invited me to give an address on Jesus and the future of the church at its annual Theological Colloquy. It was most intriguing to me that they had asked participants to read Marcus Borg's book, *Meeting Jesus Again for the First Time* in preparation. They were fascinated by the way that book had become popular in the US and they wanted an American with whom to discuss it.

Betsy and I traveled to Berlin and were driven to the centuries-old city of Brandenburg and to the grounds of its historic cathedral. The Colloquy was held at a nearby conference center and featured several German Theologians who spoke on subjects related to the theme, and lively discussion followed each and overflowed into our meals together. I was provided with a translator for the presentations in German, and since most of the participants were bi-lingual, conversation was possible and always engaging.

My presentation was scheduled near the end of the Colloquy, and I was able to have copies of it made and distributed. The text of the address is included in the Appendix, its title, *The Living Christ in the Life of the Church*. I still marvel and give thanks for the remarkable and mutually stimulating relationships we have with Christians and Churches in other nations and with other church bodies in our own. The faith, wisdom, and inspiration of our Christian sisters and brothers is an inestimable gift that we receive and that is the fruit of our ecumenical vocation.

* * * * * *

While still in the Southern Conference, an unanticipated additional opportunity was proposed just a few years after the start of our Full Communion Partnership with the Church of the Rheinland. A retired missionary couple who had spent many years in Angola, Africa, were members of our church in Durham, and seeing the success of our relationship with the EKR suggested that a similar relationship might be developed with the Evangelical Congregational Church of Angola. They had to leave there in 1975 when war broke out following Angolan independence from the colonial rule of Portugal. They had stayed in contact with several friends there, and they longed to provide support for those churches.

I contacted Dan Hoffman, the Africa Secretary of our Global Ministries Board, to see if such a partnership was possible and might be potentially beneficial to the Angolan Christians. It was clear to me that it would be of great interest to our Black churches. The Secretary responded with enthusiasm. He had a particular affinity with those churches and pastors. He had served in Brazil for the Global Ministries Board and was fluent in Portuguese, the second language of the Angolans, and he had supported them as best he could throughout the civil war which wreaked havoc on their communities.

The Evangelical Congregational Church of Angola was centered in the interior highlands of the country, in and around the city of Huambo. Congregational Church missionaries had gone there in the 1890s, converted many Angolans to Christianity, and established several churches. Over the years the numbers had grown, and schools and clinics were built, all with the support of American church folks.

The Angolan mission was part of a comity arrangement by which European and American church mission agencies agreed to do their mission work in the different ethnic/linguistic areas of Africa. The ethnic group around Huambo was designated for the American Congregationalists, the area on the coast around the capital city of Luanda was the territory of the British Methodists, and the northern region was designated for British Baptists. It seemed like a good idea at the time, and other areas of Africa were missionized in that way.

Tragically, when the Portuguese colonists left in 1975, a civil war broke out among those three ethnic groups to see who would then govern the country. What had been a sensible cooperative agreement between churches turned out to be, in a secondary sense, a religious conflict. Church buildings were among the first things destroyed in the fighting as one group made incursions into the territory of the others.

Unfortunately, the Cold War had a devastating effect on Angola as well as on Germany. The Russian government supported the group around Luanda, and military troops from Cuba's Communist government were engaged in the fighting. South Africa supported Unita, the army of the Angolan highlands, whose leader was Dr. Jonas Zavimbi. His primary and secondary educations were in mission schools near Huambo, and he was a hero to that tribal group.

The apparent prize was control of the diamond mines in eastern Angola which supplied diamonds for lucrative businesses in South Africa. US foreign policy opposed the Russian-backed armies and saw South African assistance to Unita as a proxy for America's national interests. At this same time the UCC, along with other religious groups, was boycotting South Africa because of its system of apartheid. Our mission board was working overtime to support the IEKA churches and people while decrying South Africa and apartheid. The Cold War was a curse in so many ways. The Lusaka Protocol ended the civil war in 1994, and we were the first group of Westerners to travel to the highlands afterward.

From Luanda, we were flown to Huambo by Missionary Air Service in one of its single-engine planes. There were four of us in our group, and Rev. K. Ray Hill, one of our African American pastors, was squeezed into the back of the plane, which was a problem for a six-foot-seven former basketball player. He tried the tiny seats but would have to put his legs over the back of the seat in front of him. There was more space in the baggage area. But when we arrived, we were received like a long-absent family, and he was treated like a celebrity. Angolans seemed in awe, not just of his stature, but by his buoyant friendliness and the way he spoke of his faith and our bonds to each other in Christ.

We were joined on that flight by a European mine sweeper who worked for the United Nations. His English was good, and we learned a lot about his frequent assignments in Angola. Military invaders had left land mines when they evacuated an area, and he was an expert in the dangerous task of detecting and removing them. He also stayed in the one functioning hostel in Huambo where we stayed.

Because of the many land mines, there were many people, especially children, who had lost legs to the mines. Roads and marketplaces had been swept clean, but children playing in fields were often victims. They needed prosthetics. We saw several scantily equipped clinics, and one newly opened by the church, but prosthetic legs were a pressing need, and they were only available from European aid organizations.

Many church buildings had been partially or entirely destroyed, and our Mission Board Secretary was able to provide funds for corrugated metal roofing if and when the members made bricks and built up the outside walls. The largest church building was in central Huambo. Its walls were mostly intact, and the roof was secure, but all the windows had been shot out and there were bullet marks everywhere. A large mural of Christ on one wall had been partially blown away.

We worshipped there with a large women's organization, the "Society of Joyce." It was named for Rev. Joyce Myers who had served there for years before the wars. The organization had grown through those years as women helped and comforted each other in losses and in the struggle to survive and care for their children. Their singing that day, a cappella and in three-part harmony, was haunting and beautiful: "Nobody Knows the Trouble I've Seen," and "Blessed Assurance," all in their language. It was the music that helped them through the grim years.

The elderly pastor who led the service that day thanked us for being with them and especially for our missionary efforts which included "giving us our language in writing." The early missionaries had learned Portuguese, but had to learn the language of the Ovimbundu people after they arrived in Angola. They then devised its written form and had it used in printing Bibles and hymnals. In retrospect, there were some negative results of the overall mission movement in Africa, but there were also undeniable positives that were deeply appreciated.

The Southern Conference and the Mission Board were only able to finance one return visit of Angolans to the U. S., but it was memorable. Two of the pastors were charged with buying a laptop computer and given all that could be spared from IEKA's scant funds. With it they could communicate with the All Africa Council of Churches office in Luanda and with churches and other groups. They had electricity for several hours each day, but phone service was sporadic, expensive, and undependable. The Internet could help.

I took them to a large computer outlet store, and the experience was painful. Both pastors spoke fairly good English, but the staff of the store had a hard time understanding their needs and difficulty grasping the electronic realities they described. The pastors had difficulty understanding the technical information about the equipment and were deeply worried that it would not work and that they would have spent the church's money in vain.

I am technologically challenged, unless it involves a hammer and screwdriver, so I was no help at all. They could not go home without a computer, so they chose the laptop that seemed the most durable, versatile, and most likely to work. We left with a computer and with all our fingers and toes crossed. I later learned that it did work and was useful, and I hoped that it was true, and they were not just trying to keep me from feeling bad.

We arranged several meetings at Black churches and at each one the place was packed. African American Christians in the Southern Conference had never met African Christians, particularly those with a shared denominational heritage, and they were delighted and inspired. On one memorable evening at Ebeneezer UCC in Burlington, the president of IEKA, one of the visiting pastors, after the usual introductions and expressions of appreciation, shared a profound message in a most remarkable way.

The speaker asked K. Ray Hill to stand, then asked Rev. Raymond Hargrove to stand. Then he asked both of the Angolan pastors who were with him to stand by them. Raymond, like K. Ray, was well over six feet tall, and the Angolans were well under that height. "Sometimes it is good to be short. The slave traders took the big Africans and brought them to America. None of us Ovimbundi are very tall." Everyone laughed. He continued, "Once here, they bred you to make you even bigger." There was a sudden silence, and after a pause, he said, "But we are all one in Jesus Christ."

These international partnerships provided our Southern Conference churches and members the opportunity to broaden and deepen our understanding of the sacred unity and remarkable diversity of our faith and of the Whole Church of which we are a part. In the address I gave in Berlin-Brandenburg (see Appendix I) I professed that the Spirit of Christ is what makes the Church authentically One, Holy, Catholic, and Apostolic. In Germany and in Angola we experienced together the unity that Christ gives and the holiness of our common life of servanthood. We were touched by the catholic/universal embrace of the apostolic message of faith, hope, and love in Christ.

Thankfully, our relationship with the Church of the Rheinland was carried over into my tenure at Lancaster Seminary.

15

LANCASTER AND THE LILLY GRANT

One of my most cherished memories is of a worship service in San-tee Chapel of Lancaster Theological Seminary as part of its Fall Convocation in 1999. Light streamed in from the elegant stained-glass windows and illuminated a packed congregation as we sang historic hymns of praise and thanksgiving. Another colleague and I were stand-ing in the chancel being installed as new members of the faculty. I was so grateful for the opportunity to serve in that hallowed place and with these remarkable colleagues that I thought I might burst.

The Seminary's medallion, suspended on a red, yellow, and black rib-bon, the colors of the Seminary and of the German Reformed Church that had founded it, was being placed around my neck by Seminary President, Peter Schmiechen. My eyes must have been glazed over, or I was somehow mentally transported, because Peter, in a stage whisper said, "Rollin, are you in there?" Well, yes, I was, just overwhelmed by the challenge and honor of this opportunity.

Lancaster Theological Seminary is located near downtown in the city of Lancaster, PA and across the street from Franklin and Marshall College. The college was established in the 18th Century by a major gift from Benjamin Franklin. Franklin College was joined in the early 18th Century by Marshall College, named for Chief Justice John Marshall, and it had been founded by the German Reformed Church. The sem-inary moved to the adjacent property from its original home in Mercersburg, PA in the early 20th Century. The original buildings of both institutions bear a close resemblance to academic buildings of that same era in Germany.

As Conference Minister of the Southern Conference, I had been an *ex officio* member for sixteen years of the seminary's Board of Trustees, as were the Conference Ministers of six other Conferences in the Central Atlantic region. Over that time, going to trustee meetings twice each year, or as often as I could make it from North Carolina, I came to know and appreciate Peter Schmiechen and the faculty for their academic excellence, their clear commitment to training pastors, and their genuine collegiality.

My official title was Distinguished Professor of the Alliance for the Renewal of Ministry. There was not much that distinguished me except that I had been a conference minister for seventeen years, knew my Conference Ministry colleagues very well, and was enthusiastic about the Lilly Endowment program. The purpose of the Alliance was to work with local church pastors and provide the resources of the seminary toward the renewal of their commitment and gifts as pastors. Through them, the renewal of vitality and growth of their congregations might get a jump start.

A test program had been run by the faculty with a group of pastors in nearby churches, drew rave reviews from them, and was used to draft the grant proposal to the Lilly Endowment. Our intention was to engage pastors in the seven UCC Conferences that support the seminary in three-year-long seminar groups. Each seminar would meet four times each year, twice at the seminary for two days with our faculty and, in between, twice with me in the local setting for sharing, mutual support, and planning. At the end of the three years, each pastor was to have a plan in place for the renewal of congregational life in his/her church.

Pastors were nominated for the program by their Conference Ministers, and we began with four seminar groups which had eight to twelve pastors in each. Four more were started during the third year as the first group were finishing the three-year commitment. One hundred and ten pastors participated by the end of the grant period. I met with each group in the church of one of the pastors, shared the scope of the program, and began with the mutual sharing by each of their local ministries and the issues with which they were dealing.

We focused on what the pastors wanted and needed to learn from our faculty and each other to deepen the faith and life of their congregations. Each group developed three or four key issues that they wanted to address. The "wish lists" were notably similar, and the faculty agreed to design sessions around them. Instead of teaching students, they would be working with experienced pastors, and that clearly seemed to motivate them.

Richards Hall was one of the older buildings on the campus, and it had been designed as a dormitory for the all-male student body of that generation. It was remodeled, using some of the Lilly grant money, to accommodate the fairly large groups that we anticipated for the on-campus portion of the program. Several months after the first round of group meetings, participants of all four groups arrived on campus and checked in to Richards Hall, and it was almost euphoric as they greeted one another and as they got acquainted with new colleagues.

It was no surprise that each of the groups had identified "Deeper Spiritual Life" as one of the primary needs of their congregations, and of themselves. In a seminar led by the seminary Professor of Spiritual Formation, they learned a series of traditional and current practices of spiritual discipline from Lectio Divina to Thomas Merton. More important, they were encouraged to think outside the box of Protestant, Reformed, and UCC traditions. The result was remarkable.

At the next gathering of his seminar group one pastor related a remarkable experience with his elders and deacons. When they arrived for their monthly Consistory Meeting, they found the door locked and a note indicating that they would meet on the chancel in the sanctuary. When they arrived there, they found the chairs in a circle, and a liturgical stole on each chair. There were no pastor's or treasurer's printed reports, just stoles. They were even more confused when the pastor asked them to put on the stoles. Reluctantly they did.

There was always prayer at the opening of their meeting, general and often perfunctory. Instead, the pastor gave a brief reminder about the "priesthood of all believers," the symbolism of the stoles, and the statement in the church's constitution that the Consistory, with the Pastor, provides spiritual guidance for the congregation. Then he led in a brief prayer. What followed was the first-ever conversation about their own spiritual journeys, about faith and doubt, and about the spiritual life of the church. He knew he would have to get back to the treasurer's report and the faulty furnace next month, but he was hopeful and eager to see where this experience might lead.

Another pastor was serving a very traditional church from the German Reformed heritage which still served communion at the altar rail, one group at a time. The church leaders had long discussed whether it was appropriate to serve children communion before they were confirmed, and there were strong feelings on both sides. On the next communion Sunday, he asked parents to bring their children with them to the altar.

As they came forward and knelt at the communion rail, a deacon served bread and wine to the adults and the pastor laid his hands on the heads of the children and blessed them. It proved to be deeply moving for the families and for the children, and they have continued the practice, with the families of smaller children going to the nursery to bring them for the blessing. Plus, there were no more discussions about who should be served at communion, or how.

Of course, when pastors get to know each other, the stories start to flow, including some that are thigh-slapping funny. As the seminar participants were arriving at one meeting, one pastor could hardly contain himself until he shared what had just happened at his church. A generous member had given a large gift to enable the church to buy a four-octave set of handbells. The problem was, where in the sanctuary was there space to set them up? There was no room to place them on the chancel.

The sanctuary was built in the Akron style, with several aisles converging in front of the chancel, and there was one set of four small pews on one side near the choir. If they were removed there would be sufficient space for the handbells. Only one man whose wife sang in the choir ever sat in any of those pews, and he said, no problem. The pews were removed some weeks later, the handbell tables were placed there and the congregation enjoyed that addition to their worship.

There was great sorrow in the church weeks later when that gentleman, who was loved by one and all, had a heart attack and died very suddenly. The funeral was held in the church with a huge crowd of mourners. The pastor conducted the funeral and the interment in the church's cemetery, with all attempting to comfort the aggrieved widow. The next afternoon the widow called the pastor and said, "Don't believe what anybody tells you, my husband did <u>not</u> have a heart attack because you removed his pew." Nothing travels faster through a church than a scandalous rumor.

The seminar group in the Penn West Conference was unique. Several of its pastors were licensed and not yet ordained. They served small churches in towns spread across the coal region, churches that could not support a resident pastor. They really enjoyed being together, mainly because they were so widely scattered and relished the comradery. One of our gatherings was during the week before World Communion Sunday, a time that is celebrated by churches of many denominations as a sign of our spiritual unity in Christ. Several of the pastors got tickled and were laughing together, and when I asked what was so funny they looked sheepish and finally confessed the cause of their laughter.

Their churches and their Conference leaders were of the old-school German Reformed tradition, and as Licensed Ministers, they were not allowed to consecrate the bread and wine for communion. So, early Sunday morning they had to call their Conference Minister and have the communion elements at hand, and he would say the prayer of consecration over the phone. It was not clear if they were required to hold the phone over the elements. You can't make this stuff up.

Dr. Greg Carey, professor of New Testament studies, had a unique way of introducing changes in biblical studies to our Alliance pastors in the seminars on campus. All of them had used the Interpreters' Bible in sermon preparation since their own seminary days. It provided parallel columns with the King James Version and the Revised Standard Version side by side, with exegetical comments below. Volume I had an extensive set of introductory essays by scholars on issues in NT studies and on each book of the NT.

A New Interpreters' Bible had recently been published, some 30 years after the first. Greg handed out copies of the list of scholarly articles from the introduction of both versions and pointed out that none of the subjects from the earlier version were discussed in the new version. There had been so much new research and new interpretive theories developed that the old issues were no longer relevant. He then walked them through the important changes in current NT interpretation. The pastors were excited at having a new lens for their teaching and preaching.

One of the concerns expressed by all the seminar groups was the difficulties they faced in dealing with, understanding, and helping families who were in conflict or facing interpersonal challenges. Our professor of Pastoral Care, Dr. Larry Evans, led a seminar on family systems, and as I went out of my office to get another cup of coffee, I noticed a line of seminar participants outside his office door. After lunch, there was another line of pastors waiting to talk individually with Larry.

Larry later told me that he had started the session with a discussion on birth order. When he shared statistics that showed that an unusual number of pastors were the oldest among several siblings, he noticed that several scooted forward in their chairs and their eyebrows went up. He went on to show how birth order had an effect on children's roles in the family and on their affectional connections to their parents. The pastors gained some insight into their own lives and into how they might better understand some of their families and they wanted to talk about it.

One of my most gratifying moments came as I was leaving the last gathering of one of the seminar groups in Pennsylvania. There were moments of shared joy and appreciation for the program, and then prayer. As I picked up my papers to leave, one of the pastors said, "OK, when can we meet together again?" They all got out their calendars. They wanted to continue the process. My heart was strangely warmed.

In writing the final report to the Lilly Endowment on the scope and results of the grant project, I was able to cite these and other positive experiences and to include evaluative responses from pastors that participated. In addition, members of the faculty wrote that interacting with parish pastors in this way over time had changed their perspective and the way they taught their student classes. Apparently, that report was favorably received by Lilly: the seminary received another grant to continue and expand the program.

* * * * *

My years at the Lancaster faculty were delightful both personally and professionally. Developing the Alliance program was very rewarding and proved beneficial to the participants and the school. Simply being part of the faculty was a joy in itself. There were usually 150 students enrolled full-time in our three-degree programs. There were fifteen of us faculty members, including the president, the dean, and the librarian.

President Schmiechen had established a tradition: wine, cheese, and conversation with the faculty every Wednesday afternoon after classes were over. I was received warmly and was happy to learn that it was a time of mutual sharing and support. We took turns providing the wine and cheese, and there was never a lack of conversation and laughter. Everyone stayed on the same page regarding seminary policies and student progress. There was interest in and support for each other's ongoing research and writing, as well as sharing regarding family life. In some ways, small is beautiful.

Our students were mostly "second career" folks who heard a call to ministry after serving in various professional or business capacities. For many years seminarians had come directly from their undergraduate studies, and this change had become a common pattern among seminaries. These older students brought a wide variety of experiences from their previous vocations, as well as experience as lay leaders in their churches. In some cases, the students were older than their professors, three of whom were only a few years beyond their PhD studies. It made for a very dynamic academic culture.

Lancaster County is Amish Country, of course, and tourists flock to the Eastern part of the county to visit their villages of Bird in Hand, Intercourse, and others. Horse-and-buggies are often hitched outside the local dry goods, feed-and-seed, and grocery stores, those being their primary means of transportation. One serious hazard is the danger of a car coming over a hill and being unable to stop before hitting a buggy, often with injuries to the riders and the horse.

Our students were all required to spend time as chaplaincy interns at Lancaster General Hospital, and frequently they were called on to meet with Amish patients and families in the Emergency Room. One student returned to campus, clearly shaken by having been on call when such a tragedy happened, and riders were killed. He had watched as dozens of that family's Amish community arrived, as their pastor prayed, and began with a lengthy prayer for the car's driver and that person's family. It was a powerful and lasting lesson he could not have been taught in a classroom.

The seminary was blessed and enriched by its connection to global partner churches. Students from India, Africa, Columbia, and two from the Hungarian Reformed Church studied at Lancaster through the efforts of the UCC Global Ministries to provide pastors and leaders for their churches. Also, two visiting professors joined our faculty, one for two years and another for just one, but their stories are remarkable.

Dr. Bonganjalo Goba was in exile from South Africa, where he had been a friend and advisor of Nelson Mandela. He was raised in the

Congregational Church in South Africa and was a leader in the anti-apartheid movement. After Mandela was imprisoned by the Apartheid government, Dr. Goba left the country, received his PhD from Chicago Theological Seminary, and later was sponsored to teach at LTS by a foundation grant. He was with us for a full academic year and left Lancaster to become the Africa Secretary for our Global Ministries Board.

Dr. Vijayakumar James and his family were in Lancaster for two years and he taught Hebrew Scriptures to our students. He was from our partner church in India, and interestingly, his father was a physician, while his wife, Sujata, was a physician whose father was on the faculty of the seminary in Bangalore where Vijay earned his doctorate. They regaled us with tales of their traditional Indian arranged marriage, and the subterfuge he used to get to see her before their ceremonial betrothal.

Dr. James left Lancaster Seminary to become the Southeast Asia Secretary for our Global Ministries Board. Was the seminary a holding area for candidates for Global Missions leadership positions? At any rate, our students and faculty all appreciated and benefited from this international exposure and from the ecumenical spirit that these Christians embodied. I imagine that other seminaries enjoy these same or similar experiences; I hope so.

* * * * * *

During my time at Lancaster Seminary, I received a call from the UCC National offices in Cleveland asking if I would be willing to serve as one of the UCC representatives on the Ministry Task Force of Churches Uniting in Christ (CUIC). Of course, I said yes. Christian unity had long been a commitment for me, and I had been involved in local and state councils of churches everywhere I served. I had also always followed the news of national ecumenical activities, including the formation of CUIC.

The Ministry Task Force was convened after a long and arduous forty-year process of consultations between first four, then nine, then

ten protestant denominations, with Roman Catholic and Lutheran ob-
servers, a pilgrimage that had begun in 1960. It was a process that held
out the possibility of unity in their common witness, mission, and in
cooperation in pastoral ministry for those churches. The Ministry Task
Force was asked to work out the final steps that could make that vision
a reality. It was a bold vision, and I felt honored to be part of it.

It was clear that an organizational merger to form one church was
not possible or desired, but Full Communion was. The goal and hope
was to be able to say to each and all: "Your faith is our faith, your sacraments are our sacraments, your mission is our mission, your ministries
are our ministries."

Two representatives from each of the churches would serve on the
Task Force, one a theologian, the other an administrative leader. The
first meeting was awkward, to say the least. A CUIC staff member welcomed us and, after a prayer we each introduced ourselves and shared
our perspectives. We were then asked to select a chairperson and a secretary. There was silence. We did not know each other well enough to
suggest a nominee, and no one would have the audacity to nominate
themselves or a colleague from their own denomination. It might have
been funny if it wasn't so weird.

Finally, someone had the wit and good sense to nominate Phil Hau-
gen, the Lutheran Bishop of Nebraska, one of the Participant Ob-
servers, and the only person there who did not have a stake in the
outcome. We then got down to business through a long discussion in
which we tried to come to a fuller understanding of our task. Through
these exchanges, it became clear that some were committed to developing the necessary procedures to facilitate our unity, while some were
principally concerned that nothing would be done that would compromise their own church's basic principles. These would turn out to be
difficult discussions.

At that point in the process, the five years of funding by the Lilly Endowment program was ending and I had passed my 66th birthday, the
time of my intended retirement. My final report to the foundation and

request for an additional five years of funding had been favorably received and the extension was approved. Betsy and I began finalizing our retirement plan, which involved moving back to North Carolina, and I agreed to continue on the Ministry Task Force of CUIC.

There was a brief "Hail and Farewell" moment at the year-end student and faculty dinner. I boxed the books that I wanted to take with me and notified the faculty and students to take any they wanted that were left; the rest were donated to a library sale. Betsy and I had purchased a one-acre lot on the river in Hillsborough, NC before we moved to PA. Our architect son-in-law, Scott, had designed a house for us and construction would begin that summer. It was all working out as planned.

We looked forward to a relaxing year in Lancaster while our house was being built in Hillsborough. We drove down periodically to check on the progress of the construction but mostly enjoyed being with our friends. CUIC met three times each year and I was able to give more time and energy to that process. I fully intended to play tennis twice each week with my faculty tennis buddy, John Payne. However, the fickle finger of fate intervened. The day after my retirement, we went to the courts, and during warm-ups, I tore a meniscus in my left knee. It was the beginning of "old guy" issues with arthritic knees, a persistent reminder of my finitude. I kept moving, albeit more slowly, and we headed for North Carolina.

16

OUT TO PASTURE – SORT OF

We moved into our new home in Hillsborough in August 2004. It was an election year and within a few days, we put out our yard signs for John Kerry and John Edwards, the Democratic candidates for president and vice president. There was an almost audible sigh of relief among our new neighbors. They had heard that the guy moving into the new house on their cul-de-sac was a retired preacher, and they were nervous that I might try to save their souls. The yard signs gave them some comfort.

As we quickly learned, they were all liberal folks who shared our political views. Two were high school teachers who bonded with Betsy immediately, one was a journalist, one an architect, and one a social worker. Our kind of folks. They had a wine and cheese get-together to welcome us and it was a laughter-filled, rollicking affair. We thought it was just short of having died and gone to heaven.

The town of Hillsborough was itself a joy. Founded in 1745, it was the inland sub-capitol of the Carolina Colony, New Bern, on the coast being the colonial Capitol, with its palatial Governor's Mansion. There are a few oft-restored buildings from the 18th century in Hillsborough, and several from the early 19th. The stately courthouse was complete with a clock tower and working 19th-century clock, a feature of local pride.

One block west of the courthouse is the Colonial Inn where British General Cornwallis was quartered during his campaign in the Carolinas during the Revolutionary War. His troops laid a flagstone sidewalk from the Inn to the Courthouse to keep his boots from getting muddy, and it has been maintained ever since. The Inn and houses on either side date from the 1700s and are designated historic sites. The town is a history buff's dream.

Hillsborough is situated on a bluff above the Eno River, lazy and shallow except after a rainstorm. Our new home was on a bluff on the other side of the river, within walking distance of town.

We joined the United Church of Chapel Hill, in part because the pastors, Rick and Jill Edens, had been close friends since I was their conference minister. Both are good preachers, good pastors, and kindred spirits. One attraction was the choir: good voices, kind people, singing good music, both classical and modern. I was eager to join the choir, but Betsy said, "No way. You were always on the platform; now you can sit with me." I did.

I contacted friends at the NC Council of Churches and volunteered to help in any way they thought appropriate. They asked me to act as chairperson to resuscitate a Christian Unity Committee that had not met for over a year. I was still meeting with the Ministry Task Force of CUIC, so it seemed an apt additional focus. Both proved challenging and those two activities ran on parallel tracks for several years. My ecumenical juices were flowing, big time.

One of our Christian Unity Committee members was Dr. Teresa Berger, a professor of theology at Duke Divinity School, a Roman Catholic who had doctoral degrees from Catholic and Protestant universities in Germany. One of our meetings in 2005 was held just days after Joseph Ratzinger, a German Cardinal, was chosen as the new Pope. Dr. Berger was a little late for the meeting, and when she arrived, everyone wanted to know how she felt about her new Pope. Her response was classic: "I now have a German Shepherd; I must teach him to sit and to heel."

In a later meeting, the Board of Directors of the Council of Churches hit a bump in the road. One of its long-time members and supporters moved that it change its name to the NC Interfaith Council and invite representatives of all the faith groups in the state to take part. It was a surprise, but everyone knew it was a critical issue. We were all aware of the rapidly growing numbers of persons of other religions who were then in our state and realized the importance of developing positive relations with them. But, to take that action immediately seemed precipitous so, of course, they referred it to a committee, namely, the Christian Unity Committee, and asked for a recommendation.

Our committee met and recommended that the Council of Churches continue as currently constituted (changes to the Constitution and Bylaws would take a while anyway), and our committee would initiate a program of Interfaith Dialogue. We could then determine what, if any, next steps to take. That recommendation was affirmed, and we began a long and fascinating process of convening dialogue groups in four cities in NC.

Someone recalled that following the 2001 destruction of the Twin Towers in New York City, a group of 200 prominent Muslim Imams had taken out a full-page ad in the NY Times titled, "A Common Word Between Us and You." It was a request for dialogue between Muslims and Christians, and it cited passages from Hebrew scriptures that advocated for peace and harmony, passages that are revered by Muslims and Christians alike.

We used that ad as a template and sent invitations to all the leaders of Islamic groups whom we knew. Since we could not discuss Hebrew scriptures without involving Jewish leaders, we invited friends who were rabbis as well as Christian leaders that we were confident would respond. Four groups were organized, and in each, it was clear that many knew each other and the meetings were cordial . . . initially.

The first meeting of every one of the interfaith dialogue groups was difficult. After greetings and introductions, within twenty minutes the focus turned to Jerusalem, the right of Palestinians to return to their former homes, the intifada/uprisings, and ongoing disputes and conflicts in Israel/Palestine. The good news is that the discussions in every group were calm, thoughtful and empathetic. The other good news was that all groups agreed that we needed to keep on talking and planned further meetings.

With that difficult conversation still hanging over the groups, they all decided within months to invite leaders of other faith groups. Interfaith dialogue might not resolve all questions, but the interchanges were valuable and getting to know each other was important. Three of the four groups are still meeting, and one has become incorporated and sponsors, among other things, regular interfaith youth events that draw a hundred kids. Be still my heart!

* * * * * *

North Carolina has always been a conservative state with pockets of urban diversity and liberal college and university towns. The political and cultural differences were getting more pronounced, and some conservative folks in rural areas and small towns were becoming Tea Party advocates and were increasingly vociferous.

Betsy and I were surprised, however, when a first-year member of the State Legislature introduced a bill that would enable his county to declare that it was a "Christian County." The bill was assigned to a committee and died there, but it was an "O my God" moment for us. We met with some friends and began talking about the separation of church and state. Others were invited and joined us, usually in our living room.

The national president of Americans United for Separation of Church and State, Rev. Barry Lynn, was a friend with whom I had worked decades before, and with his help and encouragement we formed a local chapter of that organization.

I was able to wrangle opportunities to speak at several organizations in Chapel Hill, including a large Reformed Jewish congregation, and we began attracting additional supporters, including people who had knowledge and skills that were beyond mine. We secured a speaking engagement for Barry Lynn at an Ethical Culture group and the place was packed. AU provided brochures, papers and audio-visuals that helped us share the history and importance of church-state separation.

It became clear that while people generally agreed that church and state should be separate, few knew much about the issue and just assumed that they were separate and would continue to be; hey it was the first clause of the First Amendment to the US Constitution. I visited with pastors of several churches who were happy to talk about the issue and were in agreement, but who made it clear that they did not want to deal with it openly in their churches.

Many of us are reticent to acknowledge and deal with an issue until it is in our laps. Very soon it was. The general election of 2016 was a stunning shock in many ways, but it energized us because of the emergence of a heretical Christian Nationalism. Soon thereafter, however, Betsy's health caused us to make a decision to relocate. That was painful. My ecumenical involvements were still in high gear and occurring simultaneously.

* * * * * *

Our CUIC meetings were getting very dicey. Episcopal committee members suggested that for Ministers of Oversight/Bishops from other denominations to be fully reconciled with theirs, they would need additional consecration by three bishops in historic apostolic succession. They cited a "cannon" (rule) from the Council of Nicea, 325 AD, which required that. Good grief. It seemed bizarre to me, but it was deeply serious for our Episcopal friends.

In response, a Presbyterian member pointed out that their Book of Order required that all Ministers of Word and Sacrament/Ordained Ministers be ordained through the laying on of hands by other clergy and by Ordained Lay Elders. That would also need to be required. Someone mused that we could hold a huge once-and-for-all event where all Bishops/Ministers of Oversight of all ten communions might gather for a mutual laying-on-of-hands by and for all. We could rent Yankee

Stadium. It was borderline crazy. Plus, the thought of Episcopal bishops being re-consecrated by the laying of hands by Lay Elders elicited gasps and giggles.

The Ministry Task Force continued trying to move toward a final statement on the Reconciliation of Ministries. It would complete the agreement that could make possible the reconciliation of our orders of ministry, and hence the unity that had been dreamed of and pursued for over 50 years. But it was not to be.

The three African Methodist Churches raised the obvious and perplexing concern that CUIC did not adequately address racism, and it showed. The proposed Reconciliation of Ministries put them at an extreme disadvantage because some of their ordained pastors did not have college and/or seminary training, higher education having not been available to them for decades. They would be excluded from serving in other denominations. It was an affront. The fact that this did not occur to us earlier is testimony to what happens when white folks write the rules for everyone.

The *coup de gras* however, came when one of the African Methodist bishops announced that his church might withdraw its previous formal recognition of the authenticity of the Episcopal Church because it had consecrated Rev. Eugene Robinson, an openly gay man, as bishop. It was also prepared to take the same step regarding the United Church of Christ because it had authorized its pastors to officiate at same-sex marriages.

The United Methodists would not move forward in this effort without the participation of the African Methodist Churches, since they longed to reunite with them, and CUIC would be a step in that direction. The entire process was suspended while leaders tried to deal with the issues of racism and homophobia. CUIC ground to a shuddering halt.

The pain of the final meeting of the Ministry Task Force still hangs heavy on my heart. We had worked for two days on a final statement of our reconciliation and were near the time for adjournment. The draft included a sentence, "We honor the history of the orders of ministry of all our churches as we move forward into a new era of unity." An Episcopal member said, "We cannot accept the word 'honor' in that sentence." There was a moment of confusion, then a Presbyterian member said, "We cannot accept the document if that word is not there." A lot of centuries old ill-will is behind that exchange.

I was the chairperson, and my mind spun at warp speed trying to find a way to hit a reset button on the discussion and find some way to proceed. The silence was deafening. Then someone else said, "I have a plane to catch. I move we adjourn." There was a second to the motion. Another long pause as my heart sank and everyone looked at their watches. I said the only thing I could as chairperson, "Is there further discussion?" There was none. Then, "All in favor say 'Aye.'" The meeting adjourned, and never met again. It was a gut-wrenching moment as I felt the entire fifty-year effort at creating a monumental act of unity crumble around us.

* * * * * *

Within the first year of our retirement Betsy had been diagnosed with Parkinson's disease. She had never had tremors, but was walking one day with a friend who asked, "Betsy, when you walk your left arm swings, but your right hangs straight down. Are you doing that on purpose?" Of course, she was not. We remembered other seemingly benign symptoms and decided to see a neurologist. Thus began a long learning curve, finding out more than we ever imagined about Parkinson's disease.

At that first meeting, and after the diagnosis had been made, we were sitting at a table with the doctor and a person who was doing research on Parkinson's patients. They began asking typical questions: have you ever had a stroke.., heart trouble .., has anyone in your family ever . . . ? Then Betsy was asked, "do you smoke or have you ever smoked?" When she answered, "no," a knowing look passed between them.

I said, "Wait a minute. What was that look about?" The researcher responded, "Smokers rarely get Parkinson's." They did not know why, just that it was a Parkinson's disease anomaly. They hastily said, "Don't start smoking, you'll die of lung cancer or heart disease."

We started reading books and articles and visiting websites about Parkinson's and going to local support groups. Betsy was still fully functional and always trying to remember to swing both arms when walking. We continued our active life with neighborhood friends, her with her women's book group, and both with our frequent wine and cheese gatherings. I continued with the CUIC meetings, interfaith efforts, and both of us with regular participation in our church.

Then Betsy began to fall occasionally, and later, with greater frequency. There were no injuries, and I was always able to help her up; thank goodness she is fairly small. We started with home care assistance for a few hours, three days each week, and it soon became obvious that that was not enough.

Reluctantly, we began thinking of moving to a more secure setting. Our friends were great, but this was becoming an everyday, hands-on matter, more than we could ask of them. Our younger daughter, Amy, is a family practice physician in Asheville, four hours away in the NC mountains, and she suggested that we look at a senior center near her. Two of her patients lived there and they were enthusiastic about it. It had independent living, assisted living, and memory care facilities. It seemed like a good idea.

We moved there, enjoyed our few years at the adult complex and made new friends there. But, as Betsy's Parkinson's became more and more difficult to care for, and dementia began to erase her memory, even the highest level of care there was inadequate. Amy and her husband, Michael, owned a house near them where Michael had his psychiatry office. They remodeled an apartment for us there and the whole family moved us to our current residence where we are blessed to have skillful home care aids daily.

Now I live with the anticipatory grief that is so well known by count-less others as I watch my best friend, lover, and companion of sixty-three years slowly decline. I try to stay healthy so I can do my part in caring for her, and I ponder the life story we have lived together.

Though in this telling the story is almost entirely about my pastoral vocation, Betsy was a remarkable person in her own right. A Phi Beta Kappa scholar, she earned a master's degree in French and had a distin-guished career as a high school teacher. I now wonder, had she not fol-lowed her heart and the prevailing cultural expectations, what might her life and career have been?

These too late in life reflections have helped me realize at a deeper level, something I knew in my head: our culture and its institutions and ethos were constructed by and for white, middle-class, straight men. As a child it never occurred to me that I might not go to college and proba-bly graduate school in some field.

I had summer jobs every year after I was sixteen, all provided at busi-nesses run by friends in our church. I went to a church-related college, on scholarships from the church, and when in seminary lived in hous-ing provided by the church, paid my rent by serving student internships which had been arranged by the dean. As a graduate I stepped into a pastoral placement system designed for guys like me. The cultural and church systems were designed for me and guys like me.

Now I look back with chagrin and some degree of guilt. I am a slow learner. I had a brilliant wife, two daughters and a gay son who helped me begin to understand. My experiences with Black pastors and friends and my work and friendship with Christians in other countries added to that growing awareness. Clueless for decades, a slow learner: I confess. Blessed beyond my ability to imagine: I give thanks.

* * * * * *

A retired pastor, friend and neighbor in Texas, when we were mov-ing to North Carolina, gave me a slim volume of poems that he had written in the 1930s. Rev. Herman Johnson had spent his career serving small town Congregational churches in the mid-west. The poems were all sonnets. One in particular has embedded itself in my mind and heart, a truth that I often reached for but only briefly ever attained.

> Look not at me, my humble, silent sheep,
> With patient eyes your furtive, sad reproof.
> I know I dumbly gazed from floor to roof
> And mumbled prose. I know I did not keep
> Your weary heads from nodding off to sleep.
> My sermon trudged along too much aloof
> From heartache. Neither did I offer proof
> That if you scatter you will always reap.
> Go not haughty from the temple door.
> God has been here. In me his mighty thought
> Struggled for utterance and made me quake,
> Threshed me, convulsed me, threw me to the floor.
> For you a miracle has here been wrought:
> A man has been a fool for Jesus' sake.

17

ACKNOWLEDGMENTS

This memoir would not have come to fruition were it not for the encouragement, guidance and wisdom of Conrad Kanagy. I am deeply grateful to him for his enterprising vision and work to establish Santos Press and to guide reluctant, would-be writers like me to take the plunge, ponder our writing in new ways and work toward publication. The cohort of writers who assembled at his urging provided gentle, probing questions and support that enhanced my writing while Conrad's technical guidance made the book a reality. Thank you, Conrad, and all.

The focus of the memoir is on my life and career in pastoral ministry, but one crucial dimension is missing. In every phase of this story our family was blessed to have delightful friends who kept us laughing, kept us honest, brought us joy, and with whom we shared hard moments as well as happy ones. A few have been mentioned in various incidents, but most have not, and their love, kindness and support are what kept us going and kept us relatively sane.

In Charlottesville, Julian and Mary King, and Dr. Vernon Mc-Casland; in Harrisburg, the Butkofsky family and Don Royal; in Houston, Ben Reid, Marilyn Mehaffey, Ann Wheeler, Randy Hilsher, and Donna Howenstein; in Fort Worth, Ruth and David McCreath, Joe and Charlotte Henry; in Austin, John and Ellie Towery, Mel and Pat Oakes, Harold and Sue Dowler, and Jim and Mary Tomasek; in Liberty Hill, Omer and Zona Galle and Herman and Selma Johnson; in Burlington, Ervin Milton, Lucinda Graves, Mike and Bonita Hooper,

Larry and Karen Small, Steve and Susan Balog; in Lancaster, John and Nancy Payne, Julia O'Brian, Greg Carey, Peter and Jan Schmiechen; in Hillsborough, Gerald and Kathleen Ponder, Barry and Ann Brown, Kelly Allen, Tim and Martha Crowley, Jerry and Janie Morris and Joe and Kaye Crawford, Renee Price and Michael Carmichael, Andrea Shapiro and Jenny Ratcliff; all have been a blessing to us.

My long-term friends from Seminary and their wives have been a special gift: Malcolm and Joanna Carnahan, Bob and Linda Stiles, George and Jane Depee, Gabe and Sandy Campbell, Micky and Emily Miller, Bob and Diana Keck; plus, a long-time friend from New Orleans, Bob Patton, whose conservative views I tried hard to change but could not. Friends and clergy colleagues in the UCC were and are a blessing: Bruno and Linda Schroeder, David and Karlyn Stephens, Yvonne Delk, Charles and Carol McCullough, Paul and Mary Sherry. The grace we have received through all these friends is truly amazing. Of course, there are pastors and church members who have been kind and supportive over the years, and whose names I could never adequately remember or report.

I am insanely, probably sinfully proud of our children and grandchildren. My older daughter, Bethany Baker, is a remarkable drama teacher, director and actor; son, Stephen Russell, is a research sociologist and professor at the University of Texas; younger daughter, Amy, is a family practice physician in Asheville. Grandkids Margit Briggs, Emma Finch, Ben Finch, Austin Baker and Ryan Russell are delightful and on their way to fruitful lives.

"My life goes on in endless song. How can I keep from singing?"

APPENDIX A: THE LIVING CHRIST IN THE CHURCH

Berlin Brandenburg/Penn Central Conference
Theological Colloquy
January 17, 2002

In planning my remarks for this occasion, I initially began with the usual greetings from your friends, colleagues and ecclesiastical siblings in the Penn Central Conference and at Lancaster Theological Seminary. It immediately occurred to me that all the greetings would have been sufficiently conveyed by now, and that what would be in order would be expressions of thanks and appreciation.

Getting In Focus

My responsibilities at Lancaster Seminary are entirely focused on our Alliance for the Renewal of Ministry, a program funded by the Lilly Endowment, Inc., a foundation which has provided generous financial support to theological education in the United States for the past generation. The purpose of the grant is to allow the seminary to provide programs which will renew the church's ministry, as well as identify and recruit its next generation of ministerial leaders. The latter dimension of our activity is under the direction of our Office of Admissions. The former aspect is addressed in our Leadership Renewal Program, which I direct.

In the Leadership Renewal Program, I convene seminar groups of seven to twelve pastors who commit themselves to meet four times per year for a period of three years. Twice each year there are two- or three-day seminars with members of our faculty on theological subjects requested by the seminar groups. The other two sessions are one day/all day sessions which I lead, and which are focused on the sharing of personal and professional joys, difficulties and issues, and mutual coaching as each pastor seeks insight on how to provide better leadership to her/ his congregation. Each is committed to having a plan in place for the renewal of the congregation he/she serves and to begin the implementation of that plan by the end of the three-year period. We believe that collegial interaction and mutual support over time are critical to pastoral morale and to effective ministry.

The theological basis for our approach to the renewal of the Church and of the churches is our conviction that where churches are moribund the problem is spiritual, not organizational. Further, we believe that "the presence of Christ in the life of the church is the touchstone for authentic spiritual renewal." Our intention is to discover together how "our own ministries might embody a faithful witness to Christ" and hence be a catalyst for the experience of the presence and reality of the Spirit of Christ in the life of the Christian community.[1] The issue, of course, is how we can understand, experience, articulate and share that foundational Christian reality. I am therefore very pleased with the subject and focus of this colloquy, and I eagerly accepted the opportunity to prepare this presentation. We have much to learn from each other in this regard, and such sharing is at the heart of our ecumenical partnership.

I was also pleased and somewhat surprised that the preparatory reading for this colloquy is Marcus Borg's *Meeting Jesus Again for the First Time.* The surprise is because I would not have expected German scholars and theologians to take much interest in an American scholar's work on the historical Jesus, since the literary and historical study of that subject originated and has flourished here, to the great benefit of the whole Christian community. I am pleased at the selection because I find Borg's work so personally edifying, and I believe it is a significant contribution to the reawakening of interest in the person and ministry of Jesus among Christians and among the unchurched in America.

Marcus Borg and the Jesus Seminar, of which he is a founding member, are a remarkable phenomenon in American culture. Not only are he and several of his Jesus Seminar colleague's bestselling authors, the seminars and workshops which they lead draw large crowds of eager participants, hungry for the insights of these otherwise very private scholars. My own evaluation is that thousands of church folk have discovered through reading Borg and others an image of Christ, an understanding of Jesus of Nazareth, which makes sense to them in ways in which the churches' traditional teaching does not. They meet a Jesus in those books and seminars whom they find compelling, and an image which kindles or renews both their faith and their enthusiasm for Christian community.

There is the problem, of course, that most of the churches to which these people belong do not very closely resemble the vision of faith and shared life in God's Realm which Borg and his colleagues describe. That is why we are addressing this theme, and why the Jesus Seminar is so controversial among church leaders. When John Dominic Crossan was a guest lecturer at Lancaster Seminary in the early 1990's we were picketed by some deeply concerned church folks of a more fundamentalist perspective. Jesus is an *issue* in American culture! Main line church leaders and teachers are less demonstrative but no less hesitant to accept the image of Jesus, which is portrayed by Borg, *et al.* for a variety of reasons. Some of those are already clear from our discussions over the last few days, and I will cite others. Suffice it to say at this point that I find the issue very engaging and stimulating, and I believe that our exploration of it is crucial.

Rev. Dr. Arthur Peacocke, the 2001 Templeton Prize winner for Progress in Religion made a very astute observation in his address on "Science and the Future of Theology" at the New England Center for Faith and Science Exchange. His thesis was that the "bridge between science and theology" no longer exists because a bridge needs two solid piers to sustain it. While the "science pier" has suffered some damage in recent decades, including acknowledging the human factor in experimentation and interpretation, the "theology pier" has essentially crumbled, at least in relation to science and the intellectual standards which pertain to it. Peacocke goes on to reflect that human beings in western culture have developed cognitive processes which have allowed them to flourish, processes which are "not purely deductive, nor purely inductive, but a composite of a particular kind, namely, inference to the best explanation (I.B.E.). He then challenges theologians to use the criteria of I.B.E.: *comprehensiveness, fruitfulness, general cogency and plausibility, internal coherence and consistency, and simplicity* in their research and writing.[2]

Who Is This Jesus?

I cite this long reference in order to illustrate one of the realities we have to face squarely in our secular culture. People today, including our church participants and we ourselves, are hard wired with those criteria. We evaluate every new idea and perspective in terms of these criteria, and then "infer to the best explanation." And that is precisely why Marcus Borg's portrait of Jesus and the conclusions he draws for the Christian life resonate as so authentic. They meet, better than most theological or scholarly renditions, and certainly better than the churches' traditional doctrines, the criteria by which we judge truth. These may not be the only criteria, and we could discuss that at length on another occasion, but they are fundamental to the way we think and how we perceive reality, and they are a kind of filter for evaluating plausibility in any inquiry.

The perspective of Marcus Borg and his colleagues meets, nearly as any approach in a long time, these criteria, and it strikes a positive chord in our souls. This portrayal of Jesus is plausible and powerful in ways many Christians never before imagined possible. Yet it does not reduce Jesus to an inspired prophet and teacher but rather preserves his uniqueness as one who opens new windows on the Holy, the sacred dimension of life and of our lives. Further, it does so in ways which make space for the authenticity of other religions and faith traditions, and it holds new possibilities for engaging them.

Of course, there are other scholars who have other perspectives, some of them consistent with Borg's, others highly critical. I want particularly to cite John Dominic Crossan, a co-founder with Borg of the Jesus Seminar. Crossan's portrait of Jesus is somewhat different from Borg's, though not incompatible. What I appreciate about Crossan is the way he describes his methodology, very much in the terms of Peacocke's criteria, and then follows it by "inference to the best (for him) explanation." The handout pages are from the appendix to his book, *The Historical Jesus: The History of a Mediterranean Jewish Peasant.*[3]

First, Crossan arranges all the relevant textual sources according to their antiquity. He then identifies four strata or periods of probable composition of those 52 documents (Appendix I, A.). Then he arranges all the passages according to their number of multiple, independent attestations, i.e., the number of times a particular passage is cited in sources which are independent of each other, and the relative antiquity of those sources (Appendix I, B.). I have copied a portion of the first stratum which includes 65 items which have at least triple independent attestation out of a total of 186 which have multiple attestations, and which comprise the basis of Crossan's picture of Jesus.

There are a number of areas where his method can be debated, but it is clear and plausible, and through it he arrives at a coherent image of Jesus. Some detractors challenge the dates assigned to some texts, particularly the early dating of portions of the Gospel of Thomas; others debate the strata he finds in the "Q" material; others challenge the discounting of such a large portion of the canonical Gospels. He has repeatedly responded, in effect: I have laid out my method and followed it; show me your alternatives and we can talk. Again, it seems to me that such an approach has struck a spark in American religious circles precisely because it closely satisfies the criteria of Peacocke's I.B.E.

Using this methodology Crossan draws a picture of Jesus, his message and his program. The focus is first on healing, the touching of the sick, poor, untouchables, and hence the breaking of the generally accepted social and religious taboos of that culture. The second emphasis is on "open commensality," the sharing of food at table with all comers, again in defiance of the scrupulously regulated practices regarding eating and cleanliness. In this he echoes and develops Borg's "politics of compassion" in opposition to the conventional wisdom's "purity system."

Yet Crossan's methodology is one key point of tension. By following such a methodology, Crossan, Borg and others are able to dismiss as secondary all the apocalyptic passages which are attributed to Jesus and construct their portrait of Him without them. That is a point of serious contention for other scholars, among them, Bart Ehrman. In his book, *Jesus: Apocalyptic Prophet of the New Millennium*, Ehrman denies the early dating of Thomas and the selective use of Q passages and concludes, "The earliest sources that we have consistently ascribe an apocalyptic message to Jesus. This message begins to be muted by the end of the first century (e.g. in Luke), until it virtually disappears (e.g. in John), and begins then to be explicitly rejected and spurned (e.g. in Thomas). It appears that when the end never did arrive, Christians had to take stock of the fact that Jesus said it would and changed his message accordingly."[4]

Ehrman goes on to sketch the portrait of a Jesus who proclaimed the end times and of one who would come, someone other than himself. But he echoes Borg and Crossan in describing Jesus' attack on the "purity system" which excluded and discounted so many people with such devastating results. He then describes how the disciples, after Jesus' death, began living in accordance with the character of God's Realm which he had proclaimed, thus becoming a unique and distinguishable movement within Judaism. This picture of Jesus is dramatically different, based primarily on the different evaluation of the sources. But Ehrman's account of the results for the Christian community are substantially the same, as he describes the process of the reshaping of the church's message in accordance with this fundamental dimension of the truth which Jesus revealed.

Other scholars seize on that same point. Many contend that we will never be able to establish with certainty the relative merits of those sources, and hence we can never reconstruct with certainty the life of Jesus. What we have to work with is the Jesus of the Church. They focus on the post-resurrection Jesus and trust that the corporate and complementary testimony of the first and second century believers, traceable in its development, is varied but not contradictory, and is reliable in regard to the only thing that really matters: their experience of Jesus with them.

Luke Timothy Johnson, in his *Living Jesus: Learning the Heart of the Gospel,* emphasizes that the fundamental experience of the earliest followers, and of their successors through the centuries, was and is a powerful knowledge of the presence of Jesus with them in their common life, their worship, and their servant ministry. He refers to the Christian pilgrimage as an "intersubjective" process of "learning Jesus." In Johnson's words, "This is not a matter of having casual opinions about who Jesus might have been. It is not a matter of reaching scientifically verifiable conclusions about who Jesus might have been. It is rather a matter of learning a living person, and through that process being transformed in one's own identity."[5]

The good news in my estimation is that we have in these scholarly offerings, though they differ dramatically on issues of historical reconstruction, compelling images of Jesus which, in differing degrees, honor the criteria for plausibility, and which are worthy of Christian devotion and discipleship. None of them fits an unreconstructed orthodox Christology, but each to some extent can be reconciled with and can helpfully correct the basic elements of the Church's historic faith. I would suggest, in fact, that the emerging new images of Jesus provide the very insights by which we should reconstruct our teaching and our proclamation. Indeed, such reconstruction is always appropriate in a reformed and reforming church, and it is in keeping with our theological tradition which has consistently sought the best explanation of faith in terms of the plausibility framework of the day.

What Is Our Message and Mission?

So, what message about Jesus are we able and should we proclaim in our contemporary, secular society? First, and perhaps most important, with Marcus Borg, we proclaim that he was ("is" comes later) a "Spirit Person," one who was so in tune with God, the Holy One, that our predecessors in discipleship came to understand that to know him was to know God. He was the holy reality of God present with them, the Spirit of God in human form (Word of God, Wisdom of God, Very God of Very God . . .). This portrayal of Jesus invites us to reclaim our heritage which knows that there is more to life and the world than meets the eye. There is a sacred dimension to life and to our lives and relationships and, though we have been misled by the cultural dogmatization of Isaac Newton and Rene Descartes, by the scientific method and rationalism, we can experience the Holy. We can view the world as God has revealed it to us in Jesus of Nazareth: through sacred eyes. In him we have new sight: the blind can see a different world and a new future

The second thing we can proclaim about Jesus, with Luke Johnson, is that He is with us, not just in our memory, but in our hearts, our relationships, our covenant life, and especially at our table. He is a living presence in the life of the church. His presence is our window to the sacred, our participation in the Holy, the very character of our communion with God and each other. Once we acknowledge the sacred dimension of life and reality and know that we can see it and share in it through the living, present Spirit of Jesus, our lives change. We are different as we begin to conform to His image: we are transformed. Kirk Hadaway, in his book *Behold, I Do a New Thing: Transforming Communities of Faith,* emphasizes over and over again that the churches must never forget their fundamental purpose: to transform persons and the world.[6] Such clarity of purpose is the key to and expresses itself in inspiring worship as well as committed service.

The third thing we have to proclaim about Jesus is that he reveals that the very nature / character of God is compassion. Each of the interpreters cited, regardless of their disagreements on method or "best explanation" of the historic material, concur that the compassion of God revealed in Jesus is in direct opposition to any system of purity, then or now. Jesus stands as divine judgment against any society or institution which excludes, denigrates, despises or discriminates against any of God's children, or which prompts anyone to count him or herself more worthy than others. He further prompts in us the love of others which manifests itself in service. Hence the compassion we know in Christ transforms us into persons of love, acceptance, humility, reconciliation and servanthood.

The fourth thing we have to proclaim about Jesus is that he draws us into loving relationships with each other, into a community of mutual sharing and support. And it is in the genetic code of this community that we celebrate our new life together and the liberated joy it gives us in worship and mutual caring. Out of this same impulse we invite and welcome all who would come into this new and sacred covenant life, and we represent in the culture at large the good news of a new way of justice, unity, inclusiveness and peace. In a society that is radically individualistic and is characterized by isolation and competition, this joyous, purposeful Christian community is good news indeed.

Re-forming the Church

Dr. Robert Paul, one of my teachers and mentors, was fond of saying that the form and order of ministry is derived from the doctrine of the church, and the doctrine of the church is derived from the doctrine of Christ. The way we see Jesus Christ will determine how we live and order our life together as a church, and how we minister. Or, to put it another way, since we confess that Jesus is the direct revelation of God, how do we show ourselves to be the people of that kind of God? Given the above reflections on the church's message about Jesus, it is appropriate to reconstruct the church's life, message and mission accordingly. And we should not be surprised to find that such a reconstruction actually conforms to the historic marks of the Church.

* Because we affirm that God was in Christ reconciling the world to Godself, we also affirm the fundamental unity of the Church. It is an alternative way of living which embodies "the unity of the spirit in the bonds of peace." This unity extends beyond any human concept of community and it encompasses the whole ecumenical Church. **The Church is One.** It is worth noting that pastors in the L. R. P. seminars express a deep longing for a more authentic unity within their own congregations, and they covet for their members a rich experience of unity and sharing in and with the whole Church. My guess is that such a longing is not a stranger to pastors in Germany.

* Because we know the living Jesus in our midst, in him we know and see with sacred eyes the deeper dimensions of the Spirit. Our worship and sacramental life is rich and vibrant, the outward, corporate celebration of our inward transformation. We live as servants to each other and

to all in need. **The Church is Holy.** Our local leaders identify spiritual formation as the primary need of their churches. Thus, we focus our prayers and energy on inviting and encouraging church members "to comprehend, with all the saints, the breadth and length and height and depth, and to know the love of Christ which surpasses knowledge, so that (we) may be filled with the fullness of God" (Eph. 3:18-19). We seek to reclaim the churches' authentic piety in terms of this transformed life and community.

* Because we know the compassion of God in the life of Jesus, we are a welcoming community, open to all, where diversity of race, nationality, age, gender or sexual preference is not a problem to be solved but a gift to be embraced. We long to see and we live toward the multi-racial, multi-cultural vision of the future God has promised. **The Church is Catholic.** There is no more critical issue in the church's life and mission in a multi-cultural society than its isolation along ethnic and socio-economic class lines. To be truly catholic is a gargantuan task, a transforming one for ourselves, and a sign of God's purpose for our world. To be truly catholic in this sense is to meet our sisters and brothers of other faiths as equals, to share the grace we have received and to acknowledge the gifts they have received from God. Authentic interfaith dialogue is thus possible.

* Because Jesus envisioned, described and proclaimed the new reality of God's Reign, a time of justice, unity and peace, we cannot rest while injustice, division and strife prevail. We are committed to give ourselves, in continuity with faithful witnesses from the apostles to this day, in the fulfillment of God's mission. **The Church is Apostolic.** Of course, apostolic zeal is probably the churches' most obvious deficit. The transformation of our lives and our societies toward Jesus' vision of God's Realm should mightily inspire us as it did our forebears. Such an apostolic zeal and faithfulness, in this context, is not a barrier to interfaith dialogue because it does not presume to have the whole truth, or a superior wisdom. It rather prompts us to listen earnestly and with humility to those whom God wishes to embrace with us in the new Realm which Jesus proclaimed and inaugurated.

* Finally, because we live in a changing world where there is a constantly expanding body of knowledge and experience, the churches' teachings and sense of mission will always be changing. That is good news, not bad. Our vocation as pastors, teachers and leaders in the church is to fulfill our role in the ever unfolding story of God's redeeming power through the presence of the living Christ. **The Church is Reformed and Reforming.** The church always exists between gospel and culture: between a constantly reinterpreted gospel and a rapidly changing context. We are therefore always reforming, and continually praying that the living presence of Jesus will be our guide and strength in this sacred vocation.

One final note: I am quite aware that I have not done justice to the several scholars I have cited. I have gleaned from each of them elements which I find insightful and helpful in a Christological reconstruction which might assist churches seeking re-formation and clarity of mission and message in our secular culture. I offer these reflections and we pursue these conversations as an affirmation of "the responsibility of the Church in each generation to make this faith its own in reality of worship, in honesty of thought and expression, and in purity of heart before God.[7]

******

1. Quote from L.R.P. Curriculum description of the "Seminar on Christology."

2. Arthur Peacocke, "Science and the Future of Theology", *Research News and Opportunities in Science and Theology,* Vol. 2, No.5, Jan. 2001.

3. John Dominic Crossan, *The Historical Jesus: The Life of a Mediterranean Jewish Peasant* (Harper San Francisco, 1991).

4. Bart Ehrman, *Jesus: Apocalyptic Prophet of the New Millennium* (Oxford University Press, Oxford, 1999), p. 134.

5. Luke Timothy Johnson, *Living Jesus: Learning the Heart of the Gospel* (Harper, San Francisco, 1999), p. 201.

6. C. Kirk Hadaway, *Behold I Do A New Thing: Transforming Communities of Faith* (Pilgrim, Cleveland), 2001.

7. *The Constitution of the United Church of Christ*, Preamble, paragraph 2, Executive Council, Cleveland, p. 2

Appendix B: TRUTH AND CONSEQUENCES

Rollin O. Russell
Bishop's Day Apart, Nashville, NC
September 15, 2008

It is a real pleasure to be with you, especially to address the subject of Ecumenism, its current state and paths into the future. It is a subject that is dear to my heart and has to a considerable extent shaped my ministry and professional life. Hence, I am delighted to be among friends with whom I have worked over the years in the North Carolina Council of Churches, members of this United Methodist Conference that has been a major supporter of the Council through the years, as well as of almost every commendable inter church activity in this part of the state.

Ecumenism, or at least the North American Protestant version thereof, is part of my DNA. My father was a pastor in the Christian Church (Disciples of Christ) and I grew up intoning Alexander Campbell's motto: "The Church of Jesus Christ on earth is essentially, intentionally, and constitutionally One." My Dad was one of the founders of the New Orleans Federation of Churches (one dare not call it a Council of Churches in the early '50's), and he was always active in the Louisiana Council of Churches. So, I am an "ecumaniac" and I come by it naturally.

One peculiar ecumenical incident occurred at St. Charles Avenue Christian Church in 1958. A fire broke out in the sanctuary and the roof collapsed into the nave and chancel. Firetrucks from all over the city came and pumped hundreds of gallons of water into the building before the fire was extinguished. Fire Chief, Edmund O'Brien, doing his inspection afterward, fell into the full baptistery, then stumbled down the front steps soaking wet and good Catholic that he was, said to the gathered reporters, "I don't know who these people are, but I think I am one of them." Another fireman who was with the Chief commented, "When he came up, he was not saying 'Glory Halleluia.'"

My seminary education was at Vanderbilt University Divinity School where I got up close and personal with Methodism and had a set of crucial experiences that also shaped my life and ministry. The founding of the United Church of Christ as a merger of the Congregational Christian and Evangelical and Reformed Churches was big news when I started in 1958. Then in 1961 Eugene Carson Blake spoke at Grace Episcopal Cathedral and initiated activities that resulted in the beginning of the Consultation on Church Union. These were the biggest ecclesiastical stories of the day, and they confirmed my ecumenical sense of vocation.

Then the sit-in movement came to Nashville during my middle year. I was a classmate of James Lawson and eventually became a member of the Student Non-Violent Coordinating Committee. Those were difficult but heady and formative days for me, a Southerner, as they were for many. Racial justice became a core conviction and commitment for my ministry. Thus, social and racial justice shaped my life and work, as did a commitment to Christian unity, and I have been involved in a variety of Christian unity and interfaith organizations as well as social justice and community ministries through the years, as have all of you.

An important mentor during my early ministry was Dr. Robert S. Paul, at that time a professor of Church History at Austin Presbyterian Theological Seminary. He was a participant in the Faith and Order Conference in Lima, Peru which produced *Baptism Eucharist and Ministry*, and had been a well-known author and ecumenical leader of his generation. So, when I was asked to represent the United Church of Christ on the Ministry Task Force of Churches Uniting in Christ I accepted the responsibility gladly, and I have served on that working group and on the Coordinating Council of CUIC for the past six years. It is from the perspective of my experience in both "conciliar ecumenism" and "faith and order ecumenism" that I will address the subject for today.

* * * * * *

In 1947 there was a great celebration marking the founding of the Church of South India. Bishop Leslie Newbigen, one of the leaders who had labored tirelessly since 1919 for that momentous landmark achievement, was asked by an interviewer why it took nearly thirty years. He responded, "Because we were in such a terrible hurry!" Ecumenism is the work of decades, the work of generations. It seems slow and difficult, even tedious, until we consider the enormity of the task.

The issues and concerns that divide the human family are, in many cases, so deep and so pervasive as to seem almost implacable. In some cases, they are wrapped up with fundamental assumptions about life which seem impossible to modify, much less to change. Whether it is the centuries old conflict between Sunni and Shi'a in the Arabian Peninsula, the animosities that fueled hatred between Croatian and Serb in the Balkans, the centuries old animosities between Catholic and Protestant in Belfast and Ulster, or the ongoing struggles of Hindu and Muslim in India, the human capacity for bitterness, vengeance and animosity, especially when they are fueled by religion, seems limitless.

Ultimately, that is what ecumenism is really about: healing the brokenness of the Body of Christ as a foretaste and sign of the healing of the brokenness of God's beloved humanity. Even in the case of the Church of South India, the divisions reconciled there go back to the Seventeenth Century divisions in the Church of England, exacerbated by the denominational struggles and competition of the Eighteenth and Nineteenth Centuries. All of these churches were and are noble traditions of religious faith attempting to be true to the Gospel of Jesus Christ as they understood it. But none of that meant anything to the vast majority of people in India. As another leader remarked at the time, "How can we invite all persons of every culture to recognize Jesus as Lord, if the confession of his name comes from people who have not themselves found in Him a sufficient center for their own unity?"

That hurts, and it hurts because it clarifies a painful fact: other loyalties, reasonable, commendable, cherished though they be, have stood in the way of our sole loyalty to Christ and to the unity He intends. There are cherished traditions, hallowed theological standards, held by each of our churches, traditions and standards that have mediated meaning and grace to our lives. What is at stake in Christian Unity, for all of us, is truth as we know it. It is not just difficult to compromise these cherished traditions, it is impossible to do so in good faith. It is therefore a great danger to the search for unity if it focuses on compromise. Willem Visser't Hooft put it this way:

> Genuine ecumenical dialogue must be understood as a spiritual battle for truth . . . although, it is a common battle against error and not a fight between partners based on the assumption that one is already right and one wrong. Ecumenical Christians should be so committed to living the whole truth that they readily confess that this truth is far greater than any of the separated witnesses.

So, the ecumenical task is not: how can we achieve a broader compromise in order to encompass the ever-growing diversity among Christians? Oskar Cullman has taught us that diversity is God's gift to us so that our unity may be worthy of God's all-encompassing love for humankind (*Unity Through Diversity*, 1986). The question really is: how can we become mutual seekers for the truth of God revealed in Jesus Christ which is above and encompasses all our truths? The very diversity of authentic truths affirmed by other Christians has the effect of forcing us to focus on the one Truth we hold in common: Christ.

Thus, ecumenism and conciliarism are more than a series of meetings, documents, programs, and worthy organizations to which we send dutiful delegates. They are not enterprises in which we participate hoping that the result will be a variety of mutual benefits. It is a fundamental mutual belonging in which each is forced by the very authenticity of the others, in the full variety of our diversity, to look beyond ourselves and our own traditions to Christ. We find our identity and our hope in the fact that *together* we belong to Him. We are God's gift to each other so that we all may come more fully to Christ. It is by our unity in Him, that the world may see that God's power to reconcile is more limitless than our human power to alienate.

That is the cluster of theological affirmations that are elegantly articulated in the Princeton Proposal, and that is the basis of all Faith and Order efforts, including the bi-lateral and multi-lateral dialogues and partnerships of Full Communion in which most of our churches are involved. "Conciliar ecumenism" has characteristically been guided by the judgment of earlier generations that "doctrine divides, but service unites." And that was clearly the case in the early 20th Century and for many decades before. Hence, Councils of Churches set the discussion of theology aside in order to be able to do together the things on which they could agree and which could more effectively be done in concert. Thank heaven for the results in terms of the relief of human suffering, the advocacy for the last and the least in society, and the care of God's creation.

But success in both these areas, faith and order partnerships as well as direct Christian service, have had as one negative effect the reduction of the sense of urgency that motivated Leslie Newbigen and should be just as compelling to us all. Peter Steinfels points out that,

In the eyes of many, thanks to the understanding and fellowship generated by dialogue, what was once the scandal of division now looks more like the virtue of diversity. The diversity of Christian traditions has kept neglected facets of the faith alive . . . . Sociologists of religion have argued that Christianity has flourished, in fact, where a diversity of church forms and practices have met the needs of different social groups.

This increase in fellowship, cooperation and dialogue has also had the effect of making it difficult for the plethora of diverse ecclesiastical bodies to maintain any clear sense of their distinctive identity at all. The result, as the Princeton Proposal so clearly points out, is a denominational emphasis on the distinctive characteristics of each, almost invariably to the detriment of our focus on the Good News of Jesus Christ and our common mission of proclaiming God's Reign.

* * * * * *

So then, how do we engage the sacred conversation on Christian unity as mutual seekers for the truth of God revealed in Jesus Christ which is beyond all our cherished glimpses of it? The task is the mutual pursuit of truth; but that effort has consequences. What follows is not so much an answer to that question of "how," but some candid reflections on the efforts that have been and are being made, and some thoughts on how the effort might be nudged forward.

The title of our discussion for today is "Challenging Pluralism: The New Way Forward for Christian Unity." I take the word "pluralism" here to indicate the grudging, or in too many cases, all too happy acceptance of the status quo in our secular and religious culture, where each of us tends to our own turf and has little sense of common purpose or "common good." "Diversity," on the other hand, implies the varieties within a shared and larger whole. It is not an "ism," not an ideology as pluralism is sometimes represented to be. The ecumenical task is to keep reminding ourselves that the whole is equal to more than the sum of its parts, that we belong to each other because we belong to Christ, and to find the synergy that makes that visibly so.

I was also nurtured on a second of Alexander Campbell's mottos: "In essentials, unity; in non-essentials, liberty; in all things, charity." They did not tell me in my Disciples home church that that quote has been attributed to a number of others, several of whom predated Campbell. It is a useful guide in ecumenical discussions until, of course, we run upon disagreements about what is essential. Conciliar efforts, by and large, have declared doctrine to be a non-essential and thus see diversity in that regard as appropriate. Councils of Churches have found unity in some very important essentials, as we know: service, mission and witness, and churches and church people all over the nation and world have learned to respect and admire each other in the process. But doctrine, the reflection on and teaching of the churches' faith, cannot be set aside and ignored. It is at the core of who we are both separately and together.

So, what are the essentials of the Christian faith on which we cannot agree? Gratefully, the list is being narrowed in some regards. Lutherans and Roman Catholics have officially come to agreement on the doctrine of justification. Wow! Lutherans and Methodists are nearing an agreement on the doctrine of sanctification. Wow! Yet all of us know the issues on which we still disagree, and all of them are internal to each of our churches. Some regard Biblical interpretation, including particular approaches to that discipline, as an essential while others do not. Some regard reproductive rights/right to life as an essential while others see it as a non-essential question on which we can live with diverse perspectives. The same is true for issues pertaining to homosexuality. Some on both sides of the matter view them as essential, while others will tolerate differences. These are not the particular focus here, but they have a profound impact on all current discussions of Christian unity, as we shall see very clearly.

In the area of faith and order ecumenism we are dealing with a different set of disagreements regarding essentials. In all of our bi-lateral agreements, as well as in an ecumenical milestone like *Baptism, Eucharist and Ministry,* and in multi-lateral conversations like Churches Uniting in Christ, we have been able to assume an emerging level of agreement and unity around the basic affirmations of our common faith as expressed in the historic ecumenical creeds and confessions. But it is precisely around our understandings of the nature and ministry of the Church that we see the consensus unraveling. We all believe in our hearts and confess with our lips that the Church is One, Holy, Catholic and Apostolic. But we interpret each of those standards of ecclesial authenticity from decidedly different and historically conditioned perspectives, and that has come to haunt us.

From the Dessert Fathers to the Cathari, from the Monastic movement to the schisms of the Reformation and Radical Reformation, and most certainly today, the Church's unity, its Oneness, has been challenged by those who have seen it as insufficiently Holy. Its Oneness and the character of its Holiness have both been challenged through the centuries by its Catholicity, as Christian communities all over the globe develop forms of worship, ministry, mission and piety that speak to their own contexts, and thus, multiply the diversity of thought and expression, including doctrine. This very catholicity is the result of the success of the Church's Apostolicity, its apostolic zeal for the propagation of the faith, on the one hand, and for its faithfulness to the apostles' teaching and leadership on the other. And that very question of apostolicity, whether we should emphasize the apostolic mission or apostolic succession, is itself a serious challenge to unity.

Conciliar Ecumenism, as we well know, has set much of this conundrum aside in order to do what we can together, and thank God for it. Faith and Order Ecumenism, as we have seen, cannot do that because this definitional formula, "One, Holy, Catholic and Apostolic," contains the very nature and essence of the Church and of our ministry. Hence, we struggle together for insight and for the Truth that transcends our truths, a unity in faith that could transform the power of our witness. To address Christian unity at this depth we must take a hard look at some very difficult barriers to our Oneness in Christ. Let me use my experience with Churches Uniting In Christ as an example which illuminates a number of these issues, the consequences, if you will, of "truth telling" at a deeper level.

* * * * * *

CUIC, in its previous form as Consultation on Church Union, had developed a seven-chapter consensus that wasn't. The then nine communions all accepted the first six chapters as sufficient grounds regarding faith and mission that enabled the churches to proceed toward Full Communion. But the seventh chapter, the one on Ministry, was rejected by two of the member church bodies. Thus, a Ministry Task Force was charged with the effort to redraft the articles on ministry in a way that would make it possible to reconcile our ministries and enable the Ministers of Word and Sacrament to serve in any of the partner churches upon invitation in a relationship of Full Communion.

The three-fold pattern of ministry articulated in *Baptism, Eucharist and Ministry* was the template, and we tried to embody the pattern of that document and apply it for our North American context and to the realities of our participating communions. We failed in that task. I served as the third chairperson of that Task Force, and in my report to the Plenary in January I cited the reasons for that failure and proposed a way forward.

** The office of Bishop was a difficult problem. No surprise here: the Princeton Proposal indicates (#54) that agreement on the theology of ministry was not possible. That, of course, is precisely what is at stake. In the CUIC discussions the Episcopal Church could not agree to any description of the office that did not include Historic Episcopal Succession. Churches of the Reformed tradition could not agree to any description of the Ministry of Oversight that did not honor and conform to its view of Corporate Episcope: equal numbers of laity and clergy making all decisions of oversight. Churches of the Methodist tradition could not agree to any description of Bishop that did not honor the ministry and authority of their bishops as fully and historically authentic.

Of course, the Devil is in the details. The initial proposals for implementing a Ministry of Oversight in Full Communion among these churches involved a gathering for a "mutual, representative, laying on of hands." But the canons of the Episcopal Church required that three bishops in historic succession lay hands on any persons who were to be set apart as bishops. The orders of the Presbyterian Church required that an equal number of lay and clergy Ordained Elders lay hands on any persons who were to be set apart. Neither could change their requirements without altering basic constituting documents, and neither was interested in doing so anyway. There are, of course, ten communions involved who would have representative leaders engaged in this celebratory act. We would need the planner of the opening ceremony at the Bejing Olympics to pull it off. The image was bizarre.

** The Interchangeability of Ministers of Word and Sacrament was, similarly, a difficult problem. Reservations regarding differing standards for educational preparation were strong and cut both ways. Churches whose students had been the object of discrimination for generations on the basis of race or gender wanted to be sure they were not excluded, while those with characteristically high standards feared a diminution of those standards. The fact that there are ordained persons in the partner communions who are gay or lesbian, and in some churches, openly so, also created problems, of course. The proposed solution was to make serving in a partner communion possible at the sole discretion and under the discipline of the receiving church body after demonstrated competence in the history, polity, faith and worship of that communion. Not totally satisfying.

Further, this last question led to a more basic and very crucial realization. One of the communions, in its official response to the Reconciliation of Ministries proposal stated that it was reconsidering whether it could remain in fellowship at all with a communion that consecrated a bishop who was openly gay and another which had passed a resolution in favor of marriage equality for gay and lesbian couples (The Episcopal Church and the United Church of Christ). This was a game breaker, and it takes us back to the question of 'essentials,' and of 'oneness vs. holiness.' Are these issues more important to us than the witness to our unity in Christ? CUIC was so stunned by the suspension of participation by that communion that it suspended its own operations until participation could be restored.

Not only were the matters of unity and apostolicity at stake in the centuries old debate regarding the office and role of bishop, the partner communions' unity, and understanding of holiness were at stake in the question: with whom may we be in ministry? In typical organizational fashion the Ministry Task Force was asked to propose a way forward. I will never forget that meeting. The Task Force devised recommendations on how we might step back and engage in conversations regarding each of the latter issues in hopes that prayerful efforts might find a way through. But when it came to the question of *episcope* the discussion hinged on one word, and we could not get agreement.

The Presbyterian Church, unique among its Reformed tradition cousins, holds that its practice of Corporate Episcope is "pre-Ignatian," that it pre-dates the office of bishop as having oversight in a large geographic area, as that office has been practiced since St. Ignatius, and therefore predates the regional expression of *episcope,* and is more or at least equally authentic. In that view the earliest Christian communities set apart bishops who served in ministry to a single gathered congregation. Who knew? The Presbyterians know, and they are probably right about the history, if not, necessarily about the conclusions they draw. "Bishop" is therefore, one of the terms that can be applied to the Minister of Word and Sacrament in each local congregation. It's in their Book of Order.

So, the Task Force proposed that "since there are multiple forms of the exercise of Episcopal oversight that have been faithfully carried forward and are present in the polities of the CUIC member churches, . . . we will explore in greater depth these historic manifestations, and that such a study and conversation will lead to the possibility of respecting multiple manifestations of episcope." Sounds good. But what was left out after hours of debate was the word "honor." The representative of the Episcopal Church could not agree to recommending "the possibility of respecting *and honoring* the multiple manifestations of *episcope*" of our partner churches. This is not to beat up on Episcopalians nor on Presbyterians. It is rather a measure of how we have, by our historic and deeply cherished traditions, painted ourselves into various corners of the household of God.

The way forward? Sometimes we just have to wait and let the paint dry; ecumenism is the task of decades and generations as we have seen. But, for now, we must keep on talking internally and with our partners about all the issues that divide us, and we must be willing to open our hearts to each other's perspectives. Second, the bilateral conversations and partnerships between our communions seem to be achievable, energizing, and going ahead nicely. The ELCA may have it right: as I understand it, they work only bilaterally—one set of problems at a time. And we should all become familiar with the solutions devised in bilateral agreements that do not involve our particular denomination on the sure and certain knowledge that the Holy Spirit is active among those folks too.

Third, of course, we must support local, statewide and global conciliarism: it is an authentic expression of our vocation of servanthood, and that is a large part of my understanding of piety and what it means to be Holy. Finally, we must continue to support multilateral efforts at "faith and order ecumenism," because the more voices of committed Christians that we have at the table, the more likely we are to be faithful to the God who made us all and to the Christ who makes us One. In our faithfulness to this ecumenical vocation to which we were all ordained, we will do well to remember Reinhold Niehbur's counsel:

Nothing that is worth doing can be achieved in our lifetime; therefore, we must be saved by hope. Nothing which is true, or beautiful or good, makes complete sense in any immediate context of history; therefore, we must be saved by faith. Nothing we do, however virtuous, could be accomplished alone; therefore, we must be saved by love. No virtuous act is quite as virtuous from the standpoint of our friend or foe as it is from our own; therefore, we must be saved by the final form of love, which is forgiveness.

1.   . Quote from L.R.P. Curriculum description of the "Seminar on Christology." ↑

2.   . Arthur Peacocke, "Science and the Future of Theology", *Research News and Opportunities in Science and Theology,* Vol. 2, No.5, Jan. 2001. ↑

3.   . John Dominic Crossan, *The Historical Jesus: The Life of a Mediterranean Jewish Peasant* (Harper San Francisco, 1991). ↑

4.   . Bart Ehrman, *Jesus: Apocalyptic Prophet of the New Millennium* (Oxford University Press, Oxford, 1999), p. 134. ↑

5.   . Luke Timothy Johnson, *Living Jesus: Learning the Heart of the Gospel* (Harper, San Francisco, 1999), p. 201. ↑

6. . C. Kirk Hadaway, *Behold I Do A New Thing: Transforming Communities of Faith* (Pilgrim, Cleveland), 2001. ↑

7. . *The Constitution of the United Church of Christ*, Preamble, paragraph 2, Executive Council, Cleveland, p. 2 ↑